THE ROMAN EMPIRE AND WORLD HISTORY

How do we fit the Roman Empire into world history? Too often the empire has simply been thought of in terms of the West. But Rome was too big to be squeezed into a purely European model; her empire bestrode three continents. Peter Fibiger Bang develops a radical new world history framework for the Roman Empire, presenting it as part of an Afro-Eurasian arena of grand empires that dominated the shape of history before the forces of globalization and industrialization made the world centre on Europe from the eighteenth century onwards. It was a world before East and West. The book traces surprising cultural connections and societal similarities between Rome and the other vast empires of Afro-Eurasia. Whether we look at war-making, slavery, empire formation, literary culture or inter-continental trade and rebellion, Rome is best approached in its Afro-Eurasian context.

PETER FIBIGER BANG is Professor of Roman History at the Saxo Institute at the University of Copenhagen. He has been in the vanguard of attempts to develop a new comparative and global history perspective on the Roman Empire for the last three decades. His previous books include *The Roman Bazaar* (Cambridge, 2008), with Dariusz Kolodziejczyk (eds.), *Universal Empire* (Cambridge, 2012) and with C. A. Bayly and Walter Scheidel (eds.), *The Oxford World History of Empire, 2 Vols.* (Oxford, 2021).

KEY THEMES IN ANCIENT HISTORY

EDITORS

P. A. Cartledge
Clare College, Cambridge

G. Woolf
Institute for the Study of the Ancient World, New York University

EMERITUS EDITOR

P. D. A. Garnsey
Jesus College, Cambridge

Key Themes in Ancient History aims to provide readable, informed and original studies of various basic topics, designed in the first instance for students and teachers of Classics and Ancient History, but also for those engaged in related disciplines. Each volume is devoted to a general theme in Greek, Roman, or where appropriate, Graeco-Roman history, or to some salient aspect or aspects of it. Besides indicating the state of current research in the relevant area, authors seek to show how the theme is significant for our own as well as ancient culture and society. It is hoped that these original, thematic volumes will encourage and stimulate promising new developments in teaching and research in ancient history.

Other books in the series

Science Writing in Greco-Roman Antiquity, by Liba Taub
978 0 521 11370 0 (hardback) 978 0 521 13063 9 (paperback)

Politics in the Roman Republic, by Henrik Mouritsen
978 1 07 03188 3 (hardback) 978 1 107 65133 3 (paperback)

Roman Political Thought, by Jed W. Atkins
978 11 07 10700 7 (hardback) 9781107514553 (paperback)

Empire and Political Cultures in the Roman World, by Emma Dench
978 0 521 81072 2 (hardback) 978 0 521 00901 0 (paperback)

Warfare in the Roman World, by A. D. Lee
978 1 107 01428 2 (hardback) 978 1 107 63828 0 (paperback)

Slaves and Slavery in Ancient Greece, by Sara Forsdyke
978 1 107 03234 7 (hardback) 978 1 107 65889 9 (paperback)

Roman Law in Context (second edition), by David Johnston
978 1 108 47630 0 (hardback) 978 1 108 70016 0 (paperback)

Risk in the Roman World, by Jerry Toner
978 1 108 48174 8 (hardback) 978 1 108 72321 3 (paperback)

For a full list of titles in this series go to www.cambridge.org/series/key-themes-ancient-history

THE ROMAN EMPIRE AND WORLD HISTORY

PETER FIBIGER BANG

University of Copenhagen

Shaftesbury Road, Cambridge CB2 8EA, United Kingdom

One Liberty Plaza, 20th Floor, New York, NY 10006, USA

477 Williamstown Road, Port Melbourne, VIC 3207, Australia

314–321, 3rd Floor, Plot 3, Splendor Forum, Jasola District Centre, New Delhi – 110025, India

103 Penang Road, #05–06/07, Visioncrest Commercial, Singapore 238467

Cambridge University Press is part of Cambridge University Press & Assessment, a department of the University of Cambridge.

We share the University's mission to contribute to society through the pursuit of education, learning and research at the highest international levels of excellence.

www.cambridge.org
Information on this title: www.cambridge.org/9781316516102

DOI: 10.1017/9781009031868

© Cambridge University Press & Assessment 2025

This publication is in copyright. Subject to statutory exception and to the provisions of relevant collective licensing agreements, no reproduction of any part may take place without the written permission of Cambridge University Press & Assessment.

When citing this work, please include a reference to the DOI 10.1017/9781009031868

First published 2025

Cover image: Istanbul, Hagia Sophia. lucky-photographer / Alamy Stock Photo. Dedication page: Persian calligraphy courtesy of Saqib Baburi.

A catalogue record for this publication is available from the British Library

A Cataloging-in-Publication data record for this book is available from the Library of Congress

ISBN 978-1-316-51610-2 Hardback
ISBN 978-1-009-01372-7 Paperback

Cambridge University Press & Assessment has no responsibility for the persistence or accuracy of URLs for external or third-party internet websites referred to in this publication and does not guarantee that any content on such websites is, or will remain, accurate or appropriate.

For EU product safety concerns, contact us at Calle de José Abascal, 56, 1º, 28003 Madrid, Spain, or email eugpsr@cambridge.org

For Jingyan

Suave is the breeze when we sit on the balcony,
You and I
Two faces and two bodies, but one of breath,
You and I
Soon the stars of heaven shall be coming out to look at us
And we will be their moon
You and I
You and I, without a 'you' and an 'I', we shall be together
from the height of joy
Happy and free from worrying prejudice,
You and I
In the sky, swallows are playing
while we laugh with them,
You and I
Isn't it even more a marvel that you and I can be here in
one corner
And at that very same time, you in the West and I in the
East,
You and I
(Rumi, freely translated from the Persian by the author)

Contents

List of Figures		*page* viii
Preface		xi
1	Rome and Pre-colonial World History	1
2	The Expanding World of Warring States: Ecology, State Formation and Slavery	28
3	Among Empires: The Universal Realms of the Afro-Eurasian World	56
4	The Imperial Cosmopolis: Courtly Literary Languages and Monotheist Religions	86
5	Premodern Globalization? Transcontinental Trade and the Rituals of Consumption in the Afro-Eurasian Arena	119
6	Resistance, Rebellion and Renewal	153
	Conclusion: Beyond Globalization – The World Histories for Rome	177
Bibliographical Essay		187
Bibliography		190
Index		223

Figures

1.1 Neo-Roman monumental rivalries of European nations during the long nineteenth century: (a) Brandenburger Tor; (b) Arc de Triomphe; (c) Trafalgar Square, with the Nelson Column; (d) Altare della Patria. *page* 3
1.2 The Roman imperial mosques of Constantinople/Istanbul: (a) the Blue Mosque, facing Hagia Sophia; (b) the grand cathedral of Justinian the Great, converted to a mosque. 6
1.3 The Afro-Eurasian arena of universal empires: (a) the arena dominated by the Qing, the Mughal and the Ottoman Empires around 1700 CE; (b) the arena by the second century CE. 24
2.1 Poros medallion, British Museum. 29
2.2 The expanding world of Afro-Eurasian state making. 54
3.1 Sasanian triumphs over Rome in the third century CE: (a) relief at Naqsh-e Rostam of Shapur the Great and Roman emperors Philip the Arab and Valerian; (b) the rock at Naqsh-e Rostam with Sasanian relief near Achaemenid royal graves. 59
3.2 The Afro-Eurasian arena of universal empires, second century CE (Rome, Parthia, Kushans and Han dynasty). 63
4.1 Orpheus on the Alexandrian coinage of Antoninus Pius, 141–142 CE. (a) Autokra(tor) Kais(ar) Adr(ianos) Antoninos Se(bastos); (b) Orpheus playing his lyre surrounded by wild animals. 90
4.2 A specimen of a Roman Orpheus mosaic: polychrome, with Orpheus in the centre, surrounded by a host of wild animals. 93
4.3 Illustrations of universal kingship in the illuminated manuscripts of Mughal India: (a) Majnun surrounded by the peaceable animals; (b) philosophers debating in front of Alexander, (c) Plato playing the organ for the animals. 95

4.4 Orpheus in the Delhi Hall of Public Audience of the Mughal emperor Shahjahan, king of the world: (a) the Hall of Public Audience in the Red Fort of Delhi, mid seventeenth century; (b) the Florentine pietre dure *Orpheus Playing to the Animals*, inlaid in the wall behind the throne. 97
5.1 Map of Dunhuang, the Jade Gate, the Tarim Basin and the Ferghana Valley. 120
5.2 Celebration of exotic animals as providential omens of universal empire and benign rule: (a) *Qilin in Beijing* (painting by Chen Zhang, Qing dynasty version of a Ming painting); (b) mosaic of a camelopard in Roman Syria; (c) Dürer's *Rhinoceros*, woodcarving, published in Nüremberg. 126
5.3 Imperial tributes: the celebration of tributes offered by subject peoples, from late Roman Constantinople, Mughal Shahjahanabad (Delhi) and Qing Beijing: (a) the so-called *Barberini Diptych*, ivory carving, showing a late Roman emperor protecting his subjects and receiving tributes; (b) Mughal Emperor Shahjahan at his court, receiving gifts or tributes from Europeans; (c-e) images of Chinese tributary peoples, produced for the Qianlong emperor by Xie Sui, second half of the eighteenth century CE; (c) official and lady of the people of Siam; (d) people from Poland; (e) the Gurkhas (headman and servant). 128
5.4 Some important locations in the history of premodern world trade. The map does not purport to be a full map of ancient world trade, but offers a guide to the places mentioned in this chapter. Map by Peter Fibiger Bang and Wolfgang Filser. 139
5.5 Picture of a Silk Road map in the Archaeological Museum of Lanzhou, Gansu Province, China. 150

Preface

> *As a result, most people understand everything in isolation, each thing apart from the others. Real wisdom lies in connecting everything together – that's when the true shape of things emerges.*
> Olga Tokarczuk, *The Books of Jacob*[1]

There is a growing sense of the need for, even the urgency of, change in the study of the Greeks and Romans. A feeling of crisis is often voiced. Some call for a move to 'decolonize'; others simply want to 'burn down' the classics.[2] This book offers one way of effecting change and renewal, a turn to world history. To be honest, it has been clear for quite some time that change was required. The postmodernist movement of the 1980s vigorously embarked on a project of deconstruction. All the 'big' narratives of Western academia, one after the other, were torn apart and taken down. The underlying assumptions of past certainties and established frameworks were laid bare, relentlessly questioned and found wanting. However, postmodernism was itself unable to substitute any alternative story. Born out of irony, its critique was reactive, wedded to its object and therefore never really able to transcend the intellectual horizon of what it criticized. Students were, so to speak, asked to continue to inhabit the ruins of a house that their own theories had destroyed. In the long run, that situation was untenable. If, for instance, we cannot any more really believe in the old narrative of Greece and Rome as the foundation for the rise of the West, where does that leave the study of the classics? How does the Roman Empire then fit into world history? Those are the big questions that this book sets out to answer.

---

[1] Olga Tokarczuk, *The Books of Jacob*, Book I, chapter 3, p. 866 (in the Polish edition), p. 856 in the English 2021 translation by Jennifer Croft, here slightly modified by this author on the basis of the original Polish.
[2] For example, Poser 2021; Yaffe 2021; Ram-Prasad 2019; Vasunia, Blanshard, Leonard et al. 2020.

The task may sound ambitious, perhaps too ambitious, but in fact it requires much less of a leap into the great unknown than might be thought. It does, however, demand an adventurous mind and curiosity beyond one's own specialism. Over the last generation, a new world history has grown out under the shadow of the postmodern. Not satisfied to leave the world in fragments, its practitioners have been busy fleshing out a new and better alternative. We need big, overarching narratives to make sense of the world, and arguably more expansive ones than at any time before. Even as politicians are beginning to curtail some of the effects of the last decade of hyperglobalization, our world will remain more interconnected than ever, while the ability of the US and even more so Europe to call the tune will be increasingly challenged. As the French philosopher Alain Finkielkraut already observed years ago, 'the world is all the time becoming more modern and increasingly less Western.'[3] We simply must seek to understand how the societies of our globe and *their histories* relate to each other. How else would we be able to comprehend and navigate the world that we live in? The new world history is, in that respect, fundamentally comparativist, an exercise in contextualization and recontextualization. As the old narratives have broken down, Western history has had to be recontextualised and better related to the histories of Asian, African and American societies. That goes also, I might even say especially, for the Roman Empire.

If this book then speaks to the current crisis of classics, its intellectual project was born out of sheer excitement, enthusiasm and joy at the widening horizons. Half a career ago and absorbed in debates on the ancient economy, I embarked on a project to compare Roman and Mughal taxation and trade. Yet, working on this problem, I realized that I had unwittingly stumbled on a much wider Afro-Eurasian history of empire. Excavating it would require me to get to know not only about the Mughals in India but also about a host of other Indian, Muslim and Chinese Empires. Together they constituted an experience that could help illuminate the Roman Empire far better than any Western colonial experience would ever be able to. The referents and customary analogues in Roman history had to be changed.[4]

Perhaps the Afro-Eurasian parallels found in this book may at first strike the reader as strange and arcane. Most Roman historians, after all, will feel more confident alluding to European history. This, however, is simply a reflection of the illusory certainties of habit and convention. European history may be more superficially familiar to Roman historians, but they do

---

[3] Finkielkraut 2005: 265 (my translation).   [4] I gesture here to Jenco 2015.

not really have so much greater 'archival' experience or in-depth command of the European past that they could not acquire a level of knowledge of other cultures easily able to match what they possess of Europe. No matter what, in order to advance beyond the merely superficial and frivolous, comparison requires us to engage in dialogue with the work of colleagues in other fields. Much of what is unfamiliar and seems incomprehensible at first in a foreign culture, as Kwame Anthony Appiah reminds us, merely requires readjustment and getting used to. Once this threshold is passed, we can relate to other cultures as well as to those seemingly more familiar.[5]

For the purposes of this book, a good start would then be to keep in mind a series of Asian empires – beyond the various Persian dynasties so familiar to the ancient historian – and their chronologies. Consider the Islamic Caliphate, especially the dynasty of the Umayyads reigning from Damascus (661–750 CE) and the Abbasids from Baghdad (750 till the tenth century CE), and the Ottomans, governing from Constantinople, modern-day Istanbul, since 1453 till the aftermath of the First World War. In the greater Indian world, especially important are the Mauryan dynasty under Chandragupta and Ashoka (321–185 BCE), the Kushanas (late-first till third century CE), the Guptas (fourth to mid sixth century CE), as well the great Mughals, defined by Babur, Akbar, Jahangir, Shahjahan and Aurangzeb (1526–1739/1858). Finally, in China, the reader will find frequent allusions to the dynasties of the Qin (221–206 BCE), the Western and Eastern Han (206 BCE–220 CE), the Tang (618–907 CE), the Ming (1368–1644 CE) and the Qing (1644–1911 CE).

To be sure, this may seem like a dramatic demand to expand the horizon of our historical imagination. Yet the path has been well prepared for us. Two of the most productive developments in the previous generation of scholarship cleared the way. In the *World of Late Antiquity* (originally 1971), Peter Brown pushed open the doors to a much wider conception of the Greco-Roman world. His late antiquity charts a cultural universe far beyond the classical heartlands to move places such as Syria, Armenia, Egypt, North Africa and Arabia with the rise of Islam, to the centre of the age's developments. Soon the example of Brown was followed by a renewed interest also in the Hellenistic period. In *From Samarkand to Sardis*, Susan Sherwin-White and Amelie Kuhrt taught us to appreciate the contribution of both Iran and Central Asia to the evolution of Hellenistic civilization.[6] Venturing far beyond what has traditionally been considered

---

[5] Appiah 2006, chapter 5 (on the primacy of practice).
[6] Brown 1971b; Kuhrt & Sherwin-White 1993. See also Østergaard 1991.

the canonical regions of the Greeks and Romans, the next logical step, if we are to learn from these works, will be to reach out for a global and Afro-Eurasian framework. In a certain sense, we are simply completing what was begun by these visionary scholars.

Fortunately, I have not been alone in this quest but benefitted from a host of collaborators, interlocutors and fellow travellers. First of all, I must single out Walter Scheidel, with whom I have enjoyed a friendship which it feels astonishing to note is already in its third decade, formed around our various collaborative enterprises in comparative history and 'seasoned' by a shared joy of playful high cuisine and wine. How times flies in good company. It was, in fact, during a very inspiring stay at Stanford in 2014 that I first gave a talk on the Roman Empire and 'the challenge of world history'. Years before, Peter Garnsey and Paul Cartledge had kindly invited me to write a volume for *Key Themes in Ancient History* on how world history could contribute to the study of Rome. Evidently, it has taken me some time to complete this task. A range of collective projects has kept me from turning my full attention to it, or rather, these collaborative endeavours have helped me explore a range of ideas that I am now, as my thoughts have matured, able to put together in this volume. A decade ago, I think more work still had to be done, both by myself and by colleagues.

Among my closest interlocutors, I must also mention Chris Bayly, a historian of colonial India and nineteenth-century globalization, a dear and sadly missed friend and collaborator, and John A. Hall, the path-breaking historical sociologist. Both together and individually, they have spent many a workshop and conversation in Copenhagen discussing about how to develop a pre-colonial world history. Ebba Koch, the Mughal art historian; Karen Turner, the historian of ancient Chinese law; and Jane Fejfer, the Roman archaeologist, have equally taken part in my workshops over the years and been there as a sounding board for my own ideas. A grant from Research Fund Denmark enabled me to form my own little group at the Saxo Institute in the University of Copenhagen, where Jacob Tullberg, Karsten Johanning, Kristian Kanstrup Christensen, Lars-Emil Nybo Nissen and Martin Müller joined the conversation. I hope they have had as much intellectual fun as I had in the process. Dingxin Zhao, Yanfei Sun and Jing Li helped me organize a workshop with Chinese colleagues at the Institute for Advanced Study in the Humanities and Social Sciences at Zhejiang University about the framework I was suggesting for pre-colonial world history. This was followed by a series of global history workshops in Leiden with Miguel John Versluys and his group, in Delhi with the late Sunil Kumar and his colleagues, in Evanston with Rajeev Kinra and Kaya

Sahin, in Shanghai with Zhongxiao Wang and Donni Wang and finally in Edinburgh with Lilliana Riga and her colleagues.

Now the book was ready to be written, and the Carlsberg Foundation, with its usual vision and trust, granted me a year off teaching to launch the project. Stefan Heidemann and Sabine Panzram at the Roman/Islam Centre in Hamburg; Sebastian Schmidt-Hofner, Mischa Meier and Steffen Patzold at the Centre for Migration and Mobility in Late Antiquity and the Early Middle Age in Tübingen; and finally Peter Eich at the DFG Graduate School, 'Empires' in Freiburg, added to this a string of visiting fellowships in Germany between 2020 and 2023 that enabled me to complete the manuscript while benefitting from a set of remarkably interdisciplinary environments. Many more have invited me to give seminars and provided much appreciated discussion of my take on ancient and world history: Luuk de Ligt and Cecilia Palombo in Leiden; Frederik Stjernfeldt in Copenhagen; Trine Hass in Aarhus; Anne-Marie Leander Touati at the University of Lund; Aloys Winterling and Claudia Tiersch at the Humboldt University in Berlin; Sitta von Reden and the *Beyond the Silk Road* Group in Freiburg; Griet Vankeerbergen and Hans Beck at McGill; Jonathan Hall and Muzaffar Alam at the University of Chicago; Joe Manning at Yale; Brent Shaw at Princeton; Charlotte Shubert in Leipzig; Sven Günther in Changchun; Shaoxiang Yan at Capital Normal, Beijing; Igor Santos Salazar in Vitoria Gasteiz; Liang Cai at Notre Dame; Jon Lendon and Krishan Kumar at the University of Virginia; Lisa Hellman and the Nordglob Network; Leonora Neville in Madison, Wisconsin; Kaya Sahin in Bloomington, Indiana; David Potter in Ann Arbor; Anne Kolb in Zürich; Babett Edelmann-Singer in Regensburg; John Weisweiler in Munich; Nils Arne Sørensen and Jesper Majbom Madsen at the University of Southern Denmark; Sabine Hübner in Basel; Olivier Hekster in Nijmegen and Antoine Borrut, Jennifer R. Davis and Samuel Collins in Maryland.

Apart from plenty of discussion, I have also been blessed by good readers and efficient assistance. Bjarke Bach Christensen has been a model of a research assistant, helping me consolidate and standardize the bibliography when I went into the footnoting stage. Birthe Miller of the Royal Library in Copenhagen expedited many a book request with kind and humorous efficiency. As the manuscript got under way, Kenneth Pomeranz and the 'Empires and the Atlantic' forum at the University of Chicago generously read and commented on Chapter 1. John A. Hall has kindly read through several full versions of the manuscript during recent visits to Copenhagen and finally managed to persuade me that it was ready for the editors. Greg Woolf then took over and challenged me to push even further, while the attentive eye of Paul Cartledge helped make numerous improvements.

I also must not forget the many colleagues who kindly offered advice on literature and helped with access to museum archives or with images of monuments and objects or permissions to use their images and materials, especially Giovanni Salmeri, Phiroze Vasunia, Michael A. Smith, Gojko Barjamovic, Vincent Gabrielsen, John Healey, Ebba Koch, Claudia Tiersch, Wolfgang Flügel, Helle W. Horsnæs, Bernhard Weisser, Jan Peuckert, Kourosh Mohammadkhani, Azadeh Pashootanizadeh, Laura Hostetler, Xuemei Wu, Patricia Radder, Chang Biliang and Yu-chih Lai. The Royal Trust of King Charles, the Art Institute of Chicago and the National Palace Museum in Taipei freely provided me with images of objects in their collections. Saqib Baburi, with his expert hand, generously composed the Persian calligraphy for the dedication, while Wolfgang Filser helped me with the maps in Fig. 1.3a and Fig 5.4. At the end, the manuscript was steered safely to print by Michael Sharp, Katie Idle and the rest of the staff at Cambridge University Press.

As I come to the end of this preface and look back over the list of people who have so generously engaged with my work, it is difficult not to feel gratitude. And so many have ended up intervening in my life also to become friends. Scholarship is in every respect a deeply transformative quest. It changes and shapes who we are far more than you might expect. In my case, it even brought radical transformation. There she was, on my first trip to China: Jingyan, my Beijing Swallow. Magical conversation over a conference dinner turned into letters, as we went home each to our own university in Denmark and the US. What more is there to say? We fell in love; it had to be. Eventually we decided to defy the limitations of location, distance and border controls. Now we are married and travel to explore world history together. For the happiness she has brought me, it is but a small token to dedicate this book to her, reminding us that *true hope is swift and flies with Swallow's wings.*

CHAPTER 1

Rome and Pre-colonial World History

> When the Arab faith mingled with Persia, India, and the remnant of the classical world it had overrun, and Muslim civilization was the central civilization of the West.
>
> V. S. Naipaul (1982: 5)

1.1 The Roman Paradox

Here is a paradox: conventionally, the Roman Empire has been understood in the light of Europe. Yet the defining characteristic of the European experience is normally taken precisely to be the absence of a unifying empire, Roman style. All attempts to subject the many polities of the continent to a new universal empire came to naught. Where the Romans had once created unity, the Europeans maintained division. The history of Europe took shape in a process that Walter Scheidel has summarized with the pithy formula of escape – escape from the Roman condition.[1] To be sure, Rome has found many eager emulators through the centuries. European kings and state-building elites mirrored themselves in the glories of the Roman past, staged their appearance in an architectural language inspired by the imperial monuments of the Caesars and graced their ambience with forms of art drawing heavily on Greco-Roman models. But however much the ruling classes liked to parade their achievements against the backdrop of Roman history, they all failed to follow in the footsteps of their ancient predecessor in the most important respect: they were unable to overcome their main rivals, extend power across Europe and impose an imperial peace.

London, Paris, Berlin or Rome – during the nineteenth century all were appointed with classicizing imperial monuments such as the Arc de

[1] Scheidel 2019.

Triomphe, Trafalgar Square, Brandenburger Tor or the stupefying Vittorio Emmanuele Monument, often referred to as the *altare della patria* (Fig. 1.1). Significantly, however, these iconic landmarks were erected as proud proclamations of national unity, modernization and greatness. In an extraordinary reversal of the historically predominant pattern, conquest and empire had been pushed to the margins. Colonies were something that nations of the European metropolis sought primarily in overseas territories far from home.[2] By contrast, ancient Rome had expanded by defeating and absorbing their closest and strongest rivals. The road to Roman world rule went over the fall of mighty Carthage and the Hellenistic successor monarchies that had emerged out of the glorious trail of conquests cut through Asia by Alexander. Nineteenth-century monuments, on the other hand, celebrated the capacity of nations to hold their own in the main theatre of military conflict and communicated their willingness to assert their position among the other great metropolitan powers of the day. In the competition of nations, no one wanted to be seen as falling behind their neighbours. If Paris saw the construction of grand symbolic architecture, London quickly answered. If a unified Germany was to be ruled by a Kaiser, the British queen would soon find herself proclaimed Imperatrix Indiae. The European neo-Romans of the nineteenth century were busy consolidating the political fragmentation which had characterized the continent since the collapse of the Western Roman court in the fifth century CE.[3]

Occasionally the European Union is cast as a new empire seeking to impose the unity that had eluded the continent for centuries. But this is nothing more than rhetorical flourish. With or without a Brexit, the Union has been far too weak to warrant this label.[4] If anything, the fragile unity achieved by the EU rather puts into sharp relief just how much of a deviation from the historical norm the empire represents. In the experience of Europe, Rome and the empire look like an anomaly. When power ebbed away from the imperial city on the Tiber, the dwindling population, a mere fraction of its former glory, was left nestling in an oversized urban landscape of gigantic but crumbling buildings; 'Wrecks of another world,

---

[2] Bang 2021a: 65–70.
[3] Bayly 2004: 208–212 and 426–430 on the connection between imperialism, nationalist competition and the revival of historicizing imperial symbols. Kumar 2017 on the link between the nation-state and colonial empire. Bang & Kolodciejczyk 2012: 1–6 and Cannadine 1983 (on Queen Victoria as empress); Watanabe-O'Kelly 2021 more generally on the symbolism, pageantry and monuments of modern nineteenth-century emperors.
[4] As Zielonka 2006 observed, if the European Union should be understood as empire, it must be in terms of the weak, feudal and dispersed Holy Roman Empire of the Middle Ages.

1.1 The Roman Paradox

(a)

(b)

Figure 1.1 Neo-Roman monumental rivalries of European nations during the long nineteenth century.
  a. Brandenburger Tor (Berlin, 1791/1793 and 1814). Photo: Claudia Tiersch and Wolfgang Flügel.
  b. Arc de Triomphe (Paris, 1806–1836). Photo: Peter Fibiger Bang.
  c. Trafalgar Square, with the Nelson Column (London, 1840–1844/1867). Photo: Phiroze Vasunia.
  d. Altare della Patria (Rome, 1885–1935). Photo: Giovanni Salmeri.

4   1 Rome and Pre-colonial World History

(c)

(d)

Figure 1.1 (cont.)

whose ashes still are warm', as Byron would later muse.⁵ Unable to fill the void, the remaining residents were for the next many centuries able to draw on the ruins as an inexhaustible quarry to provide the materials for one phase of opulent building activity after the other. Medieval, renaissance and baroque Rome all relied on the spoliation of the imperial past.

The imperial capital had been the product of an enormous concentration of resources; it drew on a Mediterranean world empire that bestrode not merely one but three continents: Europe, Asia and Africa. Little wonder then that it does not easily map onto the European experience. Nothing in the history of pre-industrial European states quite prepares the student for ancient Rome. The imperial titan is too big, too unwieldy and simply out of all proportion to be squeezed down into a European size. Confronted with the Roman past, the compact patterns and models so familiar to students of European history frequently fall short, and their expectations serve as a poor guide to the old empire; its reality must be painted on a wider canvas. Only a turn to world history can open a reservoir of experiences and parallels of a scale vast enough to provide a match for ancient Rome.

This is what this book aims to do; it seeks to recontextualize Rome and identify a set of world-historical contexts which illuminate the ancient experience of empire. Europeans, after all, were not the only ones to reflect their experience in ancient Rome. The Ottomans, for instance, made no secret of their claim to succession from Rome. After its conquest in 1453, they deliberately chose Constantinople, the new Rome on the Bosporus, as their seat of empire. Hagia Sophia, built under Justinian as the flagship of imperial Roman Christianity, became the model for the grand mosques of Ottoman Istanbul.⁶ Once, when I had to give a talk about the idea for this book, I provided an image of the Blue Mosque for a poster that my host wanted to produce to advertise the event. Probably in a hurry and just skimming the image from a small email attachment, he expressed his delight in the fact that I had chosen 'Hagia Sophia' (Fig. 1.2). The mistake is, at least, suggestive and may be taken as a good omen for this project. Reaching in similar fashion across three continents, the Ottomans open a window to a world of Afro-Eurasian state and empire formation that represents a set of parallel, traditionally neglected but all the more illuminating experiences and contexts for Roman history.

---

⁵ Byron, *Childe Harold's Pilgrimage*, canto IV, xlvi, line 414.
⁶ On Ottoman symbolical claims to Roman imperial status, see Necipoğlu 1989 and 2005: 80–103 and 139–143; Kafadar 2007; Kolodziejczyk 2012 and Casale forthcoming. Sinan, the Ottoman master architect, claimed in his writings that in the Süleymaniye he had surpassed the dome of the Hagia Sophia (Akin & Crane 2006: 89, sections 54–58).

6 1 Rome and Pre-colonial World History

Figure 1.2 The Roman imperial mosques of Constantinople/Istanbul.
a. The Blue Mosque built between 1609 and 1617, during the reign of Ahmed I, on a location facing Hagia Sophia. Photo: Ebba Koch.
b. Hagia Sophia, the grand cathedral of Justinian the Great, converted to a mosque after the Ottoman conquest of Constantinople in 1453. Photo: Getty Images.

1.2 The Challenge of the New World History

Over the last generation, world history has been one of the most dynamic fields within the wider discipline. A spate of new works has emerged to question the shape of world history, tracing global connections and intensively debating what global and world history could mean.[7] Yet the response to this vibrant development from most classicists has been hesitant. 'Global history is a difficult topic', remarked Hartmut Leppin, perhaps sometimes even perceived as an existential threat.[8] Formerly, the study of the Greeks and Romans had nestled comfortably within the reigning narrative that used to structure knowledge in Western academic institutions. When charted on a map, world history took the shape of what might be labelled as the progressive crescent. After early beginnings in the ancient Near East, the story moved west into the Mediterranean with the rise of Greece and Rome, then curved up into France during the Middle Ages before Britain finally received the baton of progress to create the modern world. Only at this point did history begin to include the rest of the planet as it fell subject to European colonialism. World history, in short, had quickly left Asia and Africa behind to progress through stages of European development and eventual global domination. Ancient slavery, medieval feudalism, modern capitalism with its industry and colonies – these were the steps that to the nineteenth-century founders of the modern academic study of society summed up the course of historical evolution, and it belonged firmly in Europe. The rest of the world was perceived as stagnant and inert, outside the current of history. Marx thus devised the catch-all category of an Asiatic mode of production within which the societies without history could be grouped. Sumner Maine, the comparative legal sociologist, placed an ahistorical India, governed by caste and unchanging tradition, in opposition to the West where the development of Roman law had enabled rationality and contract to free society from the stifling dictates of hierarchy and status.[9]

To a modern observer, it is obvious that this nineteenth-century narrative was a self-deceptive product of the illusions created by the age of high colonialism in which Europeans, for a very brief period, seemed able to dictate events across the planet. But if this is so, the credit is in no small part

---

[7] Conrad 2016 for an overview.   [8] Leppin 2017.
[9] Maine 1861; Marx 1859, preface, and further 1964: 83 (in the stages of historical development, the Asiatic was the earliest but also the most resistant to change). Behind Marx, of course, was Hegel (e.g., 2020 [1830/31]: 1165, 1216, 1230–1238 and 1286, especially). See Chakrabarty & Saussy 2018: 310–315 for a brief recapitulation of the critique of this type of thinking.

due to the critical work of Edward Said and his *Orientalism*. In this postcolonial classic, Said led a frontal attack on the notion of the static Orient. When Western students of Oriental societies focused on ancient texts, as if they held the key to the secret of a supposedly never-changing Middle Eastern, Indian or Chinese society, they helped forge the colonial order. Their activities created a regime of knowledge which silenced the colonial populations and served to keep them in subjection. It was the scholars staffing the Oriental faculties of Western universities who had acquired the power to define the character of the societies they were studying. The people living there were left only to express themselves in the language provided by their rulers. The solution was obvious. The Orientalist institution had to be torn down, to enable the various peoples under Western hegemony to begin to speak for themselves, developing their own story instead of having it told for them.[10]

Here was a programme of liberation that passionately spoke to the conflicts, concerns and priorities of an era shaped by the dismantling of colonial empires. Decolonization had seen the emergence of a vast number of nations. Over a few decades the membership of the UN had risen from the original 51 founders in 1945 to 151 in 1978.[11] These new nations now had to find their voice and have it heard. Still, simply to leave people to tell their own story can only be half the solution, albeit a welcome and necessary one. No other continent than Europe constitutes a better warning against letting history be told solely through the eyes of one nation or ethnic group. This is a certain recipe for emphasizing the things which divide us, even elevating prejudice and bigotry to a position of truth. No one today needs to learn that we are connected across states and nations. The planet has just seen a great lockdown caused by a lethal virus spreading between societies. History has to address this dimension of human existence, too: exploring what connects us, explaining what societies have in common and seeing how they interact. How else can we understand the world which is ours? We need that kind of comparative knowledge.

Said, however, identified a significant risk in comparison and dismissed the comparative project merely as a tool of subjection, tending to narrow rather than open perspectives.[12] Too often Western thinkers had held other societies to the arbitrary standards of their own lifeworld and then found them wanting. European societies unsurprisingly in these analyses turned

---

[10] Said 1978. For a critique, see MacKenzie 1995 and Hall 2010: 364–365.
[11] See www.un.org/en/about-us/growth-in-un-membership.
[12] Said 1978: 77–79 ('codifying, tabulating, comparing'; 'to rule and to learn, then to compare the Orient').

out to be best at being, well, European. But such unreflexive Eurocentrism was not invariably and necessarily the outcome of comparison. In combatting the stereotype of the Orient as outside history and open to domination, Said perhaps substituted another – that of an omnipotent, all-encompassing and uniform Western discourse. The polarizing and uncompromising logic of the anti-colonial struggle tended to, so to speak, wipe out nuance and vastly exaggerate the power of the colonial system, the all-important enemy and overwhelmingly significant other. Yet, however much it may have been able to influence the terms of the debate, the colonial discourse never reached the position of the hegemonic and coherent monolith portrayed in Said's *Orientalism*, capable of silencing the other. Quickly, divergent and subaltern voices rose whose messages began to resonate forcefully across colonial empires – think of Gandhi and a whole string of revolutionary critics of Western power.[13]

Scholarship on the Orient did not merely confirm the Eurocentric world-view, but also pushed against its boundaries, confronting it with phenomena and truths unfamiliar to the Western public. This may be illustrated by a glance at Martin Bernal's *Black Athena*. The meaty volume forcefully brought Said's agenda into the field of ancient and classical studies with a simple and clear-cut thesis: nineteenth-century European beliefs in their own exceptionalism had excluded ancient Egypt and to some extent Mesopotamia, the Orient and Africa, in short, from the prevailing narrative about the development of ancient civilization. The freedom-loving Greeks, on the other hand, were celebrated as the originators of Europe, the West and rational civilization. This stood in stark contrast to the eighteenth century, when Europeans had generally revered Egypt as a source of ancient wisdom, as in Mozart's freemasonic opera *The Magic Flute*, and thus had been able to acknowledge the achievements of the South and the East.[14]

Nonetheless, there is something strangely distorted about this assessment. Even as the Europeans grew increasingly (over)confident of their cultural leadership and its age-old Hellenic roots during the era of relentless colonial expansion over the nineteenth and early twentieth century, their previous certainties were constantly undermined. The story of scholarship narrated on the pages of Bernal's book is also one of discovery and

---

[13] See Ballantyne & Burton 2012, introduction, for a programmatic statement of this point. See Cooper 2005, especially the introduction, for the tendency of postcolonial critique to 'flatten' European history into an omnipotent and all-encompassing stereotype. The limitations of power must also be understood; see Cooper's chapter 6. Further, see Taiwo 2022 and Thomas 1994.

[14] Bernal 1987, whose critique was prefigured by Said 1978: 86–87.

broadening horizons. For the first time in perhaps a millennium and a half, the secrets of the ancient Egyptian hieroglyphs and the Mesopotamian cuneiform script were unlocked. Voices, long since silenced, came to life again and described a hitherto unknown, fascinating past cultural universe teeming with stories of gods and priests, kings and queens, the meaning of life and the cultural background to the Old Testament. The Parthenon marbles or the Pergamon Altar, these glories of Hellenic culture, may have been the prize possessions of the collections of the British and Berlin Museums. Even so, following hot on their heels were the Assyrian palace reliefs, the Babylonian Ishtar Gate or the extensive displays of majestic Egyptian sculpture and mummies.[15] However, these treasured exhibits were only the tip of a much bigger iceberg.

In India, for instance, archaeology discovered the long-lost Harappa Bronze Age civilization along the Indus. By then epigraphers had already been able to date and trace the contours of the third-century BCE Mauryan Empire of Chandragupta and Ashoka. In the Americas, nineteenth- to twentieth-century Mayan archaeology uncovered a world of forgotten cities under the lush vegetation of the Mexican jungle. Within my own lifetime, the decipherment of their hieroglyphics has added written Mayan to the list of lost languages recovered from antiquity. Examples could easily be multiplied, but here we end with the early twentieth-century expeditions to the Tarim Basin that founded what is popularly known as Silk Road studies. Hidden in caves or under the sand dunes of the desert, texts and art works came to light that revealed a late antique social universe of Buddhists, Manicheans and Nestorian Christians unexpectedly rubbing shoulders in Central Asia. In short, the excavated stories and objects not only of Near Eastern but of world antiquity dramatically expanded and changed the (Western) view of the most ancient periods of human society. Vague myths and dim rumours gave way to certified chronologies and informed history.[16]

As the ancient past began to take on firmer global contours, the established trajectory of Western progression began to look increasingly inadequate.[17] It may be coincidental, but the most prominent attempts to tackle this issue were made by two luminaries who were originally trained as ancient historians. But if this was a coincidence, it is unfortunately symptomatic that both

---

[15] MacGregor 2021, especially 33–47, on the hierarchy of antiquities in the great museum collections.
[16] Jasanof 2005 (a portrait of French and British collection and exploration); Larsen 1996 (on the excavation of Assyrian antiquity); Ray 2007 (on the history of South Asian archaeology); Trigger 2006: 160, 177 and 503 and Bernal 1980 (on Mayan archaeology). Hansen 2012 interweaves a fascinating account of the exploratory journeys in her history of the Silk Road.
[17] Toynbee 1962–1964 [1934–1961], Vol. I: 165.

1.2 The Challenge of the New World History

have led a marginal existence inside our discipline. Both Arnold Toynbee (1889–1975) and Max Weber (1864–1920) have primarily become household names of world history and sociology, respectively. In response to the expanding panorama of world history, they developed a version that saw the course of history as consisting of the rise and decline of a long series of separate civilizations. In his multivolume *A Study of History*, Toynbee identified and analyzed the life cycle of no fewer than twenty-one civilizations. A towering figure in his own time, Toynbee is now little read and even less cited. His version of civilizational history, in spite of its novelty, remained anchored in nineteenth-century ideas. Each civilization was conceived as an autonomous organism, constituted the all-encompassing framework for the people living inside its area and followed more or less its own internal development as it went through its youthful, mature and old ages.[18] Instead of causal explanations, his pages are teaming with metaphors, verging almost on metaphysics.[19]

Max Weber, on the other hand, is anything but forgotten. His work remains a strong influence on modern social science. Most significantly he attempted to analytically establish culture as a force in societal development. Capitalism, for instance, was not merely a product of material circumstances but shaped up to become a world-transforming force only when it was combined with Puritan Protestantism during the sixteenth and seventeenth centuries in the Netherlands and Britain. Irrationally, the Puritan faith had shackled its worldly practitioners to a life of work without consumption. Profits were not to be enjoyed, only to be ploughed back into new business investment. Religious belief had come to sanctify the goal of capitalism: to use money to make more money. Money had ceased to be a means to an end but become the goal itself. If capitalism, therefore, was a rational activity, it was so only in a narrowly defined economic sense.

For the same reason, Western civilization could not be described, as it had by many, as simply rational in contrast to the other civilizations. In a vast comparative exercise studying religion in China, India and Judaism, Weber emphasized that the other world religions, the backbone of the other civilizations, were no less rational than modern European, Christian civilization. There was no absolute divide, and Weber's historical sociology is packed with comparisons based on the observation of fundamental

---

[18] Toynbee 1962–1964, Vol. 1: 147–181.
[19] For example, Toynbee 1962–1964, Vol. 1: 203–204 (yin and yang as an alternating rhythm of all civilizations, their developmental music) or p. 135 (a civilization as a tree with dying roots and eventually a dead trunk). In this scheme, the 'half millennium' of Roman Mediterranean hegemony is reduced to a dying phase when the creative impulse of Hellenic civilization is snuffed out.

societal similarities between the great agrarian civilizations of Afro-Eurasia. Nevertheless, the fundamental question to Weber remained that of modernity. Ultimately his comparisons end up stressing a number of specific features that had enabled the Western Europe of his own time to develop what he saw as rational industrial capitalism. The other great societies had lacked these few specific features, but they had developed forms of rational thought and organization along different lines.[20]

Even as Weber's work in some respects represented a challenge to the hegemonic understanding of world history as tracing an arc of Western progress, it thus still ended up reinforcing the established narrative. Written over the first two decades of the twentieth century, it probably was as far as one could push our mental horizon. European and Western predominance, after all, was a well-established fact that no one could ignore at the time. By the 1970s and 1980s, however, the nineteenth-century edifice that had held the various elements in the traditional world-historical narrative together was crumbling. Two world wars, followed by two decades of rapid decolonization, had swept away the world of European colonialism and global hegemony. Not only had empire become illegitimate; Europe had also ceased to be the obvious centre of the world. Often Eurocentrism is denounced as a moral failing. But the issue goes far beyond the question of good or bad. It has simply become increasingly difficult to make sense of world events through a conception of history that sees Europe as the centre of the planet and the end of evolution. As new nations launched their own programmes of development, it quickly turned out that the European experience of modernization could not automatically be taken as paradigmatic for others. Their development took a different path. It was, in the programmatic statement of Dipesh Chakrabarty, time to 'provincialise' the European model and treat it as just one among several referential poles. The purpose, in other words, was not to throw away the forms of scholarship pursued at the modern university but to reform and build better intellectual frameworks that were more inclusive. Not only history but all the fundamental theories of social science had to be revised.[21]

Enter the so-called school of historical sociology. In the 1980s a spate of path-breaking works set about re-examining the European historical experience which had served as the template for most macro-theories of social development. Three books, all hailing from the same research seminar at the

---

[20] Weber 1920–1921: the tension between cultural relativism and focus on explaining Western modernity is clear in the preface, Vol. 1, 11–12 (Vorbemerkung); 253–254, 258–259, 265–267. See further Salvatore 2021: 173 on the ambiguous Eurocentrism of Weberian civilizational analysis.
[21] Chakrabarty 2000; Chakrabarty & Saussy 2018.

1.2 The Challenge of the New World History 13

London School of Economics and written by Michael Mann, John Hall and Ernest Gellner, have become classics of macro-historical enquiry. In the *Sources of Social Power*, Mann embarked on a journey, spanning three decades and four volumes, to supplant both Marxist and Weberian social theory. The course of human history ought not be explained by any single fundamental cause, whether economy or culture. It was the result of an interplay of several forces: political, ideological, military and economic. What decided the progressive development of human societies was the ability to combine elements of each into institutional bundles that increased the organizational capacity of collectives.

While Mann's multivariate sociology was path-breaking and quite an eye-opener on ancient societies, his history stayed close to the dated trajectory of the progressive crescent. Empire, for instance, falls out of the narrative after the fall of Rome, only to reappear during the age of European colonialism, more than a millennium later.[22] Here his comrade in arms, John Hall, was more adventurous. His analysis of the evolution of societal power was still dominated by the rise of Europe, but his re-interrogation of the European experience took place on a background of comparative analyses of Islam, India and China. Yet each of these other great societies of the pre-industrial world were still – as a relic of the nineteenth century and Weber – treated as separate civilizations and by implication as standing outside the mainstream of history.[23] Gellner, finally, in *Plough, Sword and Book*, cut through these cultural distinctions to provide a brief sociological sketch of pre-industrial life, treating the various civilizations interchangeably as expressions of the same fundamental condition.[24]

This trinity of works quickly received company. For our purposes, most important perhaps were the contributions by historian of Islam Patricia Crone and historian of the Byzantine Empire John Haldon. Both of them added greater depth to the portrait of pre-industrial societies in books of their own. Taken together, the efforts of the historical sociologists had managed to produce a more inclusive image of the pre-industrial and pre-colonial past.[25] Still, their analyses offered mostly static portraits and left open the question posed at the time by anthropologist Eric Wolf about *Europe and the People without History*. Comparative sociology had to be complemented by a turn to world history to forge a new narrative framework instead of the old.[26]

---

[22] Mann 1986: 526 locates Rome as the last empire of significance to his story of power, before picking up the theme again with colonialism in Mann 2012, chapter 2.
[23] Hall 1985.   [24] Gellner 1988.   [25] Crone 1989; Haldon 1993.   [26] Wolf 1982.

Working both in parallel and in dialogue with the historical sociologists has been a steadily rising number of historians trying to cultivate world history as a field. An early trailblazer was William McNeill's *Plagues and Peoples* from 1976. His fascinating discussion sketched a shared Afro-Eurasian historical framework for the last 5,000 years, shaped around the dynamic balance that existed between dense agricultural human societies and their epidemic crowd diseases.[27] A decade later this was followed by Crosby's *Ecological Imperialism* and another decade on by Jared Diamond's *Guns, Germs and Steel*. The latter two shifted emphasis in the ecological enquiry to the question of why Europe had in the end been able to rise to global predominance and settle large tracts of the planet with colonists. They found the answer in the pool of germs, plants and domesticated animals that cohabited with human populations across Afro-Eurasia. When brought by Europeans to the Americas and Oceania, this so-called *portmanteau biota* represented a deadly combination to the unaccustomed Indigenous populations, which prior to contact had both fewer diseases and domesticated animals. It was these biological agents beyond the conscious control of the Europeans that had paved the way for their success, not primarily their 'superior' form of culture and organization.[28]

But when the question is about Europe's rise to world hegemony, no other book has been more influential over the last generation than Kenneth Pomeranz's *The Great Divergence*. This instant classic of global history undertook a sustained comparison of the economies of early-modern Europe and late imperial China. The result was a forceful attack on any lingering notions of inherent advantages of European societies in economic and social organization. Not until industrialization gained momentum at the end of the eighteenth century was it possible to detect a decisive gap between China and the West. Nothing in the centuries before had suggested that Europe was on a significantly different path of development. Whether one looked to market formation or the organization of production, European leadership was anything but obvious. China could normally match the economic level of the Euro-Atlantic world. Its eventual industrialization was a product of the fortuitous location of coal in proximity to the economic leading zones and the windfall gain of the Americas – in short, sheer luck.[29]

Stated like this, the thesis was perhaps pushed to the extreme. The foundation for Pomeranz's view had already been laid by Mark Elvin in

[27] McNeill 1976. [28] Crosby 1986; Diamond 1997. [29] Pomeranz 2000.

his wonderful and imaginative *Pattern of the Chinese Past* and extended by Bin Wong in the eye-opening *China Transformed*. Both these took off from the contemporary observations of Adam Smith that eighteenth-century China had possessed a well-developed commercial economy. Still, as both noted, China was not on the brink of a breakthrough to modern conditions but rather developed into the most elaborate and successful version of a stable agrarian empire in history.³⁰ In comparison, European societies went through a series of three violent and chaotic rolling revolutions in state-building and military mobilization, in science, and in world trade from around 1500. Slowly these dynamics began to reinforce each other, but it took time before the effects grew strong enough radically to upend things. When European sailors began to circle the planet around 1500, they were unable to challenge the big monarchies of Asia but had to make do with setting up shop along the margins of the Indian Ocean world. After 1750, the balance of power had begun to tilt visibly in the favour of European state-making and commercial elites. Over the following century the rulers of India, the Ottoman Empire and even the mighty Qing dynasty found themselves reeling under the relentless pressure of European commercial and territorial expansion.³¹ But where precisely one identifies the tipping point in the prior 250 years is a matter of the 'small print'. Early or late, from a world history perspective, this was a short period of time and the conclusion is clear: the European rise to global hegemony during the long nineteenth century was caused by a series of relatively late developments. That is the decisive insight to come out of the Pomeranz debate, and it has been the final nail in the coffin of the Eurocentric nineteenth-century version of world history.

But what to put in its place? Before Europe, then, one would have to think of world history differently. As V. S. Naipaul reminds us in the epigraph to this chapter, one could for instance locate the Islamic world at the centre of a pre-colonial history. Even more than Islam, the historical experience of China has come to be seen as an alternative point of reference and made to serve as a central site for efforts to rethink the shape of world history and construct a more inclusive story.³² By the time Francis Fukuyama, twenty-five years after Michael Mann, revisited the problem

---

³⁰ Bin Wong 1997; Elvin 1973.
³¹ Rieber 2014, especially chapters 3 and 5; Darwin 2007; Bayly 2004.
³² Chaudhuri 1990 for an attempt to rethink the shape of Asian history before the rise of Europe; Hodgson 1993, chapter 7, on 'the role of Islam in world history'; Bin Wong 1997 for an attempt to establish China as a comparative standard equal to Europe. Pollock & Elman 2018 bypass Europe and compare historical China and India with each other.

of social power and political order, a fundamental reorientation had taken place. Ancient China had been substituted for Greco-Roman antiquity in the narrative. With the collapse of the story of the long Western progression towards modernity, there was no preordained role for either Greeks or Romans in world history.[33] Nothing, or at most precious little, in Greco-Roman history was necessary to explain the birth of modernity, as Walter Scheidel concluded in his recent discussion.[34] This view is an obvious challenge to the field of classics and ancient history to which we must find an answer, and to do so, we must engage more intensively with the newly developing discourse on world history.[35]

1.3 Towards a New Ancient World History – and a Place for Rome

The new world history, however, is still just in the making. During a recent workshop, a Chinese colleague remarked in discussion that, to him, writing China into world history meant aligning the history of the middle kingdom to the categories of European history. This was a purely pragmatic stance, and as historian of the Qing dynasty Pamela Crossley has shown in her *Hammer and Anvil*, it is possible to get quite far with such an approach.[36] If the differences were generally small within the pre-colonial world, what is there to prevent us from extending the well-established European chronologies to embrace the rest of Afro-Eurasia? So we have seen a global early modernity, a global middle ages, perhaps even a global late antiquity, but so far few attempts to argue for a global classical age.[37] Within this framework, a strong trend has emerged to write so-called connected histories. Under the leadership of Sanjay Subrahmanyam, this group of historians reject comparison and have instead set out in the pursuit of global connections. Their stories seek to identify liminal persons that crossed civilizational boundaries and may be presented as precursors of the cultural mixture and connectivity of modern borderless globalization.[38] Inspired by the same impulse to celebrate the global ties of cultures, the notional construct of the Silk Road has received a new lease of life. Coined during the age of high imperialism by the German

---

[33] Fukuyama 2011.
[34] Scheidel 2019, in contrast to the more traditional position of Beard 2015: 15.
[35] Quinn 2024: introduction, for some further reflections on the need for a new narrative.
[36] Crossley 2019.
[37] Porter 2012 and Subrahmanyam 1998 (global early modernity); Homes & Standen 2018 and Morton & Skottki's new Routledge series 'Global Histories before Globalization' (global middle ages); Di Cosmo & Maas 2019 (global late antiquity).
[38] Subrahmanyam 1997 and 2022; Sachsenmaier 2018; Hunt 2014; Davis 2006.

geographer Ferdinand von Richthofen, fuelled by its sense of adventure and romance and vigorously promoted by China, the Silk Road attracts attention as never before. To an upbeat Peter Frankopan, it simply holds the keys to a new global history.[39] For others, it has served as a flag under which to study an ancient and medieval form of globalization built around the long-distance trade in exotic spices and rich silken fabrics running across both Central Asia and the Indian Ocean.[40] Still others have pursued the agenda of connection by looking for globalizing processes in various geographical macro-regions before the rise of Europe. The ancient Mediterranean, for instance, is then treated as showing a geographically more constricted form of globalization than the modern, culminating in the Rome Empire.[41]

But these attempts to generate a history of global reach by expanding the European experience, whether in terms of chronology or the connectivity of globalization, can only be a first step. The global drive to modernise and the pressure to conform to standards set by the most successful Euro-Atlantic powers was an outgrowth of industrialization and colonial empire building. This was one of the key insights identified by C. A. Bayly in *The Birth of the Modern World*, a path-breaking and foundational work on the global history of the nineteenth century.[42] By writing pre-colonial history on the chronological template of European history and its competitive pressures of globalization, we inadvertently extend the moment of European global hegemony back before it was achieved. If the world was ever made to march to a tune set in Europe, it was only for a brief moment. Before the age of forced convergence, the world moved to a different rhythm. To identify that rhythm is one of the most central tasks confronting the new global history at the moment, and it means transcending the ready-to-hand frameworks based on the extension of Europe.[43] Histories of global connection must be better contextualized by comparison. The problem of Roman imperial history and the problem of world history, in other words, turn out to be the same: both must be taken out of the European mould.

However, in the absence of a clear hegemonic centre, as Hervé Inglebert recently noted, there is no unifying principle immediately

---

[39] Frankopan 2015; Benjamin 2018 also organizes his history of ancient Eurasia around the Silk Road.
[40] For example, Lughod 1989; Whitfield 2018; Evers 2018; Jarzombek 2024.
[41] Hodos 2017; Pitts 2018; Pitts & Versluys 2015; Hodos 2020. Hingley 2005 and Horden & Purcell 2000 pioneered the approach.
[42] Bayly 2004.
[43] See also Berend 2023 (the need to generate concepts more attuned to the historical processes of the pre-industrial world; the global middle ages is paradoxically Eurocentric) and McKeown 2012 (connected history depends on an implicit comparison between the categories of Europe and Asia, that it was supposed to transcend).

available for pre-colonial world history. All that might seem possible is the pursuit of area studies, much as in the time of Toynbee, one culture or civilization at a time.[44] To be sure, in several recent world histories, the area-studies principle tends undeniably to crowd out attempts at synthesis, the further you go back in history.[45] But atomistic fragmentation is not the only alternative to a Eurocentric world history. Cultures are not self-reliant, autonomous wholes; they constantly borrow and adapt from each other. This is not a feature which emerged only with modern globalization. If premodern civilizations have sometimes seemed closed onto themselves, it is because of the way we study them. For very understandable reasons, language-learning assumes primacy, and later specialization tends to reinforce a focus on a restricted body of texts or a specific site or locality. How else could we pretend to unlock the secrets of a long gone past, if we do not apply ourselves arduously to study their often arcane languages and artistic idioms? Deep immersive learning has many strengths, but it also comes with weaknesses and blind angles of its own.

One of these is synthesis. No one can learn all the languages, after all. Most Roman historians do not even master all the written languages of the empire but make do with Latin and Greek – neither of which was used by a majority of the population – and normally feel most confident by sticking to one region or province. This means that the question about how Rome relates to other historical societies is rarely even posed. Still, language is not an absolute barrier and should not be allowed to function as a mental prison. Intercultural communication is clearly possible, as students of cosmopolitanism reminds us. After all, much in the world is 'utterly humanly familiar'. This pragmatic observation belongs to Kwame Appiah, who continues, 'once someone has translated the language you don't know … you will have no more (and, of course, no less) trouble understanding' than the things more seemingly familiar to you.[46] Marriage, kingship, religious cult, warfare – the list could be extended ad infinitum – are all institutions and forms of activity that are found in most societies. Some of their features will be specific to the particular society in which they are studied, but much is also shared across cultural boundaries, and for many aspects of past life, it is not even evident that language opens a particularly privileged path to understanding.

Historical demography and epidemiology would be one obvious case.[47] Another example would be the share of their produce that peasants have

---

[44] Inglebert 2018.   [45] Gehrke 2020; Benjamin 2015.   [46] Appiah 2006: 94; Fraenkel 2015.
[47] The implication, for instance, of Hopkins 2018, chapters 3–4 (two studies of the lacunose evidence from graveyards in the Roman Empire and what they could tell us about the demographic composition of the imperial population).

commonly had to hand over to landlords, city dwellers and rulers. Here knowledge of the constraints of agricultural production, practices of land surveying and the (military) power of lords to be gleaned from parallel historical experiences may well tell us more than fine-grained conceptual analysis of very fragmentary primary, documentary sources. The sceptic will object that the handling of such 'secondary' material will inevitably lead to misunderstandings, crude assessments and loss of nuance. But that is missing the point. Salman Rushdie once famously quipped that 'it is normally supposed that something always gets lost in translation; I cling, obstinately, to the notion that something can also be gained'.[48] The thing we gain is access to a wider experience, a better understanding of commonalities and the very capacity to identify shared developments, fundamental processes and broader trends. Much, therefore, speaks in favour of pragmatism. It is not a question of either/or. World history can alternate, as I will try to demonstrate in this book, between immersive study and the broader perspective obtainable only by engaging the work of colleagues in neighbouring fields and using them as our informants and translators.

In fact, we already tacitly acknowledge the necessity of such work, but then it goes under the label of theory. Classicists and ancient historians constantly draw on theory to illuminate the Greeks and Romans.[49] Yet the general insights of current theory come with one major drawback. Most theory has been developed to explain modern industrialized or even post-industrial conditions. For a time, anthropology seemed to offer an alternative. Fanning out from Western university departments at the turn of the nineteenth century, the practitioners of the discipline sought out pockets of human society as yet untouched by the forces of modernization. Most of the communities selected by anthropologists as their object were small-scale and commonly non-state. However, as such pockets have thinned out, anthropology has increasingly, as a voice of anti-modernity, turned to studying communities that have become marginalized in or fallen victim to the processes of modern development. Whichever way, the current use of theory reflects precisely the 'lack of a tenable framework of world history'.[50] Either you have to align the ancient experience to the modern as much as possible or you adopt models from much

---

[48] Rushdie 1982. For a discussion, see Majeed 2021, especially p. 360 (dealing with *shame*, where an almost identical phrase is uttered by one of the characters in the novel).
[49] For example, Bianchi, Brill & Holmes 2019; Vasunia, Blanshard, Leonard, et al. 2020.
[50] Hodgson 1974, Vol. 1: 31.

simpler pre-state societies. What has been missing is theory tailored to the explanatory needs of larger, pre-industrial societies that saw the formation of cities, states and empires.[51]

This gap was separately identified, at a remarkable intellectual conjuncture in the late 1960s and early 1970s, by Moses Finley and Marshall Hodgson. One a towering figure in the study of the Greco-Roman world, the other of premodern Islam, both pioneered reflection on the place of their pre-industrial culture in the context of world history. To overcome the limitations of theory, what was needed, they concluded, was more comparative study, not of the cultural essences of civilizations, placing one block against the other, but of specific institutions and concrete processes of complex, cited and literate, agrarian societies.[52] Here then is a challenge left to us to step out of our comfort zone and open the lines of communication to other neighbouring disciplines studying pre-industrial societies and cultures. There should be little to make us hesitate. If we are generally comfortable spanning the enormous gap between industrial and pre-industrial conditions in our use of theory, then we should also be able to tolerate generalization across societies that on all parameters are much closer to each other. Whether we look to the economic foundations, forms of technology, modes of communication, social organization and cultural manifestations, the differences among these societies are bound to have been much smaller than what separates life in our modern global village from all of them together.

To find common ground, however, experiment is necessary.[53] Different geographical and thematic contexts will have to be explored. Afro-Eurasia, the pre-colonial Americas, what backdrops of world history are most suitable – that is the question. Inspired by the efforts of the historical sociologists, a small body of work has sprouted in ancient history over the last generation to confront the unfamiliar in a search for commonalities and shared foundations between the Greco-Roman and other pre-industrial societies. Differences are here treated as less absolute but as belonging to a repertoire of potential responses

---

[51] Van Oyen 2020, for instance, is a brilliant study of the significance of household organization at all levels of the Roman economy, from province to capital, drawing on the currently fashionable actor-network theory of anthropologist Bruno Latour. But when the theory outlaws the use of concepts such as empire and hierarchy, it becomes as much a straitjacket as an enabling perspective.
[52] Hodgson 1974, Vol. 1: 31–45; Finley 1975: 118–119.
[53] Seland 2022 and Naerebout & Singor 2014 are two recent textbooks that each in their own way open the quest.

1.3 Towards a New Ancient World History

to broadly similar conditions. Finley opened the quest by focusing on Greco-Roman slavery. It is now well-established to include comparison, both with the plantation economies of the Caribbean and the ancient Near East and with other historical societies even further afield.[54]

Comparative work has also been done on the city-state. Mogens Hansen, for instance, embedded his examination of the Greek polis in a wider context of more than thirty historically attested city-state cultures.[55] Kurt Raaflaub, with shifting collaborators, embarked on a broad-spectred project to generate comparative histories for the ancient world.[56] So far, however, the formation of empires has proven by far the most fertile field spawning comparisons and interdisciplinary conversation. Archaeologists of the Precolumbian Americas and South Asia have teamed up with classicists to probe the various dimensions of imperial rule. A large European research network embarked on a project to bring historians together to examine parallels among the Romans, the Ottomans, the Mughals and other similar empires.[57] No doubt reinforced by the current great power rivalry of the US and China, attempts to match the imperial experience of ancient China and Rome have grown into a sub-trend of its own.[58]

If the current quest for comparison has successfully broadened horizons and the reach of the historical imagination, the effort has still primarily been an exercise in historical sociology: comparison of cases perceived as typologically similar but treated as separate.[59] A unified alternative historical framework has yet fully to be fleshed out. Ian Morris, for instance, in *Why the West Rules for Now*, still makes do with depicting history as a millennia-long race along a progressing Western frontier towards modernity, significantly interrupted by a long medieval interlude with China in the lead, as a concession to the revisionist historiography.[60] Meanwhile, the attempt of Sitta von Reden and her group to push beyond the Silk Roads carves out an

---

[54] Finley 1980; Katsari & Del Lago 2008; Bradley & Cartledge 2011; Lenski & Cameron 2018.
[55] Hansen 2000 & 2002.
[56] Published in the series *The Ancient World: Comparative Histories*. Some examples include Konstan & Raaflaub 2009; Arnason & Raaflaub 2011; Alcock, Bodel & Talbert 2012.
[57] Alcock, Altroy, Morrison et al. 2001; Bang & Bayly 2003; Morris & Scheidel 2009; Bang & Bayly 2011; Bang & Kolodciejczyk 2012; Duindam, Artan & Kunt 2011.
[58] Mutschler & Mittag 2008; Scheidel 2009 and 2015; Auyang 2014; Beck & Vankeerberghen 2021. A subgenre looks at philosophy, science and literary culture in ancient China and the Greco-Roman world; see Lloyd 1996; Lloyd & Sivin 2002; Sim 2007; Beecroft 2010; Lloyd & Zhao 2018.
[59] Yoffee 2015 on early cities is a good example. [60] Morris 2010.

Afro-Eurasian framework for our study of the ancient economy.[61] Out of the experiments in recontextualization, therefore, the contours of a new geographical framework and temporality are slowly becoming discernible. A unifying history may, after all, be within reach that can place the comparative examples within a shared development. But which exactly?

One of the great strengths of the pursuit of world history is its capacity to play with chronologies. Inspired by biology and geological time, big history has for instance begun to ask us to situate human society within the wider and deeper history of our planet and solar system. But for most purposes this is going too big, after all. Measured against the timescale of natural history, the human experience is but a quick flash, a day or two in the life of our planet.[62] Most societal development will be invisible from such a distant vantage point. While a scheme tailored solely to European history may be too detailed to extend across the pre-colonial world, big history is not fine-grained enough. Something in between is needed, a macro-perspective that may be able to discern some broad trends across Afro-Eurasia and the Americas before the rise of colonialism.

A survey of West Eurasian state formation from its beginnings in the early Bronze Age till the formation of the Muslim empire some three-and-a-half millennia later may point us in the right direction.[63] Whether one looks to Assur or Carthage, the pharaohs or the caliphs, it reveals a political universe of remarkably recurrent patterns. The portraits produced by historians of the many separate, individual polities that came and went over this long period of time sport surprisingly many fundamental parallels in spite of their differences. But out of this repetitive flow, two long-term trends appear that are barely perceptible on the basis of the study of each single city-state or monarchy. First, state power went through a slow but steady consolidation and amalgamation of individual polities into vast universal empires. Second, the world of state making saw an enormous expansion. Population numbers rose considerably and the extent of territory subject to state power increased several times in size. While the realm of the Egyptian pharaoh had represented the height of state power in the third millennium BCE,

---

[61] Von Reden, Dwivedi, Fabian et al. 2020, 2022 and 2023.
[62] Benjamin 2015, chapter 1, for an interesting attempt. Christian 2011 for the foundational text of big history.
[63] Bang & Scheidel 2013.

it had come to constitute but a single, if affluent, province of the Roman Empire by the first century CE.

However, this expansive pattern was in no way confined solely to the Middle East and Mediterranean; it can in fact be identified across Afro-Eurasia and traced beyond the accustomed chronological boundaries of antiquity. Listen to Abu Tauleb Hossaini:

> There are five lofty emperors whom because of their greatness people do not refer to by their names. The emperor of Hind, they call Dara, and the emperor of Rome [Rum], they hail as Kaisar, and the Emperor of Khuttun, and Chin, and Maucheen, they name Fughfoor, and the emperor of Turkestan they mention as Kaghan and they call the lord of Eran and Turan, king of kings.[64]

Penned in the Persian language by an intellectual at the court of the Great Mughals during the seventeenth century, these lines conjure a fascinating alternative vision of world history. The zone of Afro-Eurasian state making had continued to expand and is here laid out as an arena dominated by what we might loosely describe as a group of mighty imperial monarchies. The Mughals saw themselves as heirs of Teimur Lenk, the conqueror from Samarkand, and therefore ought as king of kings to govern both India and their central Asian ancestral homeland. Next to the Mughals we find the Fughfoor, the title used in Arabic to denote the Chinese emperor, and the Kaisar-i Rum, whichs although Roman in origin would have referred to the Ottoman sultan.

Here may well be the unifying world history framework called for by Finley, Hodgson and, in his own fashion, Inglebert. Hossaini's image of the world encompasses a wide geographical reach and also provides the key to give meaningful chronological shape to the history of complex agrarian society (see Fig. 1.3).[65] For lack of better alternatives, world historians sometimes speak of the Axial Age. Inspired by Hegel and his notion of the spirit of history, the German philosopher Karl Jaspers once proclaimed the centuries between 800 and 200 BCE, which saw thinkers such as Confucius, Buddha and Socrates, as a world historical breakthrough to a new stage of consciousness, an axis in the development of human society.[66] Yet it is not immediately obvious how the

---

[64] Davy & White 1783: 130 (my translation from the Persian, updating Davy's on p. 131), a passage contextualized by me in Bang, Bayly & Scheidel 2021, Vol. 2, introduction to Part VI and p. 721, in particular.
[65] See Syros 2012 for a short foray into the cross-fertilization of Indian, Persian, Islamic and Byzantine political theory.
[66] Arnason, Eisenstadt & Wittrock 2004; Jaspers 1949.

24   1 Rome and Pre-colonial World History

(a)
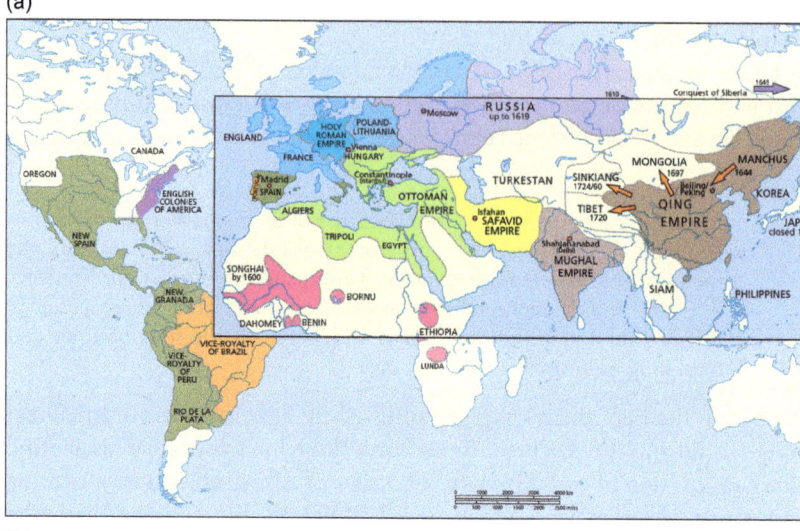

(b)
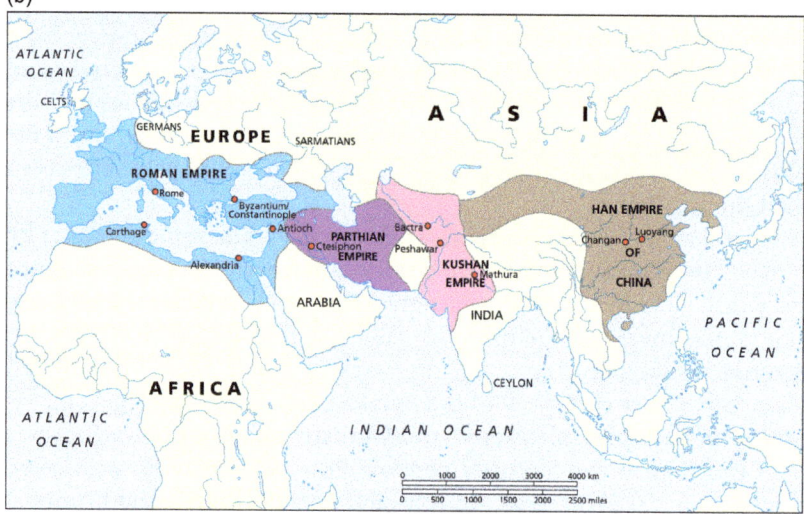

Figure 1.3 The Afro-Eurasian arena of universal empires.
a. The arena dominated by the Qing, the Mughal and the Ottoman Empires around 1700 CE.
b. The arena by the second century CE.
Source: Bang & Kolodziejczyk (2012) with grapphic modification by Wolfgang Filser.

message of Confucius in China to respect traditional hierarchies squares with the injunction of Socrates to his fellow citizens in Athens that they ceaselessly question established wisdom and customs. Whatever unity could be claimed on the basis of these thinkers is too elusive as a structuring principle for a world history. By contrast, Hossaini provides a far more concrete and materially tangible axis for a world history. The period identified by Jaspers as crucial was, more or less, the moment when grand empires begin to mushroom across the Afro-Eurasian landmass.[67]

Classical Greco-Roman antiquity finds its place within the epoch in world history where the foundations of what we might call the Afro-Eurasian arena of universal empires, sketched by Hossaini, were laid. Titles such as the Persian Shahanshah or the Roman Caesar became fixtures of state-craft in precisely this period. With the rise of the Achaemenid dynasty in the mid sixth century BCE, empire broke the bounds of the ancient Levant to reach deep into central Asia and push out towards the centre of the Mediterranean. Over the next few centuries this movement gathered force. Vast empires, with rulers who saw themselves as universal and standing above other lords, began for the first time to form in a band stretching across Afro-Eurasia, from China to the shores of the Atlantic. Why this was the case is a key question of global history, and it is one in which the Roman experience has a significant role to play. But it is also a history which the thinkers of the nineteenth century had ignored and deemed outside the main current of social evolution.[68]

Yet the complex of empires was far from the stagnant formation that they all envisaged it to be. To be sure, from one perspective one dynasty of conquerors might seem merely to replace the other. Still, under the endless succession of rulers, their societies continued slowly to grow in a glacially expanding drift and the texture of rule accumulated new layers. The Khagan, mentioned by Hossaini, was an addition to the 'club' that came at the very end of antiquity as the power of the central Asian steppe increased until it culminated in the vast and unmatched Mongol conquests of the thirteenth century CE. In antiquity, the distance was still too big between the main centres of power and the density of contacts too thin to foster a political horizon that could as

---

[67] Marshall Hodgson's 'pre-Axial', 'Axial' and 'Post Axial' here (1974, Vol. 1: 108–117).
[68] I join in this book the world historians (e.g., Bayly 2002) that use the term 'arena' to denote the historical complex of state-forming agrarian societies stretching across the Afro-Eurasian world.

a matter of course be projected across the length and breadth of the Afro-Eurasian world. A sole inscription commemorating a fledgling Kushan ruler in North India of the third century CE measures him against the Roman Caesar, the Persian king of kings, the rajas of India and just possibly one of the monarchs from the Chinese culture sphere (see Chapter 3). But that was a first. By the end of antiquity, the caliph would be able to imagine himself at the head of a procession of tributary Afro-Eurasian rulers.[69]

Even so, normally the great imperial dynasties matched their achievements against their closest regional rival(s). Most famous, perhaps, are the reliefs at Naqsh-e Rostam in modern Iran depicting the Sasanian king of kings rising in solitary glory over his defeated and prostrate Roman imperial opponents (See Fig. 3.1 further below). However, this is all that is needed. These regional rivalries serially linked up to form a loosely interconnected world of imperial rule and lordship stretching from the western to the eastern end of Afro-Eurasia and lasting from the onset of Achaemenid rule to the rise of European colonialism in the second half of the eighteenth century.[70] The following five chapters will explore how Rome may be seen to fit in and contribute to this story. We will embark on a journey that seeks to transcend the barriers to our neighbouring area studies in the hope of creating a sphere where we can meet in mutually beneficial dialogue.

Chapter 2 will look at state formation, ecology, peasantries and slavery; Chapter 3 examines the character of universal empires, while Chapter 4 will analyze the rise of cosmopolitan literary cultures and ecumenic religion and Chapter 5 tackles the character of intercontinental trade before the modern capitalism of European trading companies. Chapter 6 will then focus on the limits of this imperial order dominating the Afro-Eurasian world for centuries by studying the capacity of peasantries, enslaved people and populations on the margins to resist, subvert and possibly rebel against the sedentary masters. Finally, the conclusion will take stock of this experiment. What kind of world history has come out of this effort, how has Rome been recontextualized, what are the cracks in the story told here, what are the omissions and what are the alternatives? However we answer these questions, the following chapters will above all demonstrate the need to identify meaningful comparative contexts for

---

[69] Fowden 2004, chapter 7. There may be Sasanian precedents, but they are only vaguely attested in later Arab material, much more likely a reflection of their times than the pre-Islamic period.
[70] Bang and Kolodziejzcyk 2012.

our study of cultural connectivity. Each chapter will start with a surprising example of cultural exchange before it proceeds through comparison to identify a world history context that can invest the case with a significance beyond the merely curious, marginal and exotic, fascinating as that might be.

CHAPTER 2

The Expanding World of Warring States
Ecology, State Formation and Slavery

> *Italy first saw elephants during the war of king Pyrrhus ... but add another 7 years and Rome would view them displayed in triumph.*
> Pliny the Elder, *Natural History* VIII[1]

It was at the battle of Heraclea in 280 BCE in Southern Italy that the Roman legions for the first time confronted a herd of war elephants. Only a few years later, as Pliny noted in his *Natural History*, a victorious general would already be able to parade the fearsome quadrupeds through the streets of Rome among the spoils of his triumph. A modern historian might extend the list of dates by observing that at the time of Heraclea, it was barely five decades ago that the Greco-Macedonian army under Alexander had first encountered these giants of the battlefield at Gaugamela in Mesopotamia and most famously in 326 BCE at the battle by the river Jhelum in the Punjab against mighty king Poros.[2]

As was so often the case with Alexander, the victory won that day had epic potential. Having gone far beyond the part of the earth familiar to the Greeks, the daring Macedonian king presented himself as someone who had overcome even the forces of nature. Coins struck in Babylon to commemorate the event depict a small horse rider charging the mighty animal with its Indian monarch sitting atop desperately hurling missiles against his undaunted attacker (Fig. 2.1). Alexander brought back a large herd of elephants from the Indian campaign but never employed them in battle. However, that quickly changed after his death in Babylon in 323 BCE. Conflict almost immediately broke out among his generals and leading nobles. Who would gain control of the far-flung realm? While the Greco-Macedonian elites slugged it out over the next couple of decades, the elephants saw action in one major battle after the other. None of

---

[1] Pliny, *Natural History* VIII, 6 (my translation).
[2] Scullard 1974 collected the documentation for the war elephant among the Greeks and Romans; chapters 3–6 track the history of its use from Alexander to end of the third century BCE.

2 The Expanding World of Warring States

Figure 2.1 Poros medallion, British Museum. Source: www.britishmuseum.org/col
lection/object/C_1887-0609-1. Copyright British Museum,

the leading contenders would be without this awe-inspiring weapon if they could avoid it. Elephants quickly became an established part of the repertoire of Hellenistic warfare.[3]

In the second generation, King Pyrrhus of Epirus, who made several spirited attempts at the throne of Macedon, brought this Indian import to Italy and Sicily in his ceaseless hunt for conquest and glory. Here, if not before, the military technology was picked up by the Carthaginians, who had access to a plentiful supply of the animals in their natural habitats across North Africa. In their wars with Rome, the elephants of Carthage wrought havoc among the legionaries more than once, and it was the most renowned of their generals, Hannibal, who finally accomplished the most spectacular feat in the history of the war elephant. In 218 BCE, he set out with an army from Spain to march it through Southern France and launch a surprise attack on the Roman arch-enemy. En route, both the river Rhône and the Alps had to be crossed before the host could descend upon the plains of Northern Italy. No fewer than thirty-seven elephants are reported to have been in Hannibal's train and ready for service when the Carthaginian general defeated the Roman army that had come out to beat him back at the river Trebia close to modern Piacenza.[4]

---

[3] A feature that can simply be taken as defining of these polities (so, e.g., Kosmin 2014).
[4] Polybios, *History* III, 72–74. The elephants made it across the Alps, saw action at the first major pitched battle at Trebia, but then mostly perished during the winter.

The speed with which the institution of the war elephant careered from India to the Iberian Peninsula is the kind of occurrence that an ancient world history may be built from. Here is a prime example of ancient globalization. But it is a form of globalization driven not by trade, as we are accustomed to expect, but by warfare. Often overlooked, war has been one of the strongest connectors in human history. However, to wage war at a scale that required the maintenance and transport of sizable herds of elephants, powerful states were needed. Only they had the organizational capacity.[5] If the fast adoption of elephants in warfare across western Afro-Eurasia was triggered by the Indian invasion of Alexander, it was made possible by the centuries of state-building in the Mediterranean that had preceded the rise of the adventurous conqueror.

Some years ago, John Ma observed that with the fragmentation following Alexander's conquests, the Eastern Mediterranean had returned to the geopolitical situation of the Bronze (and early Iron) Age. Before the rise of the Achaemenids in the sixth century BCE, the Levant had been shaped by a number of regional monarchies in competition with each other, chiefly Assyria and Egypt. That situation reasserted itself under the successors of Alexander, the so-called Diadochi.[6] But this observation provides only half the story. The Hellenistic world did not simply recreate the political conditions of the Bronze Age; it had become a much bigger universe. At the formation of their empire, the Achaemenids had burst through the boundaries of the great-power system of the Near-Eastern Bronze Age, strung out between Egypt, Central Anatolia and Mesopotamia, to reach deep into Central Asia. Similarly, during the Bronze Age, the states of the Aegean had been on the very margins of the Levantine world. But by the third century BCE, state-making elites had expanded their reach much further across and deeper beyond the littoral of the central and western Mediterranean Sea. Over the preceding centuries, these state-making societies had accumulated enough weight that their interactions now began to gravitate around a new centre. With the advent of the Punic Wars, the grandest theatres of military conflict had decisively moved out of the shadow of the former Bronze Age universe. To win them, Rome had to develop a military strength that no power in the Eastern Mediterranean would be able to match.

---

[5] Trautman 2015, for a discussion of the infrastructure necessary for the support of war elephants that Indian monarchies had to establish and maintain during the centuries.
[6] Ma 2013.

This expansion of strong Iron Age states was a common feature of Afro-Eurasia in the four to five centuries preceding the victory of Rome in the second Punic War. In addition to the Mediterranean or Achaemenid and Hellenistic Central Asia, one could mention the flood plains of Northern India or the central plains of China. All these geographical regions saw the zone of state formation expand.[7] In Chinese history, these centuries are normally referred to as the 'warring states period'.[8] That is a good marker, and this is precisely what we will explore here. The aim of this chapter is to situate Rome within this expanding Afro-Eurasian world of warring states. The following section will turn to ecology and demography to examine the fundamental logic of sedentary peasant society. Then the chapter turns to state formation and war-making. The city-state has often been thought of as something particularly Greek and Roman. But there were many other city-state cultures, and the Greeks and Romans should not be seen in isolation but studied against this wider background. State formation was normally accompanied by steeper social hierarchies; this was true of the Greco-Roman world as well, where slavery grew in importance. The final section of the chapter attempts to contextualize Greco-Roman slavery within a wider global history of slavery, from the ancient Near East to the Islamic world and the colonial Americas. The peasant, the early state and the slave – these are three key components in our understanding of the Roman republic, but they all have a much wider and longer world history into which Rome must now be fitted.

2.1 Ecology, Demography and the Peasantry

At the basis of state making was the formation of relatively dense and sedentary peasant populations. Only they could produce the economic surplus necessary to sustain the ruling structure. But agriculturalists have not generally been eager to hand over their produce to others. For this to happen, they had to be trapped or, perhaps better put, find themselves caged. Early agriculturalists had to be, so to speak, turned into peasants obligated to hand over part of their resources to a ruling institution and its representatives.[9] How did that happen?

---

[7] Beattie & Anderson 2021; Burke III 2009 for the broad contours of this development. For analysis, see also von Reden, Dwivedi, Fabian et al. 2022, chapter 7, and especially p. 37.
[8] I deliberately collapse the preceding multistate spring and autumn periods into the warring states period (453–221), in order to tailor the chronology to serve world history, rather than only Chinese history; Zhao 2015a: 82–87 on the expanding world of Chinese state formation.
[9] On peasants defined by the claims of outsiders on their surplus, see especially Wolf 1966, chapter 1, and Thorner 1965; Mann 1986: 67–70 (caging mechanisms).

World historians have approached this phenomenon as a fundamental question of demography and ecology. For the first handful of millennia where human groups experimented with agriculture, they avoided capture. As Graeber and Wengrow have recently reiterated in *The Dawn of Everything*, domestication of plants and animals was just one of the many strategies that humans slowly began to employ shortly after the end of the last ice age, usually next to and in combination with hunting and gathering. The turn to farming strategies was not a one-off event in human history but was characterized for a long time, say from the tenth to the fifth millennium BCE, by pragmatic opportunism. Humans simply worked with what was available in the local environment, experimenting with plant seeds and roots that they were already gathering in the wild or finding ways of collaborating with the animals they were also hunting. Some of these experiments failed; others were probably resisted by members of the group and quite a few abandoned when alternative opportunities arose. There was no straight line from agriculture and animal husbandry to sedentary peasantries.[10]

In a classic study, the Danish agricultural economist Ester Boserup pointed out that no land should really be perceived as unused.[11] With humans around, the question was rather how intensively it was exploited. The more people, the more intensively the land had to be worked and the more elaborate the methods of cultivation. If there were few people, little effort had to be dedicated to obtaining a catch or harvest big enough to feed the population living on a given territory. Hunter-gatherers and early farmers all benefitted from abundant land and could win their daily 'bread' with only a few hours of work. Slash and burn agriculture, for instance, saw the farmers fell the trees in an area and then set it on fire. A patch, cleared in this way, could be cultivated with relative ease for a number of years. The ash provided fertilizer, and few weeds germinated in the soil to compete with the crop. As weeds began to encroach on the patch and the ash lost its effect, the agriculturalists would simply move on and clear new ground, where the process could then start over again.

There was, however, a slow-working catch to the opportunistic experiment with agriculture. It could support more people on the same piece of territory, but garden plots and fields required tending and continuous work, however light at first. Compared to a pure hunting lifestyle, the early agriculturalists became less mobile. Perhaps as an unexpected boon (but who can tell?), families were able to raise more children. The toddlers

---

[10] Graeber & Wengrow 2021.   [11] Boserup 1965.

would not have to be carried around between frequently shifting locations and could also more quickly be put to good use in the daily tasks of the family. The most important long-term effect of agriculture has been to allow human numbers to multiply.[12] Time and time again, groups of agriculturalists thus have seen their range of movement increasingly constricted. As human numbers grew, farming families found that their neighbours were coming closer. It became more difficult to move on to new lands. Instead, the period when land was left uncultivated, the so-called *fallow period*, had to be shortened and existing fields worked harder. Much more effort had to be put into soil preparation and weeding. Agricultural intensification generally, as Boserup observed, came at the price of lower productivity per work hour. Drudgery increasingly became a steady companion of sedentary agricultural life. No wonder that many human groups have sought to avoid this daily grind, if at all possible.[13]

It used to be thought that hunters and early farmers lived in fundamentally egalitarian societies. That view has been largely abandoned, disproved by anthropological fieldwork. Even among these groups, where there was little to separate individuals in terms of material possessions, some were able to claim higher authority and prestige, while others had to take orders and accept offering them their services.[14] Still, there were clear limits to social hierarchies. Sociologists talk of 'rank', rather than permanently stratified societies, and note that the small elite had insufficient powers to cage the population. People could simply move away.[15] But, as pockets of sedentary farmers began to congeal, the exit door became increasingly narrow and elites soon found themselves in a position to strengthen and solidify their position in relation to what now became the peasantry.

Beyond the sedentary core areas of peasant societies, however, the density of human population remained relatively low. This, on the other hand, opened a niche for people giving greater weight to or even primarily specializing in animal husbandry. In the more densely settled areas, the number of domesticated animals was heavily capped by the need to use the land to produce food for humans. Grazing for sheep, goats, cattle and horses was limited. The animals often had to make do with marginal lands, unsuitable for cultivation, such as forest or mountainsides. In the Mediterranean, small

---

[12] Barker & Goucher 2015, chapter 1.
[13] Boserup 1965, chapters 3–8 especially, followed most recently by Scott 2017: 95–96. Sahlins 1972 is classic on early farming and hunter-gatherer avoidance of drudgery.
[14] A point overplayed by Graeber & Wengrow 2021, chapter 1. An alternative interpretation is Chase-Dunn & Khutkyy 2021: 117–124.
[15] Mann 1986: 63–70. See further Clastres 1987: 189–218.

populations of herders developed a symbiotic relationship with the cultivators in the practice of so-called transhumance pastoralism. Taking their flocks of animals to the mountains in high summer, they would bring them down on the plains after harvest for grazing the stubble and in return fertilizing the fields with animal manure. On the expanding agricultural frontier, the pressure on the land was less intense. Here smaller human numbers and more extensive land use enabled much greater flocks of domesticated animals, whether in mixed farming arrangements or various degrees of pastoralism and nomadism.

A central theme of world history is how mobile nomadic populations developed in a balance, not always peaceful, with the slowly advancing frontier of peasant society. Especially, the enormous grass steppes of Central Asia have attracted attention.[16] In Roman history, nomadic populations beyond the sedentary agricultural zone in North Africa and the Middle East made crucial interventions. Think of the vital contribution of contingents of Numidian cavalry to the armies of both Carthage and Rome during the Punic Wars or the much later Arabic conquests. To the north, nomads on the Ukrainian steppe both clashed and collaborated with the grain-growing Greek communities establishing themselves along the Black Sea littoral.[17] Nomads living close to the agriculturalists were often able to sell their animals or products in exchange for grain or, say, metal objects produced in sedentary societies. Their easier access to horses in particular also enabled them on occasion to conduct swift raids on the sedentary populations. Fast and mobile, they could not be caged like the peasantry. In our sources, invariably written by sedentary elites, the various populations from the nomadic and extensively farmed areas are commonly portrayed as a threat. Over the long term, the movement was in the opposite direction; it was the zones of sedentary peasantries that expanded into the less extensively farmed areas.[18]

The founding question of the modern discipline of economics has been to explore how humanity could escape the drudgery of peasant life and reach modern affluence. From this perspective, agrarian society has seemed both poor and stagnant. But a turn to world history immediately makes

---

[16] On nomads in world history, Lattimore 1940 remains foundational; see more recently Anthony 2007, part II, and Golden 2011.

[17] Polybios, *History* III, 116–117 (Numidian cavalry of Hannibal at Cannae); *History* XV, 9–14 (at Zama, on both sides). Shaw 1995, chapters 7–8; Tiersch 2015. A fascinating glimpse at Greek Black Sea communities and nomad leaders is provided by Austin 2006, no. 115. More generally, see Batty 2007: 192–199, in particular, and Braund 2005.

[18] Di Cosmo 2002; Ford 2020 (ethnographies of barbarians in the Roman and Chinese empires).

clear that economics has offered a too one-dimensional perspective. Peasant society was not without growth. However, growth did not manifest itself significantly in higher incomes per capita; rather its surplus was produced in a slowly rising number of people. The effect was utterly transformative. From small beginnings, dense peasant populations continued to expand in a glacial drift across the continents. While Roman historians, under the paradigmatic influence of economics, have been absorbed in ultimately irresolvable discussions as to whether the empire might briefly have achieved some small, marginal improvements in per capita incomes, they have lost sight of this much more fundamental phenomenon. The rise of Rome and the empire belongs within the world history of expanding peasant populations and the iron logic of intensification and drudgery.[19]

Across the Afro-Eurasian landmass, as more densely settled peasant populations began supporting cities, states and elites started to evolve during the fourth and third millennium BCE. This was at the beginning of the Bronze Age, and the pockets with more intensive cultivation and dense sedentary peasantries were still quite small. First was the so-called Fertile Crescent, followed by Egypt, the Indus Valley in Pakistan and eventually the plain of the Yellow River in China.[20] Students have often been struck by the prominence of river valleys among early state-making societies. Take the Egyptian Nile. Its annual rise inundated nearby soil with a nourishing mud, killed off weeds and secured a plentiful supply of water. Add the warm and reliable climate, and you have a very benign situation for agriculturalists. They could hardly fail to multiply. But this situation manifested only within a very restricted strip on both sides of the river, beyond which was gruelling and barren desert. In short, once the peasantry started growing, it quickly became trapped in the valley. There was nowhere else to go. Indeed, a rising number of people could easily be channelled into further agricultural expansion. Soon the peasant families had by the proverbial sweat of their brow to start developing a much more labour-intensive irrigation system, digging canals, lifting water and so much more, to avoid hunger. The Nile is an extreme example, laying bare the underlying caging mechanism with particular clarity.[21] However, its strong geographical confinement of the peasantry was far from a necessary precondition for the growth of sedentary agriculture, nor was irrigation. Right from the beginning, some of the areas capable of sustaining cities and state formation depended on rain-fed

---

[19] Bang 2016: 78–79.   [20] Scott 2017, chapters 3–4; Mann 1986, chapters 3–4.
[21] Mann 1986: 108–115 (on the Nile).

cultivation. The decisive factor behind the process was the growth of population enabled by agriculture. Across the globe, examples can be found. The Americas had been cut off from the rest of humanity since the end of the last ice age. Nevertheless, broadly similar processes got started, under different environmental conditions, with different food crops and at a slightly later date. The strongest commonality was the rising density of humans.[22]

By the eighth to fifth centuries BCE, now well into the Iron Age, the clusters of densely settled peasant populations were busily extending their frontiers in a band reaching from east to west in the mostly subtropical climate zone of Afro-Eurasia. Ian Morris has dubbed this zone the 'lucky latitudes', where conditions were especially conducive to agriculture. State-sustaining peasantries had taken a vast step beyond the old Bronze Age centres. Expansion took place in the hinterland along the northern and southern coastline of the Mediterranean, further and further west, all the way to the Atlantic. In India, the Ganges plain had eclipsed the Indus as the area of the most vigorous agricultural growth. In China, the world of the Central Plains saw steady expansion, and several previously separate centres of intensification became linked up with each other. Meanwhile, large areas in Central Asia had now joined the 'club'. The emergence of Rome was part of this wider Afro-Eurasian development.[23]

Demographers guesstimate that around 5000 BCE, humanity comprised perhaps some five to ten million people, a combination of hunters, gatherers and farmers. When we reach the first century CE, this number had multiplied manifold, to perhaps as much as some 200 million. The overwhelming majority of these people inhabited the zones of more intensive agriculture, peasantries, cities and states.[24] Under hard pressure,

---

[22] Barker & Goucher 2015, chapters 8–23, offer a global survey of the varied conditions of early agriculture.

[23] Morris 2010: 85, 114–115; Woolf 2020, chapters 7–12; Gleba, Marín-Aguilera & Dimova 2021 for a recent archaeological collection surveying the westward growth and expansion of urbanism in the first-millennium BCE Mediterranean. The growth of state-forming societies, in the later stages of the development identified here, are admirably traced by the team led by von Reden, Dwivedi, Fabian et al. 2020 and von Reden, Fabian, Weaverdyck 2022. For the Central Asian and North Indian Kushans, for example, the discussion of Morris is instructive (von Reden, Dwivedi, Fabian et al. 2020, chapter 16, and von Reden, Fabian, Weaverdyck et al. 2022, chapter 13). Rather than a position of middlemen in the intercontinental trade, the rise of the Kushan Empire was enabled by the growth of more intensive irrigation agriculture. Rising population made it possible for aristocratic, monastic and imperial elites to impose higher demands on the agriculturalists.

[24] Scheidel 2013: 14; Scott 2017: 95–95, although he, a typo perhaps, at 100 million seriously underestimates world population by the first century CE. Durand (1974, table 1) estimated approximately 250 million, and McEvedy & Jones (1978: 342–345) estimated 170 million – probably a good indication of the plausible range.

2.1 Ecology, Demography and the Peasantry   37

some of these might occasionally try to move away from the most intensively cultivated areas and adopt the more extensive forms of cultivation and herding possible on the frontier of sedentary agricultural society. But that, as we will return to in Chapter 6, was only a minority option. Geographically, of course, the cultivated zones were still small compared to the entire land surface. Yet, in spite of the utopian hopes invested in the stateless frontier by the current luminaries of anthropology from James Scott to David Graeber, this vast territorial expanse could not serve as an alternative for humanity. The regions beyond intensive cultivation would not have been able to support the numbers living on the agricultural plains. Individuals and groups might still find a refuge here. As a whole, however, humanity was already caged.[25]

The long, slow and outwardly expansive growth of peasantries capable of supporting urbanization has perhaps not quite received the attention by historians that it warrants. Its significance, one of the strongest transformative forces in world history, has often been, at least partly, occluded by other concerns. Most students look only at individual societies, and as they inevitably came and went over the millennia, their collapse has often attracted far more attention.[26] A notable exception is William McNeill, who made the slow growth of peasant society with urbanization the main theme of what is probably the work that more than any other demonstrated the value of a new kind of world history: *Plagues and Peoples*, from 1976.[27] Most may still consult the book for its analysis of the rise of global pandemics. The plague of fifth-century Athens that famously claimed Perikles as one of its victims is presented in a framework that also comprised the Antonine, Justinianic and Black Death plagues. However, there was a more important story to tell behind these pandemic catastrophes, and this was a story about long-term growth enabled by the mutual adjustment between diseases and human populations.

More intensive agriculture and the rise of cities brought greater numbers of humans and their domesticated animals closer together while waste and faeces accumulated in their surroundings. This offered a perfect breeding ground for bacteria, viruses and intestinal parasites. Diarrhoea (dysentery) became one of the great killers in human society. Meanwhile, living closely together, many diseases of domesticated animals also jumped onto human hosts. Citified peasant society slowly accumulated a host of crowd diseases

---

[25] A demographic logic basically ignored by Graeber & Wengrow 2021 (so Scheidel 2022: 14) and much underestimated by Scott 2017: 135 and 253.
[26] For critiques of this habit, see McAnany & Yoffee 2010.   [27] McNeill 1976.

that depended on the accessibility of large numbers of humans (and animals) in order to spread and circulate. All in all, the disease load on city and peasant populations increased significantly. People grew shorter, a considerable number would even have been stunted. By today's standards, mortality rates were high. Many cities – where people lived in the greatest densities – would simply have had difficulties reproducing themselves and needed constant replenishment by newcomers. Urbanism depended on the ability of peasantries to produce a population surplus that could, in part, be absorbed by the cities. Sedentary peasant society generated its own migratory flows of people. While the intensively cultivated areas were filling up, some people would move further out to less densely populated zones; others would drift towards the cities in search of employment. But these flows involved much more than simply people. Malaria, for instance, followed in the footsteps of the agricultural expansion westwards across the Mediterranean.[28]

These processes were as old as the first formation of cities in the Bronze Age but stepped up into a higher gear, beginning in our age of warring states and continuing right up till today. As the zones of intensive peasant cultivation and urbanization grew decisively beyond the old Bronze Age population cores, the distances between the most densely populated regions narrowed and the chance that disease strains developed in one centre would jump onto a new population of potential hosts increased significantly. Epidemics spanning several macro-regions across Afro-Eurasia all of a sudden became possible.[29] The fifth-century BCE Athenian plague was reported to have come up through Egypt and extended all across the Achaemenid Empire before reaching the Aegean. Centuries later, the Antonine Plague was believed to have come into the Roman Empire with the legions of Verus returning victorious from campaigning in Mesopotamia.[30] It is, however, only with the Justinianic Plague of the sixth century that we can identify the pathogen that caused the disease. In this particular case, the much-feared *Yersinia pestis*, which would return in the fourteenth century to produce the Black Death, has been identified in genetic material archaeologically recovered from its victims. Other genetic studies point to an area of Central Asia as the origin of the epidemic. However, what is no less remarkable, the spread of the plague depended on the black rat that had made its entry into the Western Mediterranean from India already in the third or second century BCE –

---

[28] McNeill 1976, chapter 2 (disease, peasantries and urban society); Sallares 2014: 252–253 (malaria); Garnsey 2017; Barker & Goucher 2015, chapter 4 (Roberts).
[29] McNeill 1976, chapter 3 provides the broad outline for the rest of this section.
[30] Thucydides, *History* II, 48.1 (on the Athenian plague); Elliott 2024 (on the Antonine).

2.1 *Ecology, Demography and the Peasantry* 39

another, albeit much less celebrated, immigrant of the Hellenistic era compared to the elephants of Greco-Macedonian rulers. The way for the terrible pandemic had, in other words, been paved by the growth of societies and the closer contacts that had become possible as a consequence over the preceding millennium.[31]

If citified peasant society suffered huge strains from disease, its populations nevertheless adjusted. An infectious disease that simply kills off its host will not be successful in the long run. Over time, therefore, infectious disease and host normally develop a mutual accommodation and learn to live with each other. One form of such mutuality would see a level of immunity build up in the population while victims would be hit at a point in their life cycle where they were less vulnerable. The traditional childhood diseases are the classic example. Here a highly infectious pathogen gets to 'attack' young individuals in the crowd, causing usually little harm, and then leave behind immunity to the adults. Pre-industrial history may be punctuated by episodes of epidemic disaster that seriously brought down population numbers. Yet, in the long run, peasantries continued to produce a population surplus and expand. Disease was merely one of several unpredictable forces in their life, together with fluctuating weather, that they had to develop strategies to absorb and survive.[32]

Much as the plague of Justinian may seem to mark a caesura in ancient world history, its effects were overcome. Soon enough demographic retrenchment was followed by recovery and further expansion. If the Rhine and the Danube had marked a northern limit of urbanization in Roman Europe, by 800 CE cities could now be found as far north as Scandinavia. In East, South-East and South Asia, peasant populations were making huge inroads into the jungle. If the agriculture of the central plains of China had been based on grains such as millet, intensively cultivated rice paddies were now shifting the population centre towards the South and the Yangtze River.[33] Meanwhile, in the Sahel, just South of the Sahara, the

---

[31] Sallares 2014: 254; Yu, Jamieson, Hulme-Beaman et al. 2022: 2 and McCormick 2003 (the rat migrating from India, reaching the Western Mediterranean during the last centuries BCE); Eisenberg & Mordechai 2019 for a recent survey and discussion of the many kinds of evidence for and work on the Justinianic plague, emphasizing the uncertainty of its impact. Spyrou, Musralina, Gnecchi Ruscone et al. 2022 for a recent genetic study advocating Central Asian origins.

[32] Garnsey 1988, chapter 1, remains unsurpassed on the survival strategies of Greco-Roman peasantries. Elliott 2016 and Harper 2017 explore the impact of climate events on Roman history. But impacts are likely to have varied much locally and not always negatively. See Sallares 2014 and Haldon, Elton, Huebner et al. 2018. Analysis must be multivariate (e.g., Manning 2018).

[33] On agrarian expansion, see Moore 2000 (northern Europe) and Elvin 2004 (China; the map on p. 10 summarizes the phases of Chinese agricultural advance; pp. 167–170 discuss demographic growth in

agricultural frontier was similarly advancing. Yet here a heavy tropical disease load continued to stifle the build-up of more dense populations. Jack Goody, the anthropologist and pioneer of global history, identified this as a key divide in world history. Below the Sahara, the caging mechanisms were not strong enough. Land remained too plentiful, and therefore the Bronze Age revolution in urban and state formation could never be fully implemented.[34]

The slow but inexorable expansion of densely settled peasant populations, from small Bronze Age beginnings, represents one of the strongest forces of pre-industrial history, and it provides the context and decisive precondition for the rise of Rome. It led to the formation of a historical complex of agrarian core zones that together began to constitute an Afro-Eurasian arena of urbanization and state formation. This was a radical break in world history, not only in terms of rising population but also in the organization of society. To understand how this occurred, the chapter now moves on to state formation.

2.2 State Formation

The inability of many peasant families to easily move on to new, more plentiful lands not only subjected them to having to work their fields harder; it also confronted them with demands from evolving elites. All of a sudden new kinds of specialization became viable. One of these was the art of government and rule. State making was now possible. Max Weber famously defined the state as the organization that was able successfully to claim a monopoly on the legitimate use of physical force within a clearly demarcated territory, but he added the important qualifier that this was characteristic only of the modern state. In many cases, though, this still remains more an aspiration than an accomplished fact. Premodern and early states could certainly never hope to establish such a high degree of control. A modified definition might, instead, describe them as 'coercion-wielding organizations that are distinct from households and kinship groups and exercise clear priority in some respects over all other organizations within substantial territories'.[35] Once the notion of an absolute monopoly is shed, the question of control becomes one of degrees, and the focus is shifted to the state as a project in the making rather than an

---

a rice-growing region). This post 'classical' advancing frontier served as the basis of Lieberman 2003–2009.

[34] Goody 1996.
[35] Tilly 1992: 1; Weber 1980: 822. Scheidel 2013 for a survey and discussion of definitions of early and classical statehood.

2.2 State Formation

abstract entity with a clear checklist of characteristics accomplished once and for all. Instead, the crucial question becomes to examine the processes and methods through which state builders attempted to establish a degree of control and priority over territory.[36]

As enough people began to find themselves unable to move out of reach, caged in the lingo of historical sociology, their villages turned into targets. Warriors would gang up on the agriculturalists to demand part of their stored foods or simply kill them to take everything for themselves. The latter strategy, though, was counterproductive. If the peasants were killed off, there would be no new harvest to claim the following year. Instead, the peasantry was forced to enter into a protective bargain with the warriors. In return for a share of the annual harvest or labour services, the warriors would protect the peasant producers from rival groups of warriors and their attempts to make claims on their produce.[37]

Warriors were not the only threat in the world of the peasant. Gods and spirits, the inscrutable and irascible forces of the cosmos that were believed to control the vagaries of weather and disease under which the agriculturalists toiled, were no less awe-inspiring. Conflicts with neighbours raised questions about the social order. Priests stepped up to organize protection against divine anger and pontificate on the right social order. Costly ceremonies and rituals were crafted to placate the gods and ensure their protection of the community. The peasantry again paid with produce or with labour to the temples and priesthoods who rose to administer the divine cults.[38]

The priest or the warrior – who was the most important force? In favour of the priests is the fact that through religious cult they articulated the social order and shaped a wholly new cultural universe. Much of what archaeologists uncover from these early Bronze Age societies is constituted by objects employed in ritual contexts.[39] On the other hand, for most of history, rulers have invested far more resources in the military than in the cultural manifestations of their power. At the end of the day, we are confronted by a chicken-and-egg question. The simple truth is that priests and warriors quickly found out that they needed each other. It was out of their partnership that the early state emerged.[40] Its order was in fact not too

---

[36] Finer 1975: 85 (from static definition to the process of building).
[37] McNeill 1976: 72–73; Carneiro 1970.
[38] Crone 1986 (on the power of the gods to cage the population, although perhaps the power accruing to the priesthood, the representative of the gods on earth, is mysteriously underestimated).
[39] Yoffee 2005 points to the significance of the fundamental redefinition of the cultural order effected by early states.
[40] Mann 1986, chapter 3–4, for a multivariate analytical account of the rise of states.

far off from the ideal societal division of labour that Plato much later would envisage in the Socratic dialogue today, known under the title of *The Republic*. Like so many other Greek aristocrats of his day, the founder of the Academy sought inspiration in Sparta. An elite group of guardians, combining military and philosophical training, power and meaning, would lord it over the producers, the peasantry. Ernest Gellner, the historical sociologist and theorizer of nationalism, understood better than many Greek historians, misled by the proverbial exceptionalism of Sparta, that here was a generic template, however utopian, for most pre-industrial societies.[41]

Even so, the transition from the Bronze to the Iron Age had opened an era of experiment as well as consolidation. Students of the Bronze Age Near East remark how the Iron Age saw renovation. State formation picked up again, and the institutions of government were resurrected on firmer foundations.[42] However, the zones of state formation also expanded, into the central and Western Mediterranean, across Central Asia and the Ganges plain of India, and steadily over the central plains of China. With the number of states growing, there followed innovation. Bronze had been the preserve of a very narrow elite. Tin, a necessary component added to the copper alloy, is a very rare metal. Iron, on the other hand, was available almost anywhere and could not in the same way be monopolized. The turn to iron not only produced stronger implements; it also made high-grade weaponry more widely available.[43] Once political elites had learned to master the implications of wider dissemination, they were ready to tap its social potential. Greater numbers of people could be mobilized around the key institutions of political power, and state structures accumulated more flesh on the bones. The history both of the early Roman Republic and of the pre-imperial Qin monarchy, for instance, reveals how an old, established, narrow aristocratic stratum saw its hold on power diminish as new groups drawn from the plebeian part of the population won access to high position.[44]

The repertoire of power and its forms of organization expanded. Charles Tilly, perhaps the most influential thinker on the state in the last generation, famously remarked that 'war made the state, and the state made war.'[45]

---

[41] Gellner 1988, chapter 3, discussed by Bang 2015b. [42] Richardson 2017.
[43] Kristiansen 2018a: 10; A. Eich 2015: 125–148; Shelach-Lavi 2015: 268.
[44] Pines 2012: 15 (from aristocratic chariot warfare to peasant mass armies). See further Rosenstein 2009, section 1. In the Roman case, the story was about how the patricians had to open their ranks and share power with the leading plebeian families.
[45] Tilly 1975: 42.

If ever there was a period when this was true, it was the Iron Age. War was endemic, and communities constantly saw themselves at war, either defending themselves against their neighbours or trying to encroach on the resources of others. City walls simply constitute the best attested form of remains from the archaic Greek polis.[46] How to create a viable and orderly body politic became a key issue. Learned men explored constitutions and strategies; politicians would try out any number of arrangements. The school of Aristotle in the later fourth century BCE embarked on a project of analyzing the varieties of political order on display in the many poleis of the Mediterranean. In the Chinese area, the proverbial 'hundred schools of thought' equally bear testimony to the political ferment of the age.[47]

Beyond the Achaemenid Empire but also inside the Persian realm, governmental power was characterized by a plurality of arrangements and players. City-states, small or middling kingdoms and (in less populous regions) chiefdoms and tribes continued to coexist. The reach of military power was seriously constrained by logistics. Most soldiers had to walk on foot; a smaller elite could rely on horses. If soldiers were to carry their own supplies of both food and water, their operational range was three days' march; if only food, it was increased to nine days. But, as Michael Mann observed in a fundamental analysis, no general could risk going that far before turning back. Supplies had to be secured from local communities along the route. No reader of Xenophon's *Anabasis*, the account of how an army of Greek mercenaries marched back from the Persian heartland, or Caesar's description of the conquest of Gaul can have failed to notice, amid the repetitive setting out on marches, how the troops constantly had to resort to plunder and harvest on the go as well as negotiate with local communities, all to secure the necessary supplies. Staying within reach of rivers or the sea was also wise. Waterborne transport, especially of bulky supplies, was much less costly than land transport. No big city could develop in the pre-industrial world without access to waterways. Marching a few thousand armed men through a district would often have been the equivalent of moving a new city through an area and, for longer distances, could rarely be done without the support of water transport.[48] Across the zone where

---

[46] Frederiksen 2011, chapter 8. See Hui 2005: 149–159, Hopkins 1978: 22–37 and Finley 1983: 60–61 on the ubiquity of war in the Chinese (and early modern European) and Greco-Roman worlds, respectively.
[47] Aristotle, *Politics* (an instructive reflection of this intellectual climate); Pines 2012: 16–19 on the theoretical experimentation of warring states thinkers in China. See Sima Qian, *Shiji*, chapter 74, for a portrait of the great diversity of thinkers and policy advisers during the warring states period.
[48] Mann 1986: 138–140, building on Engels 1978. Xenophon, *Anabasis* IV, for example, 1.9–1.15, 4.5–4.18, 5.29–5.33 and 7.13; Caesar, *Gallic War*, for example, book 1, especially chapters 15–20, 23.1, 26.6, 28.3, 37.5–39.1, 40.10–12, 48.2, 49.1.

state formation was gaining traction, access was uneven and distance always an obstacle. All this meant that the basic logistical constraints often worked in favour of political fragmentation and the localization of power.[49]

Most states were small and surprisingly resilient. The wonder that the few allied Hellenic poleis of the early fifth century were able to resist the Achaemenids famously inspired the history of Herodotus and was later turned into a bedrock of modern ancient history. Yet the city-state ought not be approached as a phenomenon peculiar to the Greek and Roman world; it is a much more widespread phenomenon. Historians have, for instance, for a long time been debating how to fit premodern China into world history. Feudalism, given the influence of Marxist theory on the field, has often been the main concept employed. But to bundle some three millennia of Chinese history under the sole label of feudalism is obviously unsatisfactory. Periods of vast empire alternated with periods of fragmentation. Even in the latter case, however, feudalism is far from ideal. In medieval European history, feudalism is commonly perceived as marking an almost complete absence of state power and lack of cities, while state power and urbanism were much more of a presence in the Chinese area in the periods of fragmentation. For pre-imperial Chinese history, several scholars have begun to look to the city-state for greater nuance in their understanding of the agrarian past and use it as a conceptual bridge to ancient Mediterranean and world history. A state centred on a city with a territory that could be covered on foot in a couple of days can easily be paralleled in the early Chinese context, perhaps and increasingly combined with a few bigger regional states. A mixture of city-states, some of them growing into slightly larger entities and regional monarchies, was, in varying combinations, characteristic also of North India and the Mediterranean. In fact, a considerable number of city-state cultures have been identified, from Ancient Mesopotamia to the Mayas of Mesoamerica.[50]

In ancient Mesopotamia, the earliest states were city-states. Their forms of organization came to define a template that was used and reshaped by the many new city-states that followed in their wake across the Levant, Anatolia and eventually the Mediterranean. The practice of naming the year in the calendar after the annually switching incumbents of leading

---

[49] Braudel 1972, Vol. 1: 355–393, is classic ('distance, the first enemy'). The practical constraints in the Roman world can now be investigated through https://orbis.stanford.edu.

[50] Hansen 2000, with the contribution of Lewis on China (emphasizing regional states); Yates 1997 (on city-states in early China); Raaflaub 2011: 49 (on the parallel developments in the Mediterranean, Mesopotamia and China). See further Xin 2021, chapter 5 (for a historiographical overview of the Chinese engagement with the notion of the city-state).

magistracies or priesthoods so familiar to students of Greco-Roman culture was already custom among the Bronze Age Sumerians and Assyrians. So was the inclusion of an assembly among the governing institutions of the city.[51] The Phoenicians brought the city-state form with them as they ventured out from the coast of Lebanon across the Mediterranean on commercial ventures to the west and set up stations along the route. While the Phoenician network accumulated weight, they were soon joined by others.

In our age of globalization, it is perhaps tempting to focus on the element of trade. But as the process gathered strength, it became far more multifaceted. Most of the new communities that developed were congregations of agriculturalists, and Carthage rose to a commanding position in the Western Mediterranean through the acquisition of a large agricultural hinterland. This gave the city a resource base that few others could match in the region.[52] Techniques of statecraft began to circulate back and forth within the expanding Mediterranean networks. A written form of Greek, for instance, was crafted through a creative adaptation of the Phoenician alphabet, spawning in turn both the development of Etruscan and Latin as written languages in Central-South Italy. Groups of mercenaries, migrants and extended aristocratic networks added substance to the flows of techniques and ideas. Naukratis, a Greek city serving as a port of trade between the Mediterranean and the kingdom of Egypt, was founded to settle the Greeks who had come to the country, mostly as mercenaries in the employ of the pharaoh. More and more people became engulfed in the projects of state builders.[53]

A good illustration of the ever more encompassing dynamics and pressures of the era may be gleaned from the swashbuckling and volatile career of Duketios, a mid fifth-century leader of 'famed family and highly influential' among the 'original' population on Sicily. At the time, the island had seen rapid and vigorous, if also chaotic and disruptive, formation of city-states. At the western end of the island, Phoenician foundations were gaining strength under the influence of Carthage; at the eastern end, Syracuse, a colonial foundation from Corinth, was presiding over a mushrooming number of Greek poleis. In the pages of Diodorus, the first-century BCE Greek historian

---

[51] Larsen 2000.
[52] Ameling 2013 (Carthage); Hansen 2006: 89–95 (most poleis were constituted by the peasantry, 'Ackerbürger' in German); Osborne 1987, chapter 7 especially.
[53] On these processes, see Malkin 2011 (Greek world), Terrenato 2019 (Italy) and more broadly Woolf 2020, chapters 7–12. Specifically on Naukratis, see Möller 2000 with Herodotus, *Histories* II, 152–182.

from Sicily, Duketios appears as a resourceful noble that attempts to build up his position by adopting the new modalities of power represented by the Greek polis. The so-called Sikels, the Indigenous peoples on the island, were mobilized for war, sometimes in alliance with a Greek polis, often against another. Some cities were conquered, others refounded, still others created from scratch. At all events, lands were parcelled out to the aspiring soldier peasants. Eventually, Duketios was defeated and his power collapsed, but his state-building project was absorbed by Syracuse.[54]

A recurrent issue for the forming states of this era, whether in the Mediterranean or on the Chinese Central Plains, was the distribution of land. The name of Shang Yang, a prominent mid fourth-century reformer and minister of the Qin monarchy, has become a symbol of the efforts of the Chinese warring states monarchies to push through land reforms to stimulate the growth of peasantries, make them available for military recruitment and restrict previous aristocratic privilege.[55] A similar 'egalitarian' force comes through even more strongly in the Mediterranean. The famous call of the Roman Gracchi brothers for land reform to replenish the peasantry was only the tip of the iceberg.[56] The rise of the hoplite, a foot soldier of modest training but equipped with a long spear, large shield and short sword, and protected by helmet and body armour, might not in itself seem very impressive, especially not in comparison to a specialist warrior, perhaps even on horse. But the strength of the hoplite was not in individual skill and prowess but in the security of the collective. Massed together in large numbers, a body of such infantrymen, shielding each other, could often stand their ground against the most formidable of enemies.[57]

To survive in the incessant struggles of the 'warring states period', the aristocrats had to mobilize a larger number of people and therefore appeal to the peasant majority.[58] At the same time, like aristocrats of all ages, they were generally averse to the idea of taxation. The larger number of soldiers, just like the aristocrats themselves, had to be able to pay for their own military equipment. The peasants, in short, had to have means of their

---

[54] Diodorus Siculus, *Library of History* 11.76.3, 11.78.5, 11.88.6–90.2; discussed by Hodos 2020, chapter 3, as paradigmatic. Finley 1968, chapters 3–10, remain worthwhile and bring out well a tension between immensely destructive short-term struggles and the capacity of Sicilian communities for regeneration in the mid-term.
[55] Sima Qian, *Shiji*, 68. For the basic comparison, see Rosenstein 2009.
[56] Appian, *Civil Wars* I, 7–13. Brunt 1962 remains a classic discussion of the land issue in Roman politics and Stockton 1979 a solid introduction to the Gracchi.
[57] On the hoplite (and legionary), see, for example, Osborne 1987, chapter 7; Schwartz 2009; and further Lendon 2005.
[58] See also the expert discussion of Torelli in Hansen 2000: 189–208.

own. This meant they had to own their own land. In return for military service, the peasantry was able to claim independence from aristocratic landowners and earn acceptance as full citizens. What that meant in practice differed significantly from city-state to city-state and from decade to decade, as coups, revolutions and military defeats kept overturning the governing order. Polybios, the Greek historian of republican Rome, famously thought he could detect a cycle of constitutional arrangements behind the chaotic experience, whereby cities alternated between monarchy, aristocracy and democracy – rule by one, few or many.[59]

The emergence of a participatory form of politics in the city-states of the Mediterranean has often been celebrated by classicists, and with good reason.[60] The Athenian democracy of the fifth to fourth centuries BCE and Rome of the late Republic have left enough evidence to enable us, for the first time in history, to observe open political debate, elections and the passing of laws by majority vote-count in detail. Yet, by placing these developments in a world history perspective, explanations can move beyond the language of wonder and miracle. The widening of political participation was not so much an anomaly as one solution to the pressures of war that forced state builders from the East or West to mobilize the peasantry in massed armies. Rome is sometimes viewed as an exceptional conqueror because the Republic was led by an aristocratic collective rather than a monarch.[61] Maybe this is merely an important reminder that, wherever we look and whatever the precise arrangement, a landed elite continued to provide the leaders of the state in monarchies as well as city-states.

2.3 Slavery and Dependency

If war was a decisive force shaping states and political organization, it also contributed significantly to the growth and institution of global slavery. Perhaps the first historian to overwhelmingly establish the value of approaching the institutions of Greco-Roman society from a new and wider world history perspective was Moses Finley. *Ancient Slavery and Modern Ideology* lucidly linked the development of the Greco-Roman city-state with the growth of chattel slavery as an institution. The argument was simple. There were many societies with slave labour but few full-blown slave societies in history: the core areas of ancient Rome and classical

---

[59] Polybios, *History* VI, 3–10. Much in the same vein, Aristotle, *Politics* III, 10, 7–8, and in greater variety, book V. For analysis and discussion, see Finley 1983, chapter 5.
[60] Ober 2017, for a recent example, or Millar 1998.
[61] For example, Raaflaub 2011: 49 ('exceptional').

Greece, the plantation systems of the early modern Caribbean, the antebellum South and Brazil. It was rare that enslaved people would make up a large proportion of the population and constitute the main source of labour for the ruling elite. Until the age of modern capitalism, free wage labour had been a marginal phenomenon. Most labour for others, therefore, was dependent labour. But its forms were multiple and could be ranged along a virtual spectrum between voluntary and coerced. Chattel slavery, where a person was reduced to the legal status of a mere piece of property, to be sold at will, and permitted to establish a family only as a privilege freely revocable by the owner, represented an extreme of domination. Normally aristocratic elites could obtain their labourers with less violence and repression. Only on the relatively few occasions when these forms of subject labour had been unavailable had elites turned to slavery as the main solution.

One such example were the plantation economies of the colonial Americas. With the arrival of people from Europe at the turn of the sixteenth century, the Amerindian population had been brought into contact with the disease pool of the Afro-Eurasian arena. The east-west orientation of the latter, rather than the north-south orientation of the former, had enabled greater numbers of domesticated animals to accumulate. These were obliged to a lesser extent than in the Americas to cross climatic zones and had therefore spread more easily among Afro-Eurasian societies. However, more animals also meant adjusting to more epidemic diseases. In the Americas, this meant that catastrophic numbers of Indigenous people died as victims of the Afro-Eurasian diseases brought with the European arrivals. For the Europeans, this meant that it was easier to consolidate rule but also more difficult to turn a profit from the new conquests.[62] The demographic collapse following colonization had left the new rulers struggling to secure enough labour until a ruthless system of massive transatlantic imports of enslaved Africans had enabled the formation of cash-crop plantations in the Caribbean, Brazil and what would become the southern states of the US.

No similar shortage of people had characterized Greece and Rome, but here the struggle of the peasantry to secure full citizenship and its mobilization for military service had equally forced the aristocracy to seek alternative sources of manpower. In the core regions of both Greek and Roman society, slavery became the main system of dependent labour, used to provide the elites with both servants and farmhands. The much-celebrated freedoms of

---

[62] Crosby 1986; Diamond 1997.

2.3 *Slavery and Dependency*

the peasantry in Greek and Roman city-states had to be bought with the enslavement of others. That was the tragedy of pre-industrial, agrarian society and its constraints.[63]

Comparison with the plantation slavery of the colonial Americas, however, hardly exhausts the question. At a closer look, as Noel Lenski has pointed out in a horizon-expanding study, several other societies can be added to the list of full-blown slave societies. In antiquity, Carthage is a strong suspect. One might also add southern Iraq in the eighth and ninth centuries, where a huge community of enslaved Africans was imported and employed to reclaim marginal land in the environs of Basra. From the much better-documented nineteenth century, at least two candidates are incontrovertible: the First Nations communities on the American North-West Coast, whose potlach ceremonies have been so intensively studied by anthropologists (see Chapter 5), and the jihadist Islamic monarchies of the Sub-Saharan Sahel and Savanna that, spearheaded by the Sokoto caliphate, reached across Africa, from east to west.

Perhaps the slave societies turn out to be less exceptional than first imagined. They did not develop out of nothing, but against a background of generalized slave use. Most of the area that came to be covered by the Roman Empire could not be described as 'slave societies' in Finley's sense – not even many of the territories occupied by Greek city-states. The slave societies constituted small pockets of especially intensive use: Classical Athens and Chios, for instance, or Roman Italy, from Etruria to Campania and the province of Sicily. Outside these, the practice of slavery was nevertheless far from insignificant. In that respect, these areas of less intensively practiced slavery align with a much larger number of other pre-industrial societies. In fact, the vast majority of enslaved people over the millennia have belonged within this group.[64]

Orlando Patterson, in a study developed in conversation with Finley, pointed out that there was a global history of slavery beyond the particularly intensive zones. For much of history, elites have exploited the labour of individuals torn away from their homes and families and reduced to a status of 'social death'. Robbed of family and background, these 'socially dead' persons had become the creatures of their master and would be

---

[63] Finley 1998 (1980). Katsari & Dal Lago 2008 provide a set of essays that systematically explore this comparative framework. Following Finley, the slave economies of the colonial Americas have simply become the standard referent in the study of Greek and Roman slavery (e.g., Vlassopoulos 2021; Bradley & Cartledge 2011; Bradley 1994). See also Harper 2011: 64, suggesting a 'soft parallel' to new world slavery, but not that of the most intensive regions.

[64] Eltis & Engerman 2011: 10; Lenski 2018 and more generally Lenski & Cameron 2018.

exploited in every conceivable function from the highest to the most menial and degrading: confidential secretary, sex partner, cook, cleaner and much more, from janissaries to eunuchs.[65]

Greco-Roman slavery belongs within this wider global history. Just as the Mediterranean city-state developed from a Near-Eastern template, so its form of slavery arose in the context of Levantine societies where enslaved persons all served in important functions.[66] These also included agricultural jobs, but most importantly they involved service in the urban households of the elite and in state institutions. Even if some of the most intensive pockets saw abatement, Greco-Roman slavery never really declined. When the armies of the Islamic caliph conquered the Roman Near East and North Africa during the seventh century CE, the new rulers took over the existing institution and eventually incorporated it within Muslim law. The practice of slavery in the Islamic world constitutes another potential avenue of comparison, especially for the urban and elite household dimension.[67] But here the rulers brought slavery to a new height of intensification: military slavery. Over the centuries, Muslim monarchs began to form elite regiments of enslaved soldiers.[68] This may seem surprising and unusual, but they did so for the same reason that masters normally had recourse to enslaved persons. More than the available alternatives, slave soldiers depended on the ruler and could be trusted as loyal. In practice, of course, things were more complicated. Armed and organized, such slaves could and sometimes did turn against the ruler, just as more regular military units can be found to have done. Roman history, after all, abounds with military coups staged by generals or the prefects of the Praetorian Guard and their restive soldiers. Yet, however imperfectly, it was to reduce the risk that the soldiers would be able to forge strong bonds of allegiance with an alternative leader that Muslim monarchs had recourse to military slavery.

In a world where family and patronage networks provided most of the social infrastructure, slavery afforded the master with access to a deracinated form of labour, not tied up with alternative networks and foci of power. With links to family and external patrons cut or at least much reduced, the enslaved person was left almost wholly at the mercy and protection of the owner. The underlying principle received expression perhaps most fully in

---

[65] Patterson 1982; Bodel & Scheidel 2017, a collection of studies, offers a wide-ranging, up-to-date assessment and adds nuance to the general framework.
[66] Lewis 2018.
[67] Harper 2011: 506 hints in this direction, even if his image of a decline of slavery in the fifth- to sixth-century Eastern empire may be overdrawn. There is little reason not to extend the continuity claimed by Harper for the fourth century into the following centuries where imperial and urban society remained in place in the East.
[68] Crone 1980.

the body of the eunuch. Subjected to castration, the male servant had been deprived of the ability to produce his own offspring, and his hopes had thereby been confined within the context of the master's household. The use of eunuchs runs as a powerful undercurrent in the history of slavery and, with the horrific death rates suffered by those who underwent the procedure, adds another chapter to slavery's catalogue of gruesome practices.[69] Eunuchs people the narratives of palatial politics, whether one looks to the (late) Roman court or to most others of the big imperial formations of Afro-Eurasian history. From trusted positions close to the ruler, they played a central part in the intrigues of factional politics. These, however, we will leave for Chapter 3.[70]

If eunuchs became prized, it was not simply because they were, from the master's perspective, more trustworthy than others. Plenty of non-castrated people rose to high positions in elite households. There was also a cultural dimension. The sex-less person could be perceived as occupying a symbolically liminal position that might be manipulated in the ceremonial displays of the elite.[71] Moreover, arrested physical transformation at puberty was often prized as sexually desirable. Eunuchs, beautiful immature boys and, let us not forget, women were exploited as sex partners and prostitutes.[72] In the Ottoman Empire, the realm that almost as a replica of Justinian's and from his capital on the Bosporus dominated the eastern Mediterranean and Middle East between the sixteenth and eighteenth centuries, female slaves often even seem to have been able to marry their owner and thus leave the status of slavery behind. This, too, can be documented in the Roman world, but there the practice was less legally acceptable at first, only made more permissible over the course of late antiquity.[73] What, however, was characteristic of both Ottoman and Roman urban slavery was relatively high manumission rates. It has been customary to emphasize the unique role of manumission in Roman slavery, but evidently this practice was used as a reward to motivate enslaved servants across the Afro-Eurasian world.[74] Only when slavery became firmly linked to a racial hierarchy in the colonial Americas did this pathway significantly narrow. For a period, the contrast in skin colour between

---

[69] For example, N'Diaye 2008.
[70] Tougher 2020 for a brief monographic survey of Eunuchs in the Roman world.
[71] A point well made by Hathaway 2018, chapter 3.
[72] Harper 2011, chapter 7, for a rich discussion in relation to late Roman slavery.
[73] Harper 2011, chapter 11.
[74] Toledano 2011: 29; Mouritsen 2011 (emphasizing the absorption of many freed slaves into Roman society).

enslaved Black Africans and white populations of European descent came to define two starkly segregated social groups that made it difficult for freed people to gain entry to the society of their former masters.

To linger a little while longer with the Ottoman comparison, in the formative phase of this empire, slavery is linked to captives from numerous wars of conquest, but as expansion ground to a halt and rule was consolidated across the Balkans and the Middle East, import of enslaved people through trade became more important. The historiography of Roman slavery follows a broadly similar course. Explosive conquest gives way to trade and imports from the frontier zones of the empire as a source of newly enslaved people, in combination with the biological reproduction achieved by slave families themselves. For a long time, it used to be believed that this development would have caused the institution slowly to decline. But ancient historians are now more inclined to see continuity, and the Ottoman comparison confirms the accuracy of this assessment. Walter Scheidel has estimated the import requirements needed to sustain the slave population of Roman Italy at some 15,000–20,000 persons annually under the late Republic and early Empire.[75] The Muslim Middle East, culminating under the Ottomans, seems for centuries on end to have maintained imports from East and Sub-Saharan Africa of some 5,000–10,000 enslaved people every year.[76]

To be sure, these figures are not directly comparable. Neither number represents the total in the two respective empires, nor were their underlying population bases identical. The Roman Empire is normally considered to have held twice the number of people of the Ottoman domains. Still, the two figures indicate a phenomenon of roughly comparable orders of magnitude. The Romans would not have had to maintain relatively much higher imports than the Ottomans in order to reproduce the institution of slavery in the empire. We might see the Ottoman world as representing a baseline, of predominantly urban slavery, to which the Romans added another layer of intensification of more widespread agricultural slavery in a few select zones inside the empire.

The Greco-Roman elites found most of their supplies of slave imports from the zones beyond the Rhine and the Danube in Europe and the Black Sea. Internal slaving across the empire was also important – poor families selling off children or abandoning them, or dealers abducting or otherwise

---

[75] Scheidel 2005: 78–79.
[76] Lovejoy 2011: 25 and 46. See further Toledano 2011: 25–26 (during the nineteenth century, imports from Africa seem to have reached a level of 16,000–18,000 people, but then sources in the Caucasus and the Slav world had been cut off).

2.3 Slavery and Dependency

capturing their human 'goods'. Anatolia seems to have been an important zone of slaving, but slavers were on the prowl all over the empire. Just as in the age of the Ottoman corsairs, pirates capturing slaves were busy in the Mediterranean Sea and similarly feared. A famous letter of Augustine describes a group of slave catchers that tried to ship out from the local harbour a very sizable group of victims caught in the rural Algerian hinterland.[77] Black people could also be found among the enslaved population, but it was especially as Islamic state-craft struck roots south of the Sahara in the centuries following the first wave of conquests that East Africa and the Sahel developed into one of the main zones of slave supplies to the Mediterranean, the Middle East and India. It was, in turn, this economy of slaving that European colonizers tapped into and intensified with their much-expanded demand for enslaved people to staff the plantations of the Caribbean and the Americas, especially from the seventeenth till the early nineteenth century.[78] The history of ancient slavery, in short, is bound up with a wider world history. Comparison with the plantation economies of the Americas helps illuminate the intensive but selective use of agricultural slaves in some pockets of the ancient Greco-Roman world, while the societies of the ancient Near East and the Islamic world put the use of urban slaves in perspective.[79]

But widening the comparative horizon also makes the limits of Greco-Roman slavery clearer. As the significance of slavery as an institution of the state-making societies of Afro-Eurasia increasingly emerges, so does the need to distinguish between forms of dependent labour. A recent analysis of the early-modern Qing dynasty, for instance, documented the importance of slavery (both urban and agricultural) in the Chinese world but also pointed to other kinds of dependent labour. Most dependents were not chattel slaves but served under a less totalizing regime of domination.[80] This, too, is an observation that the Greco-Roman historian may learn from. When a recent analysis controversially opted to view the Helots, the subject peasant population toiling under the admittedly ruthless lordship of Sparta, as slaves (albeit a very special form of slave), then it is worth remembering that the choice is not binary, free or slave; peasantries often

---

[77] Augustine, *Letter 10**. On the sources of the Roman slave supply, see Scheidel 2011: 303–304 and at greater length Harper 2011, chapter 2 (with a discussion of Augustine's letter on pp. 92–95, both for its period-specific and structural aspects). On Ottoman and Arab slaving among European populations, see Clarence-Smith & Eltis 2011.
[78] Lovejoy 2011, chapters 2–3 (on the Islamic slave trade). Harper 2011: 87–91 rightly identifies Roman late antiquity as a period where the foundations were laid for the Sub-Saharan slave trade that the Arab and Muslim conquerors would then go on to intensify in the seventh and eighth century.
[79] See further and in more general terms, Flaig. 2009.   [80] Crossley 2011.

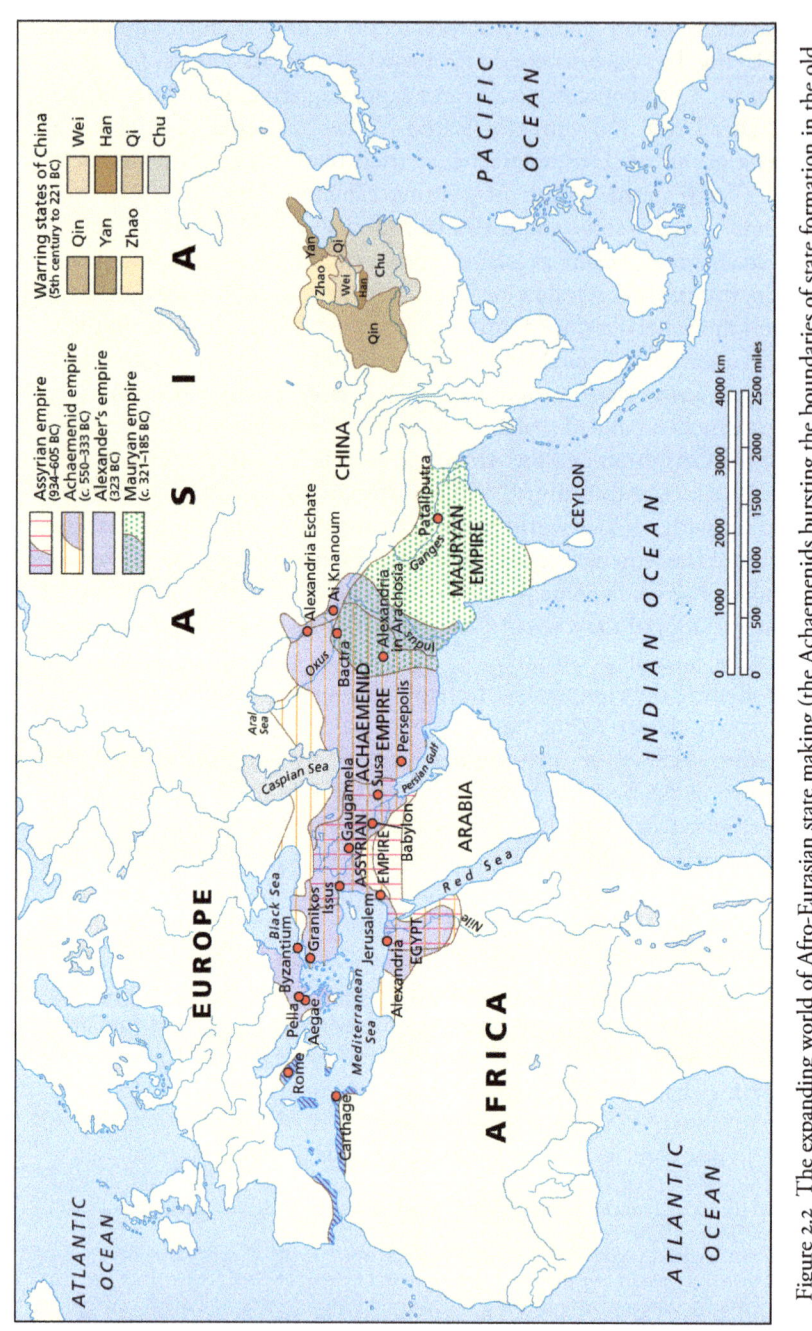

Figure 2.2 The expanding world of Afro-Eurasian state making (the Achaemenids bursting the boundaries of state formation in the old Near East, followed by the warring states of China, the Mauryan Empire, Rome and Carthage). Source: Peter Fibiger Bang and Dariusz Kolodziejczyk, eds., *Universal Empire* (Cambridge: Cambridge University Press, 2012).

existed in degrees of submission and dependence.[81] As one reads about the Helots in Strabo, 'they were held by the Spartans as "public serfs" and had been assigned their own settlements and public services and dues to render'.[82]

To understand how this became the general condition takes us from the small warring states of the Iron Age to the formation of large empires, the subject of the next chapter. So often approached as an anomaly, in some sense, classical Sparta may be taken as a premonition of the things to come. In microcosm, its order arguably prefigured the world that Rome would go on to create.[83] As for now, this chapter has identified the development of what we might term an Afro-Eurasian arena as the world history context for Rome (see fig. 2.2). It is within the expanding zones of 'caged' peasantries running in a band from East to West, across the three continents, that the emergence of Rome belongs and finds its closest parallels. Rome may simply best be analyzed as one variant of the forms of society emerging out of this Afro-Eurasia-wide development. Here the focus has been on early state formation and the institutionalization of slavery, but the process will be even clearer as we now move on to empire.

---

[81] Lewis 2018, chapter 6, followed by Vlassopoulos 2021, chapter 8 (to consider helotage as 'not "proper" slavery is deeply misleading', yet 'it is undeniable that the helots of Messenia lived effectively as communities of dependent peasants', pp. 169–170). Although not contemporary, our sources are so fragmentary that perhaps we should not disregard the first-century BCE evidence of Diodorus Siculus, *Library of History* 11.84.8, which describes how the Spartans defeated rebellious Helots and then enslaved them. This must mean they were not considered slaves before. For a further critique and nuanced discussion, see Cartledge 2024.

[82] *Strabo VIII*, v, 4 (my translation).   [83] Brilliantly suggested by Van Dam 2010: 16.

CHAPTER 3

Among Empires
The Universal Realms of the Afro-Eurasian World

> *For the life and victory of the illustrious Septimius Wahballāt Athenodoros, King of Kings and Corrector of all the East, son of Septimius Odainat, King of Kings; and for the life of the illustrious Septimia Batzabbay, the Queen, mother of the King of Kings, daughter of Antiochus. Fourteen Miles.*
>
> Healey (2010)[1]

Around the late 260s CE, this milestone would have greeted the weary traveller some fourteen miles west of Palmyra, the affluent oasis city of the Syrian Desert midway between Damascus and the Euphrates. The inscription announced the spectacular rise of a local family to the sphere of empire and high politics – but not, perhaps, in the way that a student of Roman history might have expected. The first title to meet the eye was 'king of kings', a dignity normally claimed by Persian rulers, not by a Roman 'corrector' of the eastern provinces of the empire. However, the prestige of Vaballathus, still a minor, and of his regent mother, best known to history as Zenobia, derived from the victories won by his deceased father Odainathus over the Sassanian emperor, Shapur I. The latter had become quite a triumphant bane of Roman emperors. Gordian III had lost his life on campaign into Persian territory in 244 CE, and Valerian was taken captive and would die a prisoner at the Sassanian court, after his disastrous defeat at the battle of Edessa in 260 CE. Odainathus was one of the Roman nobles who had stepped into the breach, stabilized the situation on the eastern front and clipped the victorious wings of the Sassanian Shahanshah. Here was a dynasty in the making that had finally been able

---

[1] Healey 2010, inscription 34 (giving all the surviving text, in Greek, Palmyrene and Latin, plus English translation, slightly modified by me): a milestone, found fourteen miles from Palmyra on the road to Emesa, put up between 268 and 270 CE, but recut with a Latin text added a few years after the fall of Zenobia, during the reign of Diocletian. The commentary on the 'official' publication in *Corpus Inscriptionum Semiticarum* II, 3, 3971, is still worth consulting. On a different note, the title chosen for this chapter gestures towards Maier 2007.

to match and defeat the frightening Persian foe. This was the message that the title signalled to the world. Soon, Queen Zenobia would take an even higher step and have her son proclaimed Augustus, supreme lord of the Roman Empire.[2]

Vaballathus and his regency were far from the only one to reach out for the throne in those decades. The realm was torn by civil war. From one region after the other, high aristocrats and generals rose to lay claim to the imperial purple while central power seemed to have collapsed. Writing about the so-called year of the four emperors, after the fall of Nero in 68 CE, the senatorial historian Tacitus had famously seen the shocking secret of empire revealed: the emperor could be found from outside Rome.[3] However, that turned out only to be a prelude to the events of the third century that unfolded on a much wider and much more brutal canvas. Imperial rule was based on an aggressive act of military assertion; it was a contest for supremacy, against opposing rulers as well as rival elites. Empire, in short, was a military hegemony. It depended crucially on elite formation and the cooperation of local aristocracies. No less important, Rome was not the only imperial Titan in town. In the half millennium from the late fourth century BCE till the early second century CE, a range of vast empires began to rise that bestrode the Afro-Eurasian land-mass from China in the East to the territories ringing the Mediterranean in the West. Their rulers vied with their nearest neighbours for pre-eminence, exemplified so well by the milestone inscription, but they also struggled with similar challenges of rule. To understand the underlying dynamics, Rome should be set against the general backdrop of this Afro-Eurasian arena of empire formation. A later section of this chapter will explore the question of military hegemony. Then the character of imperial elites and rule will be analyzed. But first, the chapter turns to the rise to dominance of grand imperial monarchies across the Afro-Eurasian world.

3.1 Interimperial Connectivity

If the Palmyrene milestone contained an unexpected message, a contemporary inscription put up to commemorate the construction of a well in Northern India in 268 CE is nothing short of sensational:

---

[2] For discussion, see Millar 1993: 159–173, Dijkstra 1995: 167–170 and Andrade 2018, chapter 8, pace Sommer 2018: 164–174 (the situation was chaotic and should not be expected to follow a set of well-established routines).
[3] Tacitus, *Histories* I, 4.

(During the reign) of the Mahārāja, Rājātirāja, Devaputra, Kaisara Kaniṣka, the son of Vasiṣka, in the forty-first year – anno 41, on the 25th day of the month of Jyaiṣṭha, at this date this well was dug by Samadavhara(?), of the Tosapuriya scions, in honour of his mother and father, for the benefit of himself with his wife and son, for the welfare of all beings . . . [of all sorts?]. And this dharma has been written.[4]

Much in this text will be familiar to a student of the Greco-Roman world accustomed to the practice of *euergetism* – an elite family paying for a public building project, probably in this case at a Buddhist sanctuary, with an engraving of an accompanying text to honour the benefactor and his family.

What makes the inscription stand out, even in a cross-cultural perspective, is something else: the list of titles given to the Kushan ruler, Kanishka III, 'Great king, king of kings, son of heaven, kaisar'. The first two of these titles emulated the well-known titles of the old Achaemenid emperors and their Sasanian successors. The third, *devaputra*, almost certainly equalled the Chinese imperial title of 'son of heaven'.[5] Spread out between Afghanistan and the floodplains of Northern India, the emperorship of the Kushans mirrored the great powers to their East and West, the rulers of China and of Persia – just like the rising dynasty of Roman Palmyrene nobles claimed to match and surpass their neighbouring Iranian opponent. And just like the Romans, the Kushans too had been put on the defensive by the awesome Shahanshah, Shapur the Great. This may explain why for the first time, and most surprising of all, the Roman term *Kaisar* was included in the titulature of the Kushan ruler. The Sasanians were busy celebrating and broadcasting their astonishing victories over the Roman emperors. At Naqsh-e Rostam, about thirteen kilometres north-west of Persepolis, rock-cut reliefs and multilingual inscriptions were put up, precisely in those years, to boast the unrivalled supremacy of the Iranian world conqueror; even the Caesars had to bow to him (Fig. 3.1).[6] The addition of Caesar to the Kushan titles may well have been a defiant response to the expansive Persian Empire, an attempt to shore up the shaky prestige of the Central Asian and Indian dynasty. The Kushan ruler could match his Sassanian enemy on all counts.

[4] Falk 2009, inscription 2.4 (edited and translated) on p. 28.
[5] Chen 2002 (this was the title used to denote the Chinese concept of 'son of heaven' by the Buddhist monks who from the Kushan world made their way into the orbit of Chinese rulers in this period); Falk 2015 suggests instead that it might equate to the Roman *divi filius*. But Kushan warriors did clash with military contingents from Chinse rulers (Rezakhani 2017: 62), so there is nothing improbable about a Chinese reference.
[6] Huyse 1999; Canepa 2009.

3.1 Interimperial Connectivity

Figure 3.1 Sasanian triumphs over Rome in the third century CE.
a. Relief at Naqsh-e Rostam of Shapur the Great, with the Roman emperors Philip the Arab and Valerian in tributary submission and captivity, second half of the third century CE. Photo: Kourosh Mohammadkhani and Azadeh Pashootanizadeh.
b. Overview of the rock at Naqsh-e Rostam, showing the Sasanian relief located below and in between the Achaemenid royal graves. Photo: Kourosh Mohammadkhani and Azadeh Pashootanizadeh.

As a matter of fact, Kushan power was on the wane. Among the triumphs claimed by Shapur was also the extension of Sasanian power east to Sind and Kushanshahr.⁷ However, to focus on the rhetorical bluff behind the collection of titles in the inscription of Kanishka III would miss the main point. After all, most rulers in history have liked to inflate the image of their might. The really noticeable thing about the engraved text on this stone slab is that by the third century CE it had become possible for a ruler to bundle together a set of titles that between them mapped out a zone of grand imperial power reaching from the Pillars of Hercules and the Atlantic coast of Europe to the mouth of the Yellow River in China.⁸ The Achaemenid Empire had marked the beginning of this development. When Cyrus the Great established his realm, the conquests far exceeded anything the world had known before. Until the mid sixth century CE, the limits of imperial power had been set by ancient Mesopotamia and the Levant, from Nineveh on the Tigris to the second cataract on the Nile. But the armies of the Achaemenids pushed far beyond the confines of this political universe. They would go all the way to Afghanistan, the Indus and mainland Greece, before they had to sound a modest retreat after burning down the Athenian Acropolis. The reach of the Achaemenid ruler was unprecedented. The great king stood alone in the world of states, but only for a while.⁹

In world-historical perspective, the rise of the Achaemenid Empire was merely the first signal of a broader development. Over the following centuries, a vast expansion of imperial space took place. Across the Afro-Eurasian land-mass, several zones of growing peasant populations and state formation were shaping up. Empire followed hot on the heels of the ever-widening frontier of state-making societies that Chapter 2 identified; it represented a consolidation of the power of political elites. The conquests of Alexander mark the moment when vast empire took a decisive step beyond the Achaemenid world order. This may sound paradoxical, because Alexander, the Macedonian king, was (as his allies complained) basically absorbed by the Persian Empire.¹⁰ When this 'last of the Achaemenids' then died in 323 BCE, the realm fractured as his generals fought over the spoils. From one perspective, it might even look as if imperial universalism had collapsed and rulers instead had begun to be content with smaller

---

⁷ Huyse 1999: 23–24 (section 3); Rezakhani 2017, chapter 2, and Benjamin 2021 for an overview of the Kushan Empire and its decline under Sasanian pressure.
⁸ Seland 2022: 111 (though with more emphasis on trade connections than interimperial kingship).
⁹ Herodotus, *Histories* VIII, 50–55; Waters 2021, in brief; Briant 2002.
¹⁰ Arrian, *Anabasis* IV, 7–12; Briant 2002: 2, 876.

territories whose extent was mutually bounded. Conditions had, in some sense, returned to an older polycentric world of the Bronze Age.[11] That, however, is an illusion. As we saw in chapter two, the universe of states and empires had grown far beyond the confines of the Bronze Age centres. What now happened instead was that several new imperial universalisms began to take their place next to the Persian. The monarchies that came out of the wreck of Alexander's empire continued to aspire to celebrate the model of the world-conquering Macedonian king and developed their own Hellenistic imperial culture.[12]

No less significantly, barely had Alexander sounded the retreat from the Indus valley when the Mauryan rulers of the Indian kingdom of Magadha on the Ganges set about extending their sway over Northern India. Under Ashoka, the *dhamma* or order of the Mauryan dynasty would reach to the south of the subcontinent. Further East, the Qin state was busy imposing its hegemony on the so-called Central Plains. The process reached completion in 221 BCE, when what may be called the entire Chinese culture sphere, 'all under heaven', fell under its rule. At that time, Rome and Carthage, at the western end of Afro-Eurasia, were about to enter the final contest to decide which was the stronger of the two. The winner, it turned out, had risen to stand supreme in the Mediterranean. After victory in the Second Punic War (218–201 BCE), Rome quickly moved to assert its hegemony also in the Eastern Mediterranean, where the successor dynasties to Alexander's empire were humiliated and subdued. A century and half after Alexander, vast empires had formed, for the first time, in a number of macro-regions outside the Middle East: India, China, Central Asia and the Mediterranean.

The formation of the Roman Empire was part of a world-historical trend. Over the next several centuries, grand empires continued to consolidate and expand their hold across Afro-Eurasian societies. Some ruling dynasties were toppled by usurpers; some empires fell. Yet other powers would soon step into the void left behind. The Mauryas, for instance, were at their last gasp when Rome emerged triumphant from the showdown with Carthage. But they were then eventually succeeded by the Kushans and, later still, the Guptas. By the second century CE, four empires formed

---

[11] Ma 2013.
[12] Bang 2012. Kosmin 2014 brings out well how the world of rival monarchies expanded. But the context is not a quasi-Westphalian one of bounded monarchies; rather, it explores the emergence of rival imperial universalisms. Certainly, the barely established empire of the Mauryan dynasty should not be seen as a coherent, neatly bounded entity clearly demarcated against the Seleucids. Just like that of the Seleucids, their realm consisted of a number of variously subjected territories.

a virtually continuous geographical band, running from east to west, mostly through the temperate and subtropical zones so conducive to agriculture (Fig. 3.2).

The rulers of all these empires, including the Roman, claimed to be universal and their power boundless. The empire and the world were, to play on the famous phrase of Ovid, the same.[13] Such grandiose claims have, for a long time, presented a provocation, and increasingly an enigma, to modern theorists of state power and sovereignty. The notion of a universal empire was clearly unrealistic; no one was able to rule over everything. This objection has been repeated for centuries like a litany. A state, from this perspective, is properly conceived within a clearly bounded territory, and states are equal in the sense that each one holds absolute sovereignty over its own territory. Universal empire, however, was based on a fundamentally different principle. It was not that the rulers did not know that some polities were beyond their reach. But they thought of statehood as a hierarchy and control as graduated. A universal emperor claimed to stand above all other polities, a notion neatly encapsulated in the Persian imperial title of the king of kings, the *shahanshah*. Courts took pride in the multitude of foreign peoples that came to pay homage, bringing exotic products from their home region as tribute. These gifts, which will be at the heart of the analysis in Chapter 5, served as a ceremonial confirmation of the pre-eminence of the emperor and demonstration of the vast number of subjects and polities existing in varying degrees of submission, ranging from direct control to clientage, or even a merely symbolic recognition.[14]

In practice, the grand imperial courts would rule over a combination of territories and peoples. Some were governed more directly. They would normally receive officials appointed by the court to preside over a province, region or city, and occasionally be subject to cadastral surveys to assess their tax payment capacity. The intensity of these regimes of governmentality varied enormously both inside and between the empires. But as a rule of thumb, the longer and more stable the rule, the greater the areas of such 'internal' administration. Additionally, an imperial lord would normally have a number of client rulers, princes and chieftains under his hegemony. Some would have been appointed directly from the court; others would seek its recognition once they had come to power. The Roman Caesars, for instance, had a great variety of these under their rule, such as the kings of Pontos on the northern Black Sea coast or Herod the Great, in Judaea.

---

[13] Ovid, *Fasti* II, 684.   [14] Bang 2011a and further 2014: 9–32 for a theoretical discussion.

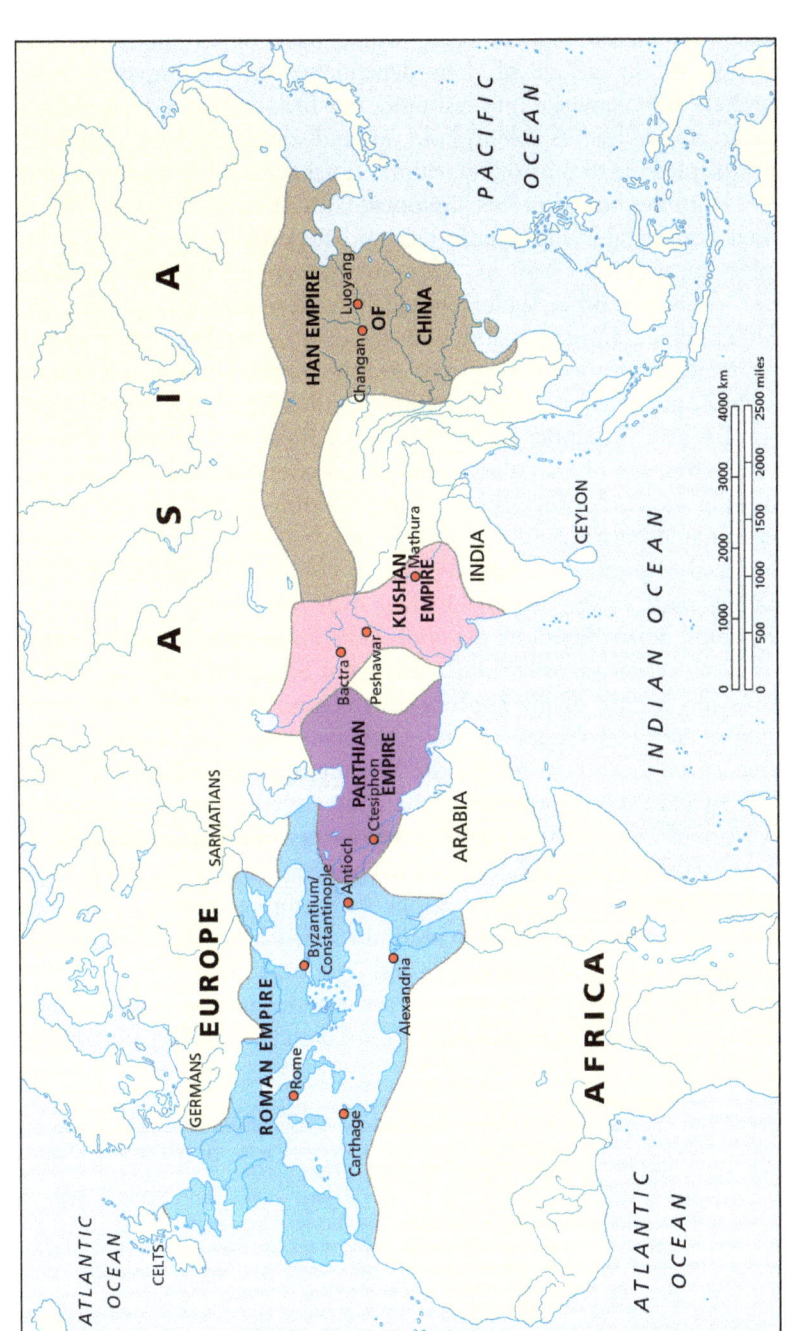

Figure 3.2 The Afro-Eurasian arena of universal empires, second century CE (Rome, Parthia, Kushans and Han dynasty).

The loyalty of these client rulers would have varied enormously, in proportion to the degree of their dependence on the imperial court. Often they might have slid into resistance in which they would have joined an 'outer' ring of leaders able to hold out and sometimes even push back against the pressure of the mighty realm.[15] It has occasionally been said that universal empires lacked proper diplomacy. But it stands to reason that it required considerable diplomatic tact and negotiation to maintain the complex hierarchical web of relations converging on the imperial courts.[16] Very few other leaders would have been able to represent any kind of credible claim to equality with the grand ruler. But they were still able to make claims on the overlord, and the most ambitious might even entertain hopes of overtaking the empire and establishing themselves as universal rulers. Alexander started his career from that position, though with the advantage of his father's solid achievements behind him, and his astonishing success continued to fire the ambitions of military dynasts for the next many centuries.

Universal empires, therefore, also had to coexist with rival powers that were able, more or less, to match their own pretensions to supremacy. There would normally not be many of these. For Roman emperors of the first to sixth centuries, only the Parthian and Sassanian ruler was in that class. As in the case of the rivalries of later universal rulers such as the Ottomans and Habsburgs, or the Ottomans and the Mughals, they attained a grudging *modus convivendi*. When pragmatic concerns dictated, they might address each other as brothers, but equality was never conceded wholeheartedly. Constantly, as the third-century inscriptions illustrate so well, they would seek to assert their pre-eminence in relation to the rival, either symbolically or militarily. While each empire, therefore, liked to pretend to constitute a world unto itself, the rivalry between the great lords also ensured a degree of convergence and interimperiality.[17]

Out of the symbolic clashes between the grand imperial courts, there developed what might be described as a set of broadly shared grammars and

---

[15] Pines & Rüpke 2021. In particular on the client kings of Rome and the character of its imperial frontier, see Braund 1984, Coert forthcoming and Whittaker 1994: 1–59 especially. Lo Cascio 2000: 13–15 brings out well the composite character of Roman imperial power.

[16] The paradigmatic case is constituted by the Chinese empire, where rigid ceremonial demands imposed by the universal emperor in the reception of embassies were often mistaken by observers as having made the court incapable of diplomatic negotiation. See the discussion by Wills 1984, chapter 7. Robinson 2021: 555–562 demonstrates the complex and intricate management of 'foreign' relations by the Ming court; Hevia 1995 by the Qing court.

[17] A concept developed by Doyle 2020. On Sasanian-Roman competitive emulation, see Canepa 2009. See Hall 2012 on universal empires as worlds unto themselves.

repertoires of universal kingship – much as Miguel John Versluys has suggested for the Hellenistic Mediterranean, only with one crucial modification.[18] The resulting languages and ceremonies of power were never welded into a homogeneous continuum. Rather, they engaged in a loosely interconnected and hybrid dialogue spearheaded by the leading courts. Each of these stood at the centre of a distinct imperial tradition but nevertheless continued to take colour, elements and shape from each other. The Roman Caesar or the Persian Shahanshah, for instance, co-evolved as models of kingship; the Confucian tradition of empire established in China was gradually combined with the Ashokan example of the universal ruler that Buddhist monks from India brought to China. Rome, in short, was part of the development that saw the Afro-Eurasian zone of more intensive cultivation and growing peasant populations turned into an arena dominated by the formation of universal empires, from East to West. The models of rulership established by these world-monarchies would continue to develop and set the standard in the world of state-forming elites over the entire course of pre-colonial world history as vast empires continued to decline and reform.[19]

3.2 Why Universal Empires?

But what made these empires come into being in the first place? That is the question now. A traditional response of historians would be to examine the character of the conquest society and then identify some cultural traits that made it particularly prone to successful expansion. Probably the most influential interpretation of Roman imperialism over the last generation has sought the explanation in the particularly rabid and relentless form of militarist expansionism cultivated by the city-state on the Tiber, prompted by fierce inter-aristocratic elite rivalry. The trouble is that most other states, at the time, were no less militarist in outlook. Even after almost a quarter century of war, Carthage still produced a Hannibal to embark on yet another two decades of all-out war against Rome. Warfare was endemic, and victory over enemies was one of the most coveted prizes available to rulers and their elites, not just among Romans or their Mediterranean enemies but in most premodern societies. Roman imperialism, Eckstein plausibly concluded, must be seen as a product of its wider state environment.[20]

---

[18] Versluys 2017. [19] Bang & Kolodziejczyk 2012. [20] Eckstein 2007.

3 Among Empires

States do not exist in splendid isolation but are surrounded by other states. As described in Chapter 2, the world of state formation had been steadily expanding. By the sixth to third centuries BCE, a number of strong clusters, within which states competed with each other over territory and resources, were maturing across Afro-Eurasia. Militarism and a desire for expansion were a product of the struggle for power and survival among such opposing states. The gain of one state immediately became the loss of its neighbours who would henceforth find it more difficult to defend themselves in confrontation with the now stronger rival. A state could not easily adopt a purely defensive attitude.

Political scientists have analyzed the consequences of this condition extensively. They see states as forming systems where they are locked in rivalry with each other.[21] Interstate politics are anarchic and rarely follow moral tenets. States cynically pursue their interests by whatever means possible. 'My enemy's enemy is my friend' will serve as a guiding principle, even if the two new potential allies had recently been at war with each other. Such considerations, according to the political scientists, ensure continued political fragmentation. States constantly change their allegiance to maintain a balance within which smaller powers team up to ensure that no single state will be strong enough to dominate them all.[22] *Realpolitik* is commonly the term used to sum up the insights of modern political science, but that also reflects the fact that its insights have been gained primarily through the study of the early modern European state system. Yet the enduring political fragmentation of Europe is far from the only possible outcome of state competition, and from a Greco-Roman perspective it is arguably a positively misleading experience.

To be sure, there is a strong intellectual-historiographical tradition that sees the fundamental tenets of international politics revealed in the history of Thucydides.[23] His account of the Atheno-Peloponnesian War (431–404 BCE) famously shows how the rise in Athenian power after the Persian wars prompted Sparta and its allies go to war; they feared that the attempts of Athens to dominate and subjugate its allies in the Delian League were transforming the city into the position of a new 'tyrant' that neither its subject allies nor its other Greek neighbours would be able to resist.[24] To prevent Athens from becoming, in the parlour of international political theory, universal hegemon, its rivals led by Sparta set out to take it down

---

[21] Watson 1992. [22] Waltz 1979; Mearsheimer 2001 for a more 'imperial' version.
[23] For example, Gaddis 2018, chapter 2; Münkler 2006: 30–34; Howse 2014, chapter 5.
[24] Thucydides I, 23.6, 122.3 and 124.2–3 (*polin tyrannon*).

before it was too late. However, the narrative unfolds against a background overwhelmingly focused on internal Greek affairs and over a very short span of time – cut even shorter by the death of the author, who did not manage to carry his account down to the end of the war. What fundamentally eludes the Thucydidean perspective is the long-term trend. If Athens failed to establish a viable hegemony, other and stronger powers would soon succeed where the moderately sized city-state had failed. In the longer run, the numerous small city-states of the Mediterranean proved unable to uphold their autonomy and resist the rise of empire. One by one and region by region, they inexorably fell under imperial hegemony until Rome sat astride a world that reached from Nubia to Scotland. The writing was already on the wall when the Peloponnesian War drew to a close. Instrumental in the Spartans' victory was the financial support of the Achaemenid imperial rulers, eager to revenge their ignominious defeats at Marathon and Salamis and to recover their tributary Asiatic subjects. Thucydides may have laid most of the blame for the defeat on the internal dissension and other 'mistakes' of the Athenians, but even he had to recognize the significance of vigorous Persian funding for the Spartan fleet. Grand empire and its hierarchical world order were already reasserting themselves.[25]

From a world-historical point of view, empire is the predictable outcome. While Athens was fighting Sparta in the last third of the fifth century BCE, a cluster or system of 'warring states' that increasingly has become the object of study had similarly taken shape in China. Military competition was ruthless. Alliances were formed and broken with the cynicism that any theorist weaned on European realpolitik would expect. Strategies of alliance building were even pursued to prevent the most powerful state from muffling the others. Little difference did it make. In 221 BCE, the Qin monarchy emerged from the contention as the sole victor. All its rivals had been overcome, and 'all under heaven' was united in a universal empire.[26] On reflection, this is perhaps not so surprising. After all, it is inherent in the logic of competition to generate eventually a winner, and during the century or more following the death of Alexander this began to happen from East to West across the Afro-Eurasian world. A related pattern can be observed also in the precolonial Americas. The absolute chronology was different, and the clusters of state-forming societies emerged along a north-south axis, from Mesoamerica to the Peruvian Andes. Even so, empires eventually began to form, culminating with the

---

[25] Thucydides II, 65, 12, with Hyland 2017: 120. See further Morris 2013.   [26] Hui 2005.

Aztecs and Incas in the fifteenth century before the arrival of the Spanish *conquistadores*.[27]

On closer inspection, strong forces work in favour of the development of a power that is able to gain momentum, gobble up the main rivals within its cluster of neighbouring societies and unite them all in a universal empire. Frederic Lane, one of the classic historians of medieval and early-modern Venice, identified the explanation in a brilliant paper in the 1950s whose significance has only slowly become clear. States, he observed, were primarily engaged in the use of violence. By far the biggest item of expenditure for premodern governments were war and armies. They also spent heavily on religious ritual and public ceremony. All of these areas of activity were important for upholding the order of the ruling class, but the resources required by the military normally outstripped the other spheres. This had profound implications for the development of states.

Let's listen at length to Lane:

> Men specializing in warfare appear very early in the history of the division of labour and were at an early date organized into large enterprises. In the use of violence there were obviously great advantages of scale when competing with rival violence-using enterprises or establishing a territorial monopoly. This fact is basic for the economic analysis of one aspect of government: the violence-using, violence-controlling industry was a natural monopoly, at least on land. Within territorial limits the service it rendered could be produced much more cheaply by a monopoly. … A monopoly of the use of force within a contiguous territory enabled a protection-producing enterprise to improve its product and reduce its costs.[28]

Subjects within the territory were made to pay taxes to the government, and that in return kept other competing violence-using enterprises from claiming payment from its population. Size mattered considerably. More often than not, a big state, able to field a correspondingly large army, would be able not only to see other rivals off but also to conquer them and add their territories to its own possessions.

Lane wrote about medieval and early modern European state formation. Although Europe has been characterized by an enduring plurality of states, the number of independent rulers and governments still fell considerably over this stretch of time.[29] Everywhere across the span of world history, the trend towards amalgamation of state-power is very pronounced. Rather

---

[27] Bang, Bayly & Scheidel 2021, vol. 2, part V and chapters 24 (Smith & Sergheraert) and 25 (Covey).
[28] Lane 1958: 402.
[29] Tilly 1992. Tilly 1985 is a Lane-inspired discussion. More thoughtful and perceptive is Steensgaard 1974.

unusually, however, in Europe this development was arrested at the level of middling-sized states. The continent was beset by periodically recurring and enormously destructive great-power wars that failed to produce a clear winner, but always curbed the most powerful player and left its imperial ambitions in tatters.[30] But that was far from the common situation. Other historical clusters of states have followed the logic of Lane all the way to its conclusion, the clear supremacy of one power over the others and the imposition of an imperial peace.

Once established, such imperial hegemonies often proved stable. The Qin dynasty fell after less than two decades of supreme power, but the Han immediately took over to consolidate an imperial rule that would endure for four centuries. This will not be surprising to Roman historians accustomed to the many dynasties that came in quick succession after the establishment of the monarchy under Augustus. Yet it was not before the Arab conquests of the seventh century CE that the Roman Empire ceased to be the predominant power of the Mediterranean. By extending their sway towards the margins of their state system, universal empires had suspended competition and thereby reduced the chance that a life-threatening challenger would emerge. Along vast stretches, their power ran out only as they reached the frontier of more densely settled areas. Beyond this zone, land was too scarcely populated to sustain state formation and people too mobile or inaccessible to be controlled.[31]

Among world historians, the peoples beyond the sedentary frontier, especially the nomads of the vast central Asian grasslands, hold a special place in the history of imperial conquest.[32] Nomadic peoples, as we have already seen, served as one of the important reservoirs of military manpower before the age of colonialism. Time and again, a conqueror would rise among them and blaze a terrifying trail of military victories through the territories of sedentary rulers. In world history, the early Arabic armies and the Mongols of Chinggis Khan are the most important and famous. In Roman history that position is claimed by Attila the Hun. Nomadic conquerors are, therefore, often seen as the strongest empire-forming force in world history. There is probably a little distortion and exaggeration at play here.

---

[30] Kennedy 1988.
[31] Bang 2021a: 48–53; Scott 2017; Hui 2005 (imperial conquest); Lattimore 1962: 469–491 (a classic on the frontier).
[32] Crossley 2019 for the most brilliant recent example; see Zarakol 2022 for an interesting example from international relations. See also Golden 2011.

Nomads were certainly a significant force, but strong nomadic empires normally rose on the back of large sedentary realms, as emphasized by Nicolai Kradin.[33] Yet nomads will nevertheless help sharpen our understanding of what constituted a successful conqueror. Mobility here was of the essence. Specializing in animal husbandry, nomads enjoyed greater supplies of horses or sometimes camels than sedentary rulers. These animals enabled swift military transport and copious contingents of forceful cavalry that could manoeuvre with ease on the battlefield. Perhaps even more fundamentally, nomads were more readily available for military service. Their mobile lifestyles meant that they were not rooted in a single location like the vast majority of sedentary populations, whose existence depended on access to farmland. Often peasants were also under an obligation to render service to an aristocratic lord. Nomadic people did not operate under these constraints and were more easily mobilized for war. Compared to most agricultural populations, their military participation ratio was very high.[34]

This puts the imperialist success of both the Qin monarchy and the Roman Republic in sharp and global perspective. The Qin is believed to have curbed the old aristocracy and made the peasantry available for service. For the same reason, the first imperial Chinese dynasty has earned a reputation for harsh, tyrannical laws in the histories penned by the lettered, land-owning aristocracy. Uncompromising ruthlessness, however, made the rulers able to field bigger armies, at lower costs than their opponents.[35] In the cases of the Roman Republic and the most successful Greek city-states, as we saw in Chapter 2, the majority population of peasants had, as Finley long ago pointed out, freed itself from aristocratic service to become full citizens.

The human costs of peasant freedom, though, were high. Slavery was much expanded, and aristocratic estates were increasingly cultivated by enslaved war captives and their offspring, complemented only in peak periods by casual free labourers. But that left the citizen peasantry available for service in war. The mobilization rates of the male citizens maintained by the Roman Republic for decades on end were astonishing, among the highest of any population in recorded history.[36] It used to be thought that the long absences of male farmhands caused many a Roman peasant family to lose their lands, ultimately a view derived from classical moralizing

---

[33] Kradin 2014: 32, 43–44.   [34] Shaw 1999.
[35] Lewis 2007, chapter 2; Hui 2005, chapter 2; Fukuyama 2011, chapter 7; Zhao 2015a, chapters 5–7.
[36] Hopkins 1978; Finley 1980.

3.2 Why Universal Empires?

histories. In fact, it may well have been that the peasant population was growing, making land increasingly scarce, and the Republic somehow stumbled on a system capable of channelling excess labour into military enterprise.[37]

While many city-states were able to call extensively on their population for warfare, most remained stuck in the expansionist tracks. The world of Mediterranean city-states, just like the normal situation in nomadic society, was politically extremely fragmented; the majority had populations numbering in the low thousands. Intense mobilization was possible normally only for small communities. A few city-states, though, were significantly larger, among them Rome. What gave the Romans their decisive advantage, however, was their ability to build an extensive war coalition of allies. Here, too, they seem to parallel the most successful nomadic warlords who all depended for their striking power on their capacity to forge the many groupings of nomadic society into one stalwart coalition. In the Roman case, the winning strategy was based on attaching their defeated Italian rivals to their cause. Instead of paying taxes, the Italian subject allies had to contribute soldiers who would go on campaign with the Roman legions and also be allowed a share in the spoils of victory. In the long run this strategy provided the Roman state with an almost inexhaustible reservoir of manpower that no other rival could match. Once a certain threshold had been reached, most other rulers and states had to rely on recruiting mercenaries, a much more expensive solution, to boost the size of the army – not so the Romans or the Qin, who could thereby grind down their enemies.[38]

The nomadic experience, finally, directs the analysis to one last aspect of the question of conquest. Conquest not only subjects the defeated society to the rule of new masters; it also works as a strong transformative force on the victors. Ibn Khaldun (1332–1406), the Arabic statesman and intellectual who late in life encountered one of the last great conquerors in the tradition of Chinggis Khan and the nomadic steppe Teimur Lenk (1336–1405), famously organized his analysis around this problem in his great work *The Introduction to History*. He had spent his active life in the volatile politics mostly of the medieval North African Maghreb. There he had seen

---

[37] De Ligt 2012 and Rosenstein 2004 are the two best argued examples of this revisionist interpretation.
[38] See Scheidel 2009: 15–17 and Rosenstein 2009: 24–34 for a basic comparison of Qin and the Roman Republican mobilization for war. Qin may look more impressive bureaucratically on paper, but the inclusion of the peasantry in the Roman citizenry made the peasants subject to recurrent censuses and call-up for war, not a meagre institutional achievement. See also Beck 2021, on this fundamental similarity, although with different emphasis.

many a ruler fall, and history gave him the explanation. Dynasties were founded by nomadic tribal conquerors. But they found it difficult to consolidate their power. Once the nomads settled down to rule, their social organization was undermined by the urban and agricultural society of their subjects. Their former nomadic lifestyle gave way to a sedentary life dependent on extracting revenue from the conquered. Soon the nomadic rulers forged links with their subjects, as they acquired property and found spouses among the sedentary population. Within a few generations, the cohesive group of nomadic warriors had been dissolved. As its members were absorbed by the host society, its military power evaporated and the ruling dynasty found that its position had become vulnerable to a new, hostile takeover.[39]

The dissipation of nomadic military power contemplated by Ibn Khaldun is only one expression of a wider phenomenon. Not only nomads but all conquerors have seen their society significantly transformed as they both got to enjoy the wealth deriving from extensive conquest and had to adjust to rule their new subjects. The Roman historians of the late Republic endlessly deplore the corruption and decline of morals caused by the acquisition of empire.[40] In the historiography of the short-lived Qin dynasty, the second emperor is presented as a corrupt and self-indulgent tyrant, walled up in his palace, totally under the spell of the chief eunuch and unaware of the state of the realm, its elites and population.[41] But while both the Roman Republic and the Qin dynasty collapsed, their imperial order survived, consolidated under a new monarchy. By contrast to the transient order of tribal nomadic conquerors studied by Ibn Khaldun, the conquest societies of Rome and Qin were anchored firmly in state organization. Once the personnel or social composition of society changed, the key institutions remained and were available to be taken over by the new powerholders. Conquests, in short, could be consolidated into a tributary empire under which a military establishment and privileged groups would get to enjoy the advantages, envisaged by Lane, of a stable imperial monopoly, subsisting on the revenues collected from the majority population.[42]

In that respect, the early Arabic empire put the solution into a short formula. Islam provided the conquering Arabs with a framework that transcended their diverse tribal allegiances. As their conquests spread and

---

[39] Ibn Khaldun, *The Muqaddimah*, trans. F. Rosenthal (1967: 123–147); Gellner 1981, chapter 1.
[40] For example, Sallust, *Bellum Jugurthinum*.   [41] Sima Qian, *Shiji*, chapter 87.
[42] Woolf 2012: 184–188 for the distinction between conquest state and tributary empire.

the Arab soldiers fanned out across the newly won territories in a network of garrison cities, more groups could quickly be absorbed within the community of the universal religion, the *umma*, and thereby consolidate the rule of empire under the caliphs.[43] Later, Islam became too widespread in itself to define a narrowly privileged class of imperial rulers. This was the reality that confronted Ibn Khaldun in the fourteenth century. Once the empire was established, as Ibn Khaldun pointed out, the egalitarian ethos of the conquest elite had to give way to a more rigid hierarchy under a monarch who was striving to elevate himself above his former peers.

As mentioned in chapter 2, Rome may seem an unusual founder of empire because it lacked a monarch. In a Khaldunian perspective, it seems more fruitful to dwell less on the formal contrast and instead note that Republican Rome represents another variety of a relatively egalitarian conquest elite. Once obtained, empire then required, as the historians of the Ottoman dynasty would later re-emphasise, that the rulers shed the ways of steppe and conquest society and transformed themselves into sedentary lords.[44] The assessment of Ibn Khaldun and his successors, here, sounds almost like an echo of the Roman transition from Republican liberty to imperial autocracy under the principate. Consolidation of imperial rule was a question of the disciplining and reformation of both army and elite. The military was turned into a professional body and placed, much as in the Arab case, in permanent garrisons along the military frontier, far from the politics of the capital. In the capital, the old Republican elite was ostensibly kept in place but radically transformed under the discipline of a court government.[45] To explore this issue, the chapter now leaves the nomadic experience behind to study the nexus between aristocratic elites, the collection of taxes and universal kingship.

3.3 From Conquest to Tributary Empire: Divine Kingship and Elite Formation

The elevated character of universal monarchies and their lofty form of courtly government have been quite an intellectual obstacle to historians, a source of both wonder and abhorrence but, either way, not easily explained. This also goes for the Roman imperial monarchy, instituted under Augustus. What to make of the introduction of cultic worship of the ruling emperor as a living god in the Greek East, or of his claim to be the

---

[43] Crone 2006; Robinson 2013; Marsham 2021.
[44] Ibn Khaldun *The Muqaddimah*, trans. Rosenthal (1967: 132–133); Anooshahr 2018, chapter 3.
[45] Bang 2021b and 2013.

son of a god, and the custom of deifying some Caesars at death in the West? Or of the centrality of the imperial household and its many slave servants for running the government? Both phenomena seem to reflect an overly personal and charismatic form of rulership, leaving subjects to suffer the caprices of one inflated individual. Such extravagance jars with the common conception of state power shaped by the normative expectation of checks and balances and the impersonal working of bureaucracy. Yet, as anthropologists from Frazer, who had trained as a classicist, to Sahlins have documented, divine kingship has been an integral element of monarchy throughout history.[46]

The world historian will then add that the centrality of divine kingship was not derived from a never-changing cultural archetype but established pragmatically through the dissemination of a number of predominant courtly styles and models. The world in which universal empires took shape was not a secularized universe, but one in which divine power to most people was real and regularly intrusive. Human and godly society were inseparable and intertwined. Any self-proclaimed ruler of the world had to demonstrate that the power of empire was consonant with the higher forces of the cosmos. Whatever the emperor – Roman, Chinese or you name it – the person was obligated to participate in an endless stream of state cultic ceremonies to guarantee that his or her reign was in alignment with divine power and the authority of emperors, as the most powerful, to most people unfathomable, person among humans, blended in with that of divinities. High above everyone else, too big to be merely human, too mortal to be unequivocally divine, they were located at an intersection, their task to mediate between gods and people. The notion of monarchical divinity, therefore, was rarely absolute but normally situational. In some contexts, the role of the ruler resembled divinity; in others it was that of a mere human.[47]

In that respect, the aristocratic elites of the Roman Empire responded to the divine claims of their autocratic ruler in a way that echoes the pattern of other grand realms. From one perspective, they would collude in the elevation of the emperor to divine status. If the emperor was superhuman, it was both easier to abide by his orders and more prestigious to serve him. From another, they insisted that the ruler was just one of them and had to show respect.[48] Chinese elites came up with the notion of the mandate of heaven. The ruler was ordained by the heavenly power to rule, but if he fell

---

[46] Moin & Strathern 2022; Graeber & Sahlins 2017; Frazer 1890.
[47] Woolf 2008; Edelmann 2007.
[48] For fundamental discussions of the imperial cult, see Price 1984; Beard, North & Price 1998, chapter 7, and Gradel 2002.

short of the moral ideals of the elite, the mandate would be revoked and passed on to a new incumbent.[49] Likewise, in Islam, the title of caliph in the beginning signified that the commander of the faithful was the deputy of God on earth. However, as Muslim power was stabilized, the (religious) elites asserted themselves to insist that the caliph was not directly appointed by God but merely the human successor of Muhammad as leader of the body politic.[50]

Everywhere the consolidation of imperial government saw the position of the monarch becoming more elevated and aloof, raised above the original conquest elite. But highness was hedged about by intricate questions of etiquette and elaborate ceremonial that served to regulate the interaction of monarch and elites. Rituals both defined and constrained the superiority of the ruler.[51] Many of the gory conflicts that enliven the histories of both Roman and other emperors sprang out of attempts by the rulers to break free of stifling ceremony and expand their room for manoeuvre.[52]

The venue where these struggles played out was the monarchical court. Contemporary writings, mostly drawn from the male aristocratic and elite layers of imperial societies, abound with disparaging remarks about life in the corridors of the palaces. Mothers, wives, daughters, mistresses, the female relations of the ruler, as well as his domestic servants, many of these played a powerful role in the politics of imperial society, because they were close to the emperor and had his ear, so to speak – much to the dismay of male aristocrats who wanted the same influence for themselves.[53] For most of history, households and families have constituted the foundations of societal power. Nowadays, we tend to frown upon this as blatant corruption that undermines the power of the state. But in the past, the state as an organization was much less pervasive. Its power could not be established against family networks but only by harnessing their resources for its purposes.[54] At the heart of court society was the household of the emperor, the richest person of the realm. Although the notion of household might be taken to imply a very simple arrangement, there was nothing simple about it. The imperial households were the result of an enormous accumulation of lands, riches and people. Servants had to be arranged in elaborate hierarchies, and extensive record-keeping was necessary to keep track

---

[49] Bielenstein 1986: 223, 230 and 259–262, and Loewe 1986: 733–740. [50] Crone & Hinds 1986.
[51] Richards 1993: 100–101. Bang 2011b, especially pp. 125–128. [52] Winterling 2003.
[53] Fejfer 2008: 368–369 especially points out how the female imperial portrait even became an important medium in the communication between ruler and elites.
[54] Haldén 2020.

of it all.⁵⁵ The imperial household served, in that respect, as the centre of governmental administration, but no less significantly as the centre of 'high society'.⁵⁶

One of the most important functions of the court was to constitute a splendid venue for the demonstration of monarchical power. Grand monumental buildings, lavish dinners parties, carefully choreographed processions – in short, pomp and pageantry – were crucial instruments of rule. They made the power of the ruler manifest, put it on display and advertised it to the world.⁵⁷ Under the Caesars, Rome was transformed into a magnificent scene for the court. No expense was spared. Ancient obelisks, for instance, were transported in custom-built ships from distant Egypt to Italy and put up to adorn the monuments of the capital. These age-old and majestic marvels proclaimed the unprecedented reach of Roman power and were part of a steadily accumulating repertoire of monuments adorning the capital. Marble temples, imperial fora, public baths, giant domes and soaring vaults and, not to forget, the sprawling palace complex on the Palatine hill, the horse race course of the Circus Maximus and the arena of the Colosseum – these are all things that continue to give Rome its special flavour, but they are also what puts it in 'league' with other grand imperial capitals. Across the Afro-Eurasian world, universal monarchies attempted to set the standard for lesser royalty and state-making elites through opulent building programmes and elaborate spectacles. The conspicuous display of wealth celebrated the great diversity of subjects under imperial rule and provided the emperors with a dazzling ambience to make the circles of power truly charmed.⁵⁸ Courtly splendour was designed to attract from near and far elites who, by offering service and submission, hoped to get to share in the power of the monarch and bask in the glory of the court.

This was necessary because even though the households of emperors were vast institutions, the imperial realms were far too big to be managed by the rulers' own administrative staff. Sometimes historians come across declarations in the sources that everything, so to speak, belonged to the

---

[55] On the administrative intricacies of the Roman imperial household, see, e.g., Lo Cascio 2000: 97–194.

[56] Elias 1969 for a fundamental sociological analysis of the mechanisms of the court and the royal household. Some historical discussions are Wallace-Hadrill 1996; Lal 2005; Spawforth 2007; Duindam, Artan & Kunt 2011 and Duindam 2015.

[57] Cannadine & Price 1987 for a pivotal collection analyzing 'pomp and circumstance' as a key dimension of premodern power, responding in part to the inspiration of Geertz 1980.

[58] Bang 2018b. For an analysis of imperial palatial and symbolical buildings, see in general Hilsdale 2021, and for specific examples, see Koch 2006 (on the Taj Mahal and the Mughals); Forêt 2000 (on the Chengde of the Qing dynasty) and Necipoglu 1992 (on the Topkapi of the Ottomans).

3.3 From Conquest to Tributary Empire

ruler. Seneca, for instance, is on record for the maxim 'Caesar omnia habet'.[59] But such statements belong to the realm of legal fiction or rhetorical flourish. In reality, power had to be shared and offices created where members of the imperial elites, themselves head of grand households, were employed to help administer the realm. One of the founders of modern sociology, Max Weber, described empires as patrimonial-bureaucratic organizations. From one perspective, they could be seen as a sprawling network of royal and aristocratic households or patrimonies; from another they displayed a hierarchy of offices and written administration.[60]

For antiquity, most historians would place Rome at the patrimonial end of the spectrum while the empire of the Qin/Han dynasty in China would customarily be located closer to the bureaucratic.[61] The number of elite administrators sent out by the 'son of heaven' to govern provincial society was considerably larger than those of the Roman *princeps*. But this contrast should not draw attention away from a more fundamental overlap. In both these and other universal monarchies across the Afro-Eurasian arena, government bureaucracies were minuscule compared to modern standards. Even the late Roman Empire and the Qing dynasty in early modern China, some of the largest, most notorious and best documented premodern bureaucratic bodies on record, made do with only some 25,000 to 30,000 officials for populations of several tens of millions.[62]

This was only possible because imperial rule relied on the service of landed aristocracies or gentry. With their stable basis in agrarian wealth, aristocrats already wielded power in society, formed part of resourceful patronage networks and possessed large households of their own.[63] The respect they commanded from the common population made them attractive tools of government but also represented a challenge. The trouble was that, when governing on behalf of the ruler, they were not simply his tools. Government office was an add-on that boosted an already substantial portfolio of power resources at the command of aristocracy and gentry. Officeholders grew their networks of connections and clients on the job, as it were, and gained access to the revenue flows of

---

[59] Seneca, *De Beneficiis* VII, 3, 6, discussed by Giliberti 1996.
[60] Weber 1980 (1921), chapter 9, 3–4, 580–653. Blake 1991 for an empirical analysis based on the Mughals.
[61] Millar 1977; Saller 1982: 111–116; Loewe 2006; Zhao 2015b. Scheidel 2009: 15–20. Beck 2021.
[62] Crossley 2021: 825 (30,000 max for the Qing and Ming); Garnsey & Humfress 2001, chapter 2 (approximately 30,000 for the late Roman bureaucracy). See further Auyang 2014: 208–211.
[63] Bang & Turner 2015.

the state.⁶⁴ The biggest and most highly placed of these creatures could aggregate power and resources to such an extent that they might become a potential rival or at least an obstacle to the monarch. The history of the Han dynasty is punctuated by the attempt of Wang Mang, the all-powerful first minister, to usurp the throne and establish his own line (9–23 CE). The number of such people from Roman history is almost too numerous to mention, but Seianus, the over-mighty praetorian prefect of the elderly Tiberius, may stand in for them all.⁶⁵

All patrimonial rulers had to practise a number of strategies designed to keep their privileged groups within bounds and under a modicum of control.⁶⁶ At their most brutal, it was far from uncommon to see a member of the very top of the imperial elite brought down and executed, or made to commit suicide, at the emperor's command if the person had become or was considered an obstacle to the monarch. The histories of the imperial courts are full of such persons. Seneca, the philosopher, teacher of Nero and perhaps the most famous Roman victim of the politics of the palace, joined a large global club of statesmen that equally fell foul of their monarch when he was forced to commit suicide (in his bathtub) in 65 CE. But taking a murderous route was rarely conducive to the good functioning of government. More often than not, it was a result of failure and breakdown in the relationship between monarch and court elite. Barely had the Qin dynasty established its rule of 'all under heaven' before its ruthless and domineering style alienated the elites of the empire. Soon a rebellion toppled the second incumbent of the dynasty and established the Han on the throne. In the daily life of court government, other strategies than blunt brutality had to be used.⁶⁷

With a metaphor half-humorously borrowed from horse breeding, two types of premodern elite may be distinguished.⁶⁸ You could have stallions or geldings. Stallions were the normal kind of aristocrat, but you could also see people rise to positions of authority that had been socially and sometimes literally castrated. The ban on marriage for Catholic priests was introduced during the European Middle Ages to prevent the property of

---

⁶⁴ As P. Eich 2015: 136–137 observes, even the late Roman imperial administration was heavily embedded in the social hierarchies of society and best understood not as a technical bureaucracy but as a kind of personal bureaucracy, absorbed by the aristocracy.
⁶⁵ Tacitus, *Annales* XV, 60–65. Bang Gu, *History of the Former Han Dynasty*, trans. H. H. Dubbs, vol. 3 (1955), pp. 470–474.
⁶⁶ On the many roles and strategies of an emperor, see Lieven 2022 (in world history) and Hekster 2022 (Rome).
⁶⁷ For example, Sima Qian, *Shiji*, chapter 87; Wallace-Hadrill 1996; Bang 2011b.
⁶⁸ Gellner 1983: 14–16.

the church from drifting into the hands of clerical families. If the clerics could not have legitimate children, they would produce no primary heirs to whom wealth could be passed on. Another method was to have recourse to either slaves or eunuchs. Both types of individuals had been deprived of their full social existence, as we saw Orlando Patterson argue in Chapter 2. Eunuchs were unable to father children. Slaves (if not also castrated) physically could, if permitted, but then the offspring belonged to the master. Either way, the capacity of these socially deracinated individuals to establish their own households and families had been severely limited, but not made completely impossible. Often they managed to forge both ties of patronage and various bonds of family. Several of the slaves of the Roman imperial household are recorded on inscriptions as having married even free citizen women.[69] But these things remained under the control of the owner and constituted a privilege that was ultimately revocable.

Paradoxically, this made slaves and eunuchs attractive as trusted servants of the monarch in running the government. They crop up everywhere across the Afro-Eurasian world of empires and monarchies, because they were, so to speak, the creatures of the ruler and could therefore, at least in theory if not always in practice, be trusted to align more closely with his interests.[70] And if they did not, they could be punished severely, without provoking the resentment that the powerful aristocratic groups usually mobilized when it was one of their own kind who got to feel the royal wrath. Quite the reverse, the normal elites would often have applauded. In their eyes, slaves and eunuchs were lowly people and had to be kept in their place, which was certainly not one that gave them command over people of the more 'worthy' sort. In that respect, the indignant scorn that a hostile tradition has relentlessly heaped on, say, the top-government freedmen of Claudius, Pallas, Narcissus and Polybius was quite in keeping with the global norm.[71] Celibates, eunuchs or slaves were an answer to the challenges of rule and control in societies dominated by patrimonial households. But they represented a special answer, not a general solution; they were confined to the, if sometimes powerful, margins of society such as the inner palace of the ruler.

Out in society, solutions that integrated the landed elites had to be devised. A quick glance at the organization of the imperial elite in the Mughal Empire will help reveal what was required. People have

---

[69] Weaver 1972, chapter 7.   [70] Hathaway 2018; Kutchner 2018.
[71] Seneca *Apocolocyntosis*, a satire over the deceased emperor Claudius, concludes by imagining Claudius as the servant of his powerful and therefore out-of-order freedmen, the ultimate mockery.

understood this Perso-Indian empire as either a bureaucratic system or a network of patrimonial households. The backbone of the imperial body was the corps of so-called *mansabdars*, drawn from elites from across and beyond the empire. This cosmopolitan ruling aristocracy was defined by service to the emperor and regulated through rank, revenue and rotation. At court, the *mansabdars* were graded into a hierarchy of numerical ranks. The rank then determined the size of the revenue grant that the *mansabdar* would receive out of the imperial taxes to maintain his own household and a contingent of soldiers. Technically speaking, a revenue grant consisted in the right to collect the taxes from a particular district. This made the aristocratic household dependent on continued service to the empire but also meant that the imperial revenue collection risked being absorbed among the other elements of the portfolio that made up the assets of the aristocratic household. The Mughal emperors therefore periodically reshuffled the distribution of the revenue grants so that the revenue holders would not continuously collect from the same district but had to move to another part of the empire.

Likewise, the *mansabdars* were regularly assigned to new postings and also saw their ranks changed. All this ensured that they remained dependent on service and did not turn the imperial grants into their own inalienable property.[72] Few other empires attempted to exert the degree of control over the landed wealth of the imperial elite as the Mughal, yet the basic principles of the *mansabdari* system were usually employed in some form or other by most premodern empires in their attempt to consolidate rule. At court an imperial elite was forged by giving it access to title and rank, as well as patronage networks and the wealth of the imperial revenues. But these benefits remained dependent on continued service. Instead of the conquest elite, the consolidation of imperial rule gradually substituted a cosmopolitan aristocracy that could be recirculated and deployed outside its region of origin.[73]

Under the Roman emperors, for instance, the old senatorial aristocracy was transformed into an imperial elite of rank and service. The number of incumbents of the highest office, the consulate, was increased. This both satisfied the ambition of more members of the Senate to reach the most prestigious rank and expanded the pool of the highest ranking that could be drawn upon for service, both in the ceremonies of the capital and in the government of the provinces. Meanwhile, a second tier of aristocratic

---

[72] Richards 1993: 58–68.
[73] Bang 2008, chapter 2, for a comparison of the Mughal and Roman aristocracies.

careers were created for the 'junior' elite of Roman society, the Equites ('knights'). Whereas it had once been the voting assemblies of the people that had served as the main arbiter of the public careers of the Roman elite, that function was now primarily in the hands of the emperor. As a result, strong provincial families were gradually included in the Roman aristocracy. Their wealth and power in provincial society made it possible for them to push to the front and gain the emperors' attention. When old established families failed to reproduce or withdrew from politics, it was increasingly from such groups that the ranks of the Roman aristocracy were replenished. Over a couple of centuries the old Roman nobility was transformed into a cosmopolitan ruling class, until provincial dynasties like Zenobia's from Palmyra had become the main contenders for the throne in the civil wars of the third century CE.[74]

In the eyes of nineteenth-century scholars, the cosmopolitan imperial elites were lacking in technical competence. Modernizing state builders were busy professionalizing administrations and armies, creating new military academies and specialized university degrees for the administration to supplant the rule of cosmopolitan aristocrats.[75] Compared to the new professionalized form of governmentality, specialization among the old cosmopolitan ruling classes was relatively limited. Sometimes attempts are made to distinguish between people of the pen and those of the sword. But these two spheres of activity did not chart clearly separate career paths. It was normal that a career would combine elements of both. Think, for instance, of the 'king' of Roman jurisprudence, Ulpian, who came to a sticky end as prefect of the praetorian guard, killed by the soldiers.[76] The ideal for the top-level aristocrat was that of the gentleman, not that of a trained professional. Frequent rotation, short tenure of offices and modestly sized staffs meant that the expert familiarity and technical knowledge celebrated by the professional were beyond the reach of such administrators.[77]

---

[74] Burton & Hopkins 1983; Weisweiler 2020. Provincial integration of the ruling class, though, remained exclusive and uneven. Some provinces could sport a considerable cohort of people who had risen to membership in the Roman senate, while others barely saw any families rise to the top. Networks of patronage were decisive. For further comparative reflections on the Roman nobility (although focused on the republic), see Vankeerberghen 2021.
[75] McNeill 1982, chapters 5–7; van Creveld 1999, chapters 3–4; Hevia 2012, chapters 1–2.
[76] Dio, *Cassius* LXXX, 2, 2–4.
[77] Garnsey & Saller 1986, chapter 2; Garnsey & Humfress 2001, chapter 2, on the principate and late Roman world. Van Berkel & Duindam 2018 for a range of studies of premodern elites, dedicated to the sword or the pen.

But this should not in itself be seen as a sign of inefficiency. While modern administrations were created around the need to optimize, rationalize and intensify the extraction of resources and expand the domains of state activity, the aims of the old empires were much more modest. Taxes were generally kept stable and moderate. The task of the elite administrator was to mediate in the conflicts of local elites and communities, broker connections between the court and the most powerful local families, and supervise the collection of taxes. One of their most important activities was simply to receive petitioners and hear cases. This made a gentlemanly demeanour and comportment much more important than specialist knowledge. Imperial officials had to embody the distant authority of the ruler, lend lustre and dignity to their office, and be able to socialize effortlessly among the leaders of local communities.[78]

In practice it was this latter class of people that had to handle the daily business of empire. Across the universal empires, local leadership was drawn mostly from affluent landowning families. Only they commanded the resources, influence and networks necessary to control their communities. Before the age of railroads, steamships and the electric telegraph, the gradient of connectivity leaned heavily in favour of local control. The channels of communication and transport kept open by beasts of burden, and sailing boats did not run fast or wide enough to enable a distant court to monitor communities closely. The ruler had to rely on the capacity of local powerholders.[79] Censuses, land surveys and record keeping were often introduced to consolidate the imperial hold, at least on the most affluent territories. Yet, as long as the lower levels of administration remained in the hands of the locals, there were clear limits to the reach of the court. Government did not substitute a copious and well-paid staff to collect the taxes, but remained crucially dependent on its local elites to provide the organizational and financial infrastructure. Local elites constituted the enabling tool, but also a screen that significantly limited the capacity of the centre to penetrate local communities.[80]

More than close control, the primary objective of the court was to maintain cordial cooperative relations with the local elites and keep conflicts to a minimum. That was sufficient to ensure the continued collection of taxes. But it also meant that net taxation was commonly quite modest, rarely increased and constantly subject to erosion. For the Roman Empire, estimates

---

[78] Saller 1982; Metcalf 1984; Meyer-Zwiffelhoffer 2002.
[79] Mann 1986, chapters 4 and 8, are fundamental on the logistical constraints of centralized premodern empires, as is Braudel 1972: 355–393, 'distance, the first enemy'.
[80] Bang 2015a. See also P. Eich 2015: 141.

hover around 5 per cent of gross domestic product (GDP). This is not quite as minuscule as it sounds. These taxes were imposed on agricultural economies, where a majority of households lived close to subsistence level. The disposable surplus over and above the bare subsistence needs of the population may well have been less than 50 per cent of the total product. Introduction of a tax demand for some 5 per cent of production in such an economy would have constituted a very considerable change, about a tenth of the surplus, and have been a significant spur to economic integration within the empires. Imperial tributes were generally consumed far from their point of collection, concentrated in lavish expenditure around the life of the court and on the armies stationed or on campaign in some of the provinces. The capitals of the rulers, whether Rome, Constantinople, Shahjahanabad (Delhi) or Beijing, invariably grew into some of the biggest cities in pre-industrial history and their armies some of the biggest military establishments.[81]

Even so, the imperial systems could not have functioned merely on what we might describe as such a bare bones budget. Most importantly, such a model would not sufficiently account for the costs of tax collection. That was expensive. Peasants commonly had to pay dues notionally far higher than what the net expenditures of the imperial governments would suggest. Both tithes and fifths, for instance, are known from the Roman Empire. The upshot of this is that the local, mostly landowning elites who managed the collection of imperial revenue must normally have kept a sizeable share for themselves.[82] How else could they be expected to organize the collection? After all, nothing really comes for free. But that, of course, also put very real limits on the share that central government could hope to claim or even receive from the agricultural economy. Demands for higher tax-payments were sure to meet with fierce opposition and resistance. In fact, arrears in tax payment regularly kept accumulating for decades on end.

Frustrated by the meagre holdings in the state treasury on his accession, the Yongzheng emperor (1722–1735), for instance, finally attempted reform. The chronic underfunding of provincial and local government in China was to be alleviated by regularizing the share of the agricultural surplus claimed by local gentry and magistrates as surcharges and what

---

[81] Bang 2008, chapter 2, for the comparative analysis, although with slightly different figures, of the Roman and Mughal Empires. But within the broad parameters of this model there was of course room for variation. Although probably underestimating the relative significance of the Roman land tax, Scheidel 2015c is surely correct to suggest that the army featured more prominently in the Roman budget; civilian officials were featured more prominently in the budget of the Han dynasty. Hopkins 1980 remains fundamental on Rome; for Afro-Eurasia in general, see O'Brien 2012.
[82] Scheidel 2015b.

have you in the name of organizing collection. From now on, such surcharges were to be part of the standard tax and be allocated to fund the operation of local government. But the reform failed, predictably, because the system continued to rely on the established power structure in agricultural communities dominated by networks of patronage, local landowners and their lackeys. They still expected to profit handsomely from their position, and they were strong enough to make good on their claim.[83]

One of the paradoxical results of the imposition of an imperial tax, therefore, was that local elites everywhere benefitted and became wealthier. Imperial backing, combined with the stability of peace, meant that landowners were able to tighten their hold on the peasant majority and gradually claim a larger part of the surplus. But even as local aristocracies can generally be seen as joining the cause of empire, rebellions were far from infrequent. Competition between rival elite groups within communities, for instance, might press one of them into rebellion. Most of the time, however, imperial courts were able to quell or contain that kind of opposition. Chapter 6 will explain why in greater detail; for now it will suffice to note that the imperial armies could generally rely on their size to defeat local opponents.

This advantage made the imperial hegemonies surprisingly stable. They could endure with isolated pockets of local resistance or, as they were often portrayed, outbreaks of banditry, while more serious regional rebellions would often be ground down. But, by the same token, local elites had considerable leeway before the army would be called in. After all, it was both an expensive and extreme measure that had to be used sparingly, as special deterrence rather than the standard method. Local aristocracies were fully aware of this limitation and ruthlessly exploited their bargaining power to better their position in imperial societies. Farhat Hasan, a historian of the Mughals in India, once remarked that the consolidation of empire saw their power subjected to a downward gravitational pull.[84] As networks between court and local elites strengthened through decades of cooperation, Mughal statecraft struck firmer roots in provincial society. However, at the same time, power was increasingly taken over by the provincial elites. Eventually, the position of the centre in Delhi or Shahjahanabad had been hollowed out, reduced to a position of a mere

---

[83] Zelin 1984, the analysis neatly summarized on pp. 306–307; for more detail, see especially chapters 6–7.
[84] Hasan 2004.

ceremonial overlord, while the empire broke up into a number of regional monarchies. Power had drifted out to the provinces. This is a scenario that no student of late antique Roman history will fail to recognize. From one perspective, the imperial state looked more extensive and imposing than ever. Yet, as the state apparatus expanded and reshaped the empire, power left Rome behind. The old capital had become a purely symbolical centre, while a number of regional courts emerged to take over as local power holders.

The state builders of the nineteenth century saw this kind of decentralization as a sign of the inherently corrupt nature of the old empires and their inevitable decline. But the regionalization of power was as much a sign of imperial success.[85] Provincial elites had been integrated into the imperial fabric and eventual took it over. Every universal empire charted its own specific course. History, after all, is not a purely mechanical process. But the underlying trend is unmistakable. Sometimes the centre managed to retain a fair amount of power, as under the late Ottoman or Qing dynasty; at other times, fragmentation was more pronounced. The development of the Arab caliphate from the seventh to the tenth century would be a good example. However, in either case, the successful developmoent of universal empire was decisively shaped by the rise of provincial elites. As they took over power, they adopted the style of the predominant court and consolidated a form of civilization. But to explore the process of imperial culture and civilization, we have to wait for the next chapter.

---

[85] Tezcan 2010; Khoury 1997; Bayly 1988: 3 and 14–21.

CHAPTER 4

The Imperial Cosmopolis
Courtly Literary Languages and Monotheist Religions

> [Alexander] then came to Hipperia, the city in Bebrycia. Here were a temple and idol of Orpheus. Both the Pierian muses and the wild animals stood placed around his statue. When Alexander took the image of Orpheus in sight, the statue began to sweat all over. Alexander then asked 'What is this sign?'. Menelaos, the soothsayer, answered him: 'King Alexander, much will you sweat and hard will you toil while subjecting the barbarian peoples and the cities of the Hellenes. And just as Orpheus, by playing his lyre and by singing, prevailed over the Hellenes, defeated the Barbarians and tamed the wild animals, so will you, by the hard labour of your spear, put all into submission.' After Alexander had heard this, he dismissed the soothsayer with great honours.
>
> *Alexander Romance*, Book 1[1]

This passage derives from the so-called *Alexander Romance*. Penned in Greek by an unknown author, most probably at Alexandria in the third century CE, the text mirrors the expansion of empire in the accomplishments of culture. Alexander the Great did not only in time serve to recall the fabulous and unmatched exploits of a great military conqueror: if his name lived on, it was because it was sung by countless poets, historians and other literati over the next many centuries. Hellenistic kings and Roman emperors all celebrated the Macedonian conqueror, but his fame travelled wider, far beyond the shores of the Mediterranean and deep into Asia. Alexander became an emblem of universal empire. Throughout the arena

---

[1] *Alexander Romance*, Book 1, 42, 4–5 (ed. L. Bergson, 1965, with subchapters by Van Thiel 1974); my translation, based on the so-called *Beta* recension, a fourth- to fifth-century CE Greek rendition of the *Romance* that presents a small but interesting variation foregrounding violence in our passage, compared to the slightly earlier third-century *Alpha* version. For comparison of the two Greek late antique and the Latin fourth-century versions, see Paschalis 2007: 76–85. The *Alexander Romance* was already in its first, third-century CE version an amalgam of many texts. Our passage has roots that can be traced to a text, preserved on a second-century Berlin papyrus (see Papathomas 2000) and, of course, develops a story also in Plutarch, *Life of Alexander* 14.8, and Arrian, *Anabasis* I, 11, 1–2.

of world monarchies that formed across Afro-Eurasia at the turn of the common era, there rose a number of cosmopolitan literary cultures.

Normally, Latin and Greek are approached solely as members of the Indo-European language family and predecessors of modern national, romance languages. However, they may equally well be studied as part of a family of cosmopolitan languages that followed in the footsteps of conquest and imperial dynasties over the course of pre-colonial world history. In this chapter, the formation of Hellenistic and Roman imperial culture and languages will be recontextualized among a number of cosmopolitan dialects that came to dominate the world of letters for centuries, spanning from Sanskrit and Arabic to Chinese and Persian. A section seeks to portray these cosmopolitan imperial cultures and identifies some common characteristics amid all their sprawling variety. The examination then moves on to probe the sociology of manuscript cultures and the dynamics that fuelled the dissemination and consolidation of imperial cosmopolitanism into monotheist religions. But first the discussion turns to explore connections between the zones of cosmopolitan imperial culture. In order to do so, it is necessary to dwell for a few pages more on Alexander, his legendary rendezvous with Orpheus and the career of his *Romance* across the Afro-Eurasian arena.

4.1 Connections

From its conception in the kingdom of Egypt, the *Alexander Romance* would go on to enjoy one of the most spectacular careers in the world of preprint books. In time, it became the most important vessel for the legend of Alexander. Quickly the Greek text began to attract translations: Latin, Armenian, Syriac, Arabic, Persian – the list kept growing century after century as the text coursed through the world of Afro-Eurasian letters. Confined to the manuscript form, even a reasonably successful book might at this time never see more than a few hundred copies produced. The *Alexander Romance* belongs to a very select group of texts that broke the ordinary bounds of scribal reproduction to travel across linguistic, cultural and religious barriers.[2] Its readers were treated to a semi-historical fable on universal kingship and rule. Alexander is the fearless and daring conqueror. His swashbuckling quest takes him to the ends of the earth, to the bottom of the sea and high up in the sky. Along the journey, wonders and wise men or women await the hero in a steady stream, while he again and again

---

[2] Stoneman, Erickson & Netton 2012; Debie 2024 (on the winding path of the Syriac versions).

proves himself destined to rule over all of humanity, assert his position at the top of the hierarchy of monarchs and collect tribute from even the most distant of peoples. Yet even this paragon of a world emperor, verging on the sphere of superhuman divinity, finds that he has to come to terms with his own mortality. Rulership also demanded that the incumbent would be a seeker after wisdom and knowledge. The exercise of power required more than mere bravado: nobility of character, generosity, an appreciation of the arts and a capacity to listen and take advice from others.

As the novelistic fable went through the hands of multiple, multilingual translators and down the generations, its story began to snowball. Anecdotes were added, episodes rebranded, and changing geopolitical landscapes registered. The text took on a life of its own, and poets included its narrative in even bigger compositions. The founding epic of (modern) Persian, the *Shahnameh* or *Book of Kings*, elaborated on the *Romance* in its song dedicated to Alexander. If its author, Firdausi (c. 935–1020), from the region of Khorasan in North-Eastern Iran, might be considered the Homer of Farsi, Nizami (1141–1203) would be the Vergil. Writing from the city of Ganja in modern Azerbaijan, he produced a set of five epics, including some of the most famous love stories of Persian literature. The longest of these epic poems is the *Eskandarnameh*, the *Book of Alexander*. Almost a millennium had passed since the original fashioning of the *Romance* by a Greek writer.

Meanwhile, the former territories of the Roman Near East and Sasanian Empire had come under the rule of Muslim dynasties. As a timeless emblem of rulership, Alexander is still presented acting in the swashbuckling style of the novel, but his exploits now also see him making a trip to Mecca, coaxing the ruler of China into submission and the payment of tribute, as well as campaigning against the Rus.[3] The expanding world of state-making elites that we met in the previous chapters finds direct reflection in the widening geographical horizon of artistic production. Where India had once marked the furthest boundary conceivable, it was now set by China and the medieval Rus.

Yet the *Romance* not only accumulated new material as it travelled further east; it also shed some elements. The episode around the statue of Orpheus with which this chapter opened dropped out of the narrative. Both the Latin and the Armenian versions have it, but the Syriac let it slip and thus kept it from entering the Arabic and Persian tradition.

---

[3] Nizami, *Eskandarname* XXVI (visit to the Kaba), LII (visit to the ruler of China), LXV (victory over Rus).

Nonetheless, its striking image of Orpheus subduing the wild animals through his music still made it into the Persianate poetic discourse, but by a circuitous route.[4]

Long before the *Romance*, the image of Orpheus had found a small niche in the pageantry and representation of Roman emperors. Among the spectacles in the Colosseum, immortalized by Martial in a set of epigrams, the audience was treated to a playful, if gruesome, mythological inversion. A host of animals had peacefully gathered around an impersonation of Orpheus. But the Thracian bard was dead, killed by a bear sent by Eurydice to fetch him down to the underworld.[5] Meanwhile, the epic poet, Roman nobleman and courtier Silius Italicus eulogized the emperor Domitian, both as a new Alexander Dionysus whose glorious victories would reach to all corners of the earth and as a force of such artistic creativity that he had surpassed even Orpheus, whose lyre had made 'the river Hebrus stand still and Mount Rhodope move on'.[6]

The tale of Orpheus playing so beautifully that it made predators and herbivores, wild as well as tame animals, come together in harmony was best understood as a parable on universal kingship, as the African senator Fronto reminded his young pupil, Marcus Aurelius, the adopted prince and future emperor, in the 140s CE. Exemplary character and eloquence, the virtues of which Orpheus was the paragon, would enable the leader to form a great following such that 'although its members were made up of diverse ethnicities, with varied cultures, they would nevertheless come to live in harmony, get accustomed to each other and associate, the mild with the ferocious, the peaceful with the violent, the moderate with the arrogant, the timid with the savage'.[7] On some of the coins of Marcus and his predecessor, Antoninus Pius, struck in Alexandria for use in the province of Egypt, the imperial profile on the front is graced by the image of Orpheus playing to the animals on the reverse (see Fig. 4.1).[8]

It may be coincidental that Orpheus is found precisely on the Roman coins of Alexandria. But at a deeper level, it is at least not surprising. Alexandria was the home of the Museum. Founded by the Ptolemaic dynasty when they carved out the kingdom of Egypt from the conquests

---

[4] www.attalus.org/translate/alexanderie.html usefully juxtaposes the Greek, Armenian and Syriac versions; see chapter 42 for the difference between the Greek/Armenian and the Syriac on Orpheus.
[5] Martial, *Book of Spectacles* (Shackleton Bailey, ed., in the Loeb Classical Library), 24 and 25.
[6] Silius Italicus, *Punica* III, 611–621 (trans. by Duff in Loeb, slightly modified).
[7] Fronto, *Ad. M. Caesarem* 4.1 (my translation).
[8] https://rpc.ashmus.ox.ac.uk/search/browse?q=Orpheus&format=tab; Jesnick 1997 gathers most Greco-Roman material relating to Orpheus, p. 15 (with further bibliography) on the coins.

90   4 The Imperial Cosmopolis

Figure 4.1 Orpheus on the Alexandrian coinage of Antoninus Pius, 141–142 CE. Obverse: Autokra(tor) Kais(ar) Adr(ianos) Antoninos Se(bastos). Reverse: Orpheus playing his lyre surrounded by wild animals. Image by Bernhard Weisser, Public Domain, Mark 1.0. Berlin, Münzkabinett der Staatlichen Museen, 18315849 (https://ikmk.smb.museum/object?lang=de&id=18315849&view=rs).

of Alexander, this academic institution led a revolution in poetic composition throughout the Hellenistic world.[9] The ancient Near East and Levant had a long-established tradition of huge royal and temple libraries.[10] To bolster their status, the new Ptolemaic rulers set up an academic institution inviting men of Greek letters to work under their patronage. The intellectual ambitions of the institution, including among others philosophy and science, history and philology, were comprehensive, and its compendious library quickly earned a reputation for being universal. This was perhaps a bit of a propagandistic stretch. Interest was focused almost solely on books written in Greek.[11] But the unprecedented accumulation of Greek books or

---

[9] Pfeiffer 1968 provides a basic and classic overview. See further Ceci & Krause-Kolodziej 2018; apart from Alexandria, only cities in Thrace, the other main 'homeland' of Orpheus, struck such coins under the empire.

[10] Barjamovic & Ryholt 2019 for the Near Eastern background of the Ptolemaic Library.

[11] Erskine 1995; Bagnall 2002. Stephens 2003: 249–251 on the universalistic ambitions of the library. The emphasis was overwhelmingly on literature in Greek, but some translated works may have entered. However, as Momigliano 1971: 6–8, 90–92 and 145 argued irrefutably, most such examples known to us are mythical fabrications. The translation of the Jewish Bible, the Septuagint, into Greek, was not a royally sponsored project. This was a claim invented by the Jewish community to gain status for their text in an overwhelmingly Hellenocentric literary culture (see also Honigman 2003: 136–143, although she unnecessarily upholds the notion of royal patronage in spite of its deeply speculative basis). Few, if any, among the literary elite (apart from the Jews themselves) ever bothered

rather scrolls facilitated the formation of a canon. The learned people at the Museum set about producing a standardized version of the Homeric epics. They also threw their energies behind sorting out the sprawling mythological tales of the many Greek communities and their temples. This was not a matter of mere book learning, however entertaining it might be. Mythology was employed as an important language of kingship and statehood. The learning of mythologists was sought to lend lustre to the claims of rulers and anchor them in an immemorial or divine past. Everything from grand pageants, court ceremonies and dinner parties could be enhanced through the allegorical language of mythology.[12]

Callimachus emerged as the leading voice of the Alexandrine mythologists. His work fashioned almost a new poetical language. Bibliophile mastery of learned, arcane references, the fruit of his tireless labours as librarian, was combined with striking, complex and often playful imagery. His poems would explore the origins of myths and employ them in artful compositions of hymnic praise to the ruling dynasty and its courtiers: 'Happy, in all things brilliant, Berenice, without whom not even the very Graces would be Graces.'[13] A complex web of meaning was spun around the royals to elevate their persons and link them to their realm and to the networks of power therein.[14] If language belongs to the repertoire of power, the Alexandrian style became the leading dialect, an idiom of unmatched refinement that for a while claimed the position of being the standard against which the rest of the Mediterranean would measure itself.

This was also the time of the rise of Rome, and as the Tiber city forcefully moved from being a local and regional power to the centre of 'the world', its elites aimed to match the sophisticated and dazzling splendour of the Ptolemaic and other Hellenistic courts. With the consolidation of imperial monarchy under Augustus, they succeeded. Luminaries such as Horace and Ovid laid under contribution the efforts of preceding generations of writers so as to transmute Hellenistic poetic genres into

---

about this text. Aspects of Near Eastern culture and symbolism are less to be found in direct translation than in the absorption of its forms of symbolism and power in the new Greek language of power. On this process in Egypt, see Stephens 2003 and Moyer 2011.

[12] Strootman 2017 situates the work of the Hellenistic poets and scholars of the Museum firmly in the context of court and royal power. Compare Silver 2008 for an illustration of the usefulness of this type of knowledge at the court of a Renaissance ruler.

[13] Callimachus, *Epigram* 51 (my translation of line 3–4). Harder 2012 now offers the most convenient entry to the fragmentary survivals of Callimachus' shorter poems.

[14] Fantuzzi & Hunter 2006, chapter 2, for a discussion, although focused on the literary aspect of Callimachus' new 'science' of aitiology, the technique of linking current phenomena to arcane local practices and their mythologies. See further the contributions to Acosta-Hughes, Lehnus & Stephens 2011.

culminating Latin idiom and give the complex mythological language of Greek literature a further boost.[15] Orpheus, too, and the capacity of his lyre to overcome the forces of nature, from dead rocks to trees and the fiercest of animals, found a place in works by the poets of Augustan court society. Among these, the prize must go to Vergil. Just as Augustus had conquered the Egypt of Cleopatra, so Vergil had set out to master Callimachean poetics in his *Georgics*.[16] This small epic was a learned tour de force. Archaic lore, myths and exotic customs of the peasantry, theoretical knowledge, all meticulously excavated from the obscure manuscript collections of the library, were woven into a delicate portrait of the passing seasons of the countryside, agriculture and animal husbandry. The entire poem was concluded by the telling of the tale of Orpheus and Eurydice, of how the Thracian bard had almost conquered death by the mesmerizing beauty of his song. This cemented the position of the figure of Orpheus in Roman aristocratic culture. In late antiquity, for instance, Orpheus playing to the animals became a popular topic both in the exuberant polychrome mosaic floors that began to decorate the stately homes of the elites and in the lavish reliefs decorating the sarcophagi that became the final resting place of some of their members (Fig. 4.2).[17]

But late antiquity also saw the transition to monotheism and Christianity in the Roman Empire. In that process, the image of Orpheus was transferred to David and Solomon, the most revered examples of royal power in the Judeo-Christian scriptural tradition. The Orphic representation of David and Solomon became an emblem of just kingship, and as such it was adopted by the followers of Islam when they conquered large parts of the Roman and Persian Empires in the seventh century. Jew, Christian or Muslim, all were considered the children of Abraham, after all.[18] When Persian was patronized by the rulers of Central Asia to become the second big literary language in the Islamic world at the turn of the first millennium, the Orphic imagery followed suit. Nizami, for instance, would portray the tormented lover, Majnun, as having moved into the desert, where the desperate calls for his beloved Laila came out as pure poetry. But if that was insufficient to overcome the separation, forced upon the couple by social conventions, his mournful song nevertheless drew a host of wild animals that began to live in peace and harmony under the inspiration of their Solomonic poet ruler.

---

[15] Heslin 2015; Zanker 1988.　[16] Nelis 2012.　[17] Jesnick 1997.
[18] Howard-Johnston 2010: 412–414 and 457–458 (Muhammad's move to write his new religion into the story of Abraham).

Figure 4.2 A specimen of a Roman Orpheus mosaic: polychrome, with Orpheus in the centre, surrounded by a host of wild animals. Tarsus, third century CE, Hatay Archaeology Museum, Antakya. Photo by DeAgostini/Getty Images.

In the epic on Alexander, the narrative of the Macedonian king was even reunited with the image of Orpheus. Towards the end of the poem, Alexander is made to preside over a debate among a range of Greek philosophers about who held the keys to the truth. Here Nizami shows himself a true heir to late antique Neoplatonism. The prophetic sage Apollonius of Tyana, to whom the Roman courtier Philostratus dedicated a voluminous biography, rubs shoulders with Porphyry and Hermes Trismegistus, as well as the more mainstream Thales, Socrates and Aristotle. But towering above them all is Plato. Against an overconfident Aristotle, Plato establishes his leadership by mastering the harmonies of the universe and so playing its music that the wild animals fall completely under his spell. The model emperor could, as in our opening example, mirror his exploits in philosophy and the arts. Like an Orpheus, David, Solomon or Greek philosopher king, his reign would usher in a paradisiacal age where harmony, peace and justice would rule among the peoples.[19]

---

[19] Koch 1988: 29–33 on Orpheus in late antique and Islamic iconography. Koch 2010 further explores Majnun, Orpheus and Persianate Solomonic kingship. O'Meara 2003 and Fowden 1986 on late antique Neoplatonism and its intellectual environment.

With the works of Nizami, the continued influence of the Alexander, Orpheus, Solomon connection was assured, and its popularity reached a new pitch in the court of the Great Mughals. From the sixteenth century they vigorously expanded their empire from Afghanistan till they reached the south of India at the end of the seventeenth. The Mughal dynasty saw itself as being in the tradition of Teimur Lenk; they were Muslims and promoted the use of Persian as the language of the court. Alexander, therefore, was one of their celebrated models of rulership, and it was not uncommon to find one of the Mughals compared to the legendary Macedonian conqueror.[20] Nizami's poetry was similarly cherished. A lavish manuscript, illustrated with one brilliant miniature painting after another, was prepared in the palatial workshop for Akbar (r. 1556–1605).[21] To posterity his fame is especially connected with the debates that he staged at his new palace at Fatehpur Sikri. Here learned men and clerics met to debate the character of God and the truth under the eyes of the emperor.[22] Against that background, it comes as little surprise that one of the episodes selected for illustration in the copy of Nizami was precisely the one where at Alexander's court Plato proves his superiority to Aristotle by playing for the animals in the manner of an Orpheus (Fig. 4.3).[23]

While the name of the mythological bard had fallen out of the Islamic and Persian cultural discourse, his imagery and courtly associations continued to resonate strongly. So far, we have followed the poetic tale through a meandering journey from Alexandria, via Rome, to the late antique Near East and the greater medieval Iranian sphere, before arriving in India and the imperial seats of the Great Mughals. At that moment, the story takes a surprising turn. Florence is suddenly joined to the itinerary. When a new palace was built in Delhi, for the grandson of Akbar, Shahjahan (r. 1628–1658), a small image of Orpheus was used as the centrepiece in the marble-decorated wall behind the throne in the hall of public audience. This image was a product of Florentine craftsmanship and has constituted quite a riddle, until the Viennese art historian Ebba Koch was able brilliantly to solve it through an admirable effort of painstaking detective work.

---

[20] Bhimsen, *Tarikh-i-Dilkasha* (ed. V. G. Khobrekar, 1972): 42. See further, Donde 2014, with thanks to Dardana Kastrioti for having pointed me to this reference.
[21] Brend 1995 offers a basic discussion of this manuscript.   [22] Moin 2012: 132–133 and 146–152.
[23] There is to my knowledge no English translation of this part of Nizami's poem. But J. C. Bürgel, *Das Alexanderbuch von Nizami* (1991), pp. 432–437, offers a German prose translation. In addition to Koch, see also Minissale 2009: 219–237, on the complex neoplatonic reflexivity of these images and the poetry of Nizami.

Figure 4.3 Illustrations of universal kingship in the illuminated manuscripts of Mughal India: Nizami's *Khamse* (British Library, Or. 12208), manuscript produced in the workshop of the emperor Akbar during the 1590s. Images by the British Library.
a. Majnun surrounded by the peaceable animals (folio 150 v).
b. Philosophers debating in front of Alexander (folio 298 r).
c. Plato playing the organ for the animals (folio 305 r).

In the Latin West, Vergil held pride of place among the poets, and so the name of Orpheus had never really vanished from cultural memory. During the Renaissance and the early Baroque, the artistic representation of Orpheus experienced quite a vogue in the courts of European rulers. But how the coloured stone image reached the Mughal court during the seventeenth century, whether as a diplomatic gift from a European delegation or procured from a Western merchant seeking to peddle his wares to the Indian emperors, is not known. This was the age when European commercial enterprise had gained a foothold in the Indian Ocean and established factories and delegations in several key locations. But it was still a very far cry from the hegemonic position that the Europeans came to enjoy with the establishment of colonial rule during the late eighteenth and nineteenth centuries. Yet the European arrival in the Indian Ocean registered in Mughal art. The artists of the court sampled several select motives and iconographies and incorporated them in their Persian style. Mughal symbolism was truly hybrid, a statement of the ecumenical reach of their power. Whereas the name of Orpheus continued to hold little meaning for the Mughals, the Florentine image of Orpheus playing to the animals could serve both as an icon of their Solomonic paradisiacal kingship and as proof of their unrivalled universalism (Fig. 4.4).[24]

The entangled history that came together in the mythology of Alexander, Orpheus and the Delhi Throne Hall decoration is difficult to fit into conventional frameworks and periodizations. From one perspective, it might be described as early modern. But that is hardly the most significant observation to make about the role of Florentine artwork in the paradisiacal ornament of the Mughal audience ritual. The global trade links had not yet grown strong enough for them to begin to force convergence among the great societies of Eurasia around the models of European culture. That moment did not arrive till the age of the long nineteenth-century era of colonialism.[25] On the contrary, the Florentine Orpheus was severed from its 'European' classical context and refitted to serve under the principles of Persianate court culture, as those had developed from the end of the first millennium CE. By then, however, the link between Orpheus and Solomon/David had long since been forged. It was a product of late antiquity. That could equally well be a label to affix to our phenomenon. Yet other candidates would be Augustan or Hellenistic. It was the era of

---

[24] Koch 1988.
[25] Bayly 2004. For an example, see Pu Yi 1987: 176–178, describing how at his installation as emperor of Japanese-occupied Manchuria, European-style uniforms took precedence over Qing dynasty attire and rituals.

Figure 4.4 Orpheus in the Delhi Hall of Public Audience of the Mughal emperor Shahjahan, king of the world.
a. The Hall of Public Audience in the Red Fort of Delhi, mid seventeenth century, constructed as a *chihil sutun*, a many-pillared hall in the style of Persepolis. Photo: Peter Fibiger Bang.
b. The Florentine *pietre dure Orpheus Playing to the Animals*, incorporated in the paradisiacal inlaid stone decoration in the wall behind the throne. Photo: Ebba Koch.

Augustus and the Roman imperial monarchy that elevated the image of Orpheus into prominence as an emblem of civilization and rule, as they wrote the history of Rome into Hellenistic court culture with its poetics of the library and learned mythology.

Early modern, medieval, late antique, Augustan or Hellenistic, many temporalities are in play. As Garth Fowden has advocated with such vigour, we need to rethink the chronology of Afro-Eurasian cultural history. His argument is to view the first millennium as one long extended period from the times of Augustus and Jesus to the mature philosophy of Persian Avicenna (Ibn Sina).[26] This millennium was characterized by the rise of the monotheistic cousins of Christianity and Islam and the development of an intellectual culture structured around key figures, including in addition to Alexander figures such as Aristotle, Plato and the Greek doctor of Roman emperors, Galen. Their texts travelled almost or just as widely as the *Romance*. However, as we have just seen, their influence lasted far beyond the year 1000 CE and had not even culminated by then.[27] Perhaps an even more radical solution is required – and one not solely based on a set of texts originating in the Mediterranean. The career of the *Alexander Romance* might usefully be placed in the context of a common pre-colonial development: the formation of a number of literary court-dominated cultures that continued to diversify and consolidate their hold across the Afro-Eurasian world, from the fourth century BCE to the rise of European colonialism.[28]

These *ecumenes*, the Greek term for a civilizational space, emerged in the Afro-Eurasian arena with the universal empires that constituted the theme of Chapter 3; as in the case of the empires, their development did not merely run in regionally parallel but separate tracks. The symbolic rivalries of neighbouring rulers, artists and learned men in search of patronage as well as the ebb and flow of territorial conquest ensured that some ideas would travel between the developing regional traditions. Sometimes the ecumenes long outlasted their founding empire or spread widely beyond its territorial confines. The court societies and their aristocratic forms of sociality had enough in common that a text like the *Alexander Romance* could find an audience far outside its place of cultural origin. This transcontinental exchange happened in a slow and thin trickle: emblematic

---

[26] Fowden 2014. [27] For example, Gommans & Huseini 2022.
[28] I reserve the term 'colonialism' to denote the era that saw the formation of European global colonial empires, spearheaded by Spain and Portugal in the sixteenth century but rising to a pitch between 1750 and 1945. Before then, 'colonialism' had primarily consisted of conquering and influencing immediate neighbours, not distant overseas territories. This is a distinction of conception that I share with Gosden 2004 (see especially chapter 4), although we differ in terminology.

objects and texts were repeatedly appropriated, repurposed and adapted in the ceremonies of power and the fashioning of elite identities. The journey undertaken by the *Alexander Romance* passed through many stopping points, proceeding in a knock-on motion, from one neighbour to the next, rather than running through the kind of continuous circuit that slowly began to connect the regions of the world with the advent of globalization, from the sixteenth and especially eighteenth century.[29]

4.2 Ecumenical Commonalities: From the Axial to the Cosmopolitan Age

Among students of world history the notion of the Axial Age has gained currency. In exploring the commonalities of the great pre-modern literary traditions of Afro-Eurasia, they have focused on the early origins. The German philosopher Karl Jaspers (1883–1969) saw the eighth to third centuries BCE as a formative period, an axis in world history. Individuals such as Socrates, Confucius and Buddha were hailed as setting the tone of a new era of reflexivity. The meaning of human existence and social life was put under scrutiny as never before.[30] It is difficult to miss the heavy Hegelian inspiration behind Jaspers's theory. To the philosopher Hegel (1770–1831), world history had been a question of the unfolding of spirit, and even though students of historical sociology have tried to put more concrete flesh on the airy bones of Jasper's Axial Age, it remains a surprisingly nebulous and abstract phenomenon. Very little seems to explain the postulated conjuncture across widely dispersed and unconnected germination points.[31] Nor ought social reflexivity be seen as the preserve of the mid first millennium BCE. No serious reader of *Gilgamesh*, the archaic Mesopotamian epic with deep roots in the third millennium BCE, can walk away unaffected by its soul-searching questions about the meaning of life and the role of humans.

Indeed, the introduction of writing during the Near Eastern Bronze Age may well have been the crucial precondition. Jack Goody famously argued that the key feature of writing was its ability to fix information.[32] In contrast to the fluidity of oral transmission, messages phrased in letters

---

[29] Bang & Kolodziejczyk 2012.   [30] Jaspers 1949.
[31] Moin & Strathern 2022: 10 and Wittrock 2015 both concede the unexplained nature of the alleged world historical conjuncture. Hegel 2020 [1830/1831]: 1197–1198 for world history as a movement through which the human spirit and its reason gain self-awareness; Arnason, Eisenstadt & Wittrock 2004 for a strong collection of historical sociological studies exploring 'the Axial Age' thesis.
[32] Goody 1986.

became stabilized. Information could now be handed down through time and remain recognizably the same. However, as the written word made the message independent of its moment of conception, it also opened up the question of interpretation. Separated from its immediate environment, the meaning of the text had to be established in the specific contexts of the readership. Did society still live up to the ideals expressed in the text? Did the king show adequate respect for the gods? Had people paid the amount of dues and taxes prescribed in the records? The questions arising from reading were manifold and instantly gave rise to a practice of exegesis in the hands of the literate few. The fact that written texts could be stored only added to the need for interpretation. As texts began to accumulate in archives and libraries, some became considered more important than others, commanding the attention of other authors who would take them as paradigmatic and begin to emulate their forms. Literary traditions took shape around the formation of canons of works deemed classical.

But the fixity of writing did not only liberate texts from the evanescent fluidity of time; it also enabled them to expand their geographical reach. If they could stay the same in time, that also went for movement through space. As long as there were people who had learned to decipher the written code and its dialect, the text could travel. Writing became a tool for transcending the constraints of local, oral society and a force of cosmopolitan integration. This is where the world shaped by the universal empires comes in. All of them relied on the cosmopolitan potential of the written word, its fixity, canonicity and translocality, to foster integration across vast geographical expanses.[33] From the third century BCE on, they presided over the spread and consolidation of a number of cosmopolitan literary languages and cultures that extended their reach far beyond the ancient Near East and the other Bronze Age centres across the Afro-Eurasian land-mass. Alexandria and its rival Hellenistic courts were among the important drivers of this development.[34] At the same time, in the East, the first imperial unification of China under the Qin dynasty in 221 BCE was quickly followed by a scriptural reform aimed to make the conventions of writing uniform. From now on, only one system of characters was to be used throughout the empire, irrespective of pre-existing regional styles of notation. The writing system which came out of this was

---

[33] Majeed 2021 for a basic discussion of literature and empire, from antiquity till postcolonial modernity.
[34] A point made by Momigliano 1977: 10 in his discussion of the Axial Age problematic.

almost a perfect cosmopolitan idiom. Chinese characters were pictograms, each standing for a word. The same signs could thus be employed across the realm, however much the spoken dialects might differ between regions.[35]

Still, it is among students of ancient India that the ancient cosmopolitan languages have recently received the most illuminating analysis. Often the languages have been approached primarily as a question of religion. But in *The Language of the Gods in the World of Men*, Sheldon Pollock has decisively revised this perception.[36] Sanskrit originated as a ritual language passed down orally within a small 'guild' of religious experts in charge of godly and sacrificial ceremonies. During the first centuries CE, Sanskrit broke out of its social isolation. Indian monarchs appropriated the arcane argot of religious ritual and made it serve as the language of court and aristocracy. To spread, the language of divine truth had to be grafted on to the strong arm of rule and politics. It was the marriage of temple and court that paved the way for the success of Sanskrit's diffusion.

In that respect, its experience stands confirmed by the two most prominent religions of the book. Both Christianity and Islam, together with their language of divine truth, rose to strength and prominence when they became the respective faiths of powerful imperial ruling groups. And as in the case of these two religions, dissemination depended on book learning; it required the use of writing. Otherwise, it would have been impossible to reach the much-widened constituency. In this process, the properties of the written language were cultivated to perfection. Sanskrit was fixed into an almost timeless and placeless idiom. Complex grammars were constructed disciplining the language into a universally recognizable form. Studied and learned vocabularies regulated the choice of words and distanced it from the sphere of fluid oral practice. The speech of the courtier was to be polished and shaped by rhetorical models. All became anchored in the *Ramayana* and the *Mahabharata*. These two great epics were established as the foundation of Sanskrit culture. They provided a set of model reflections on the challenges of kingship and noble life; their version of the language was considered classic and ideal, the standard against which every other text was measured. Their sprawling narratives of gods, royalty, intrigues and war provided a rich mythology of kingship that could be employed by

---

[35] Bodde 1986: 56–58; Sima Qian, *Shiji*, Basic Annals 6 (First Emperor of Qin, trans. W. H. Nienhauser Jr., *The Grand Scribe's Records*, Vol. 1 (2018), pp. 137 and 140.
[36] Pollock 2006.

the rulers to express their claims to power in an idiom enhanced by divine genealogy.

The metre, the words, the stories, all may have been different, yet it would be difficult for a student of Greece and Rome not to recognize the fundamental similarities of Sanskrit to the two so-called classical languages.[37] The centrality of grammar and rhetorical expression, the price put on learned and arcane vocabulary, the canon of works dominated by epics, these are all familiar mainstays of Greek and Latin – and often held against them: 'dead languages', fixed in a long gone past. But, as Wilfried Stroh argued in a refreshing history of Latin, it was the very death of the language, its frozenness in time, that had given it life.[38] As with Sanskrit, its fixity had enabled it to travel across a wide geographical expanse and down through the ages. It is not by coincidence, therefore, that Pollock in his study re-found inspiration in the Greco-Roman experience and dubbed the expansive movement of his language across South and South-East Asia as the 'Sanskrit cosmopolis'. At that point, however, the dialogue was broken off. The Greco-Latin formation in the Mediterranean was denounced as a counter-cosmopolis. Greek and Latin had been spread only at the point of a spear, a product of naked militarism, lauded by Vergil in the famous opening lines of his *Aeneid*, 'Of arms and a man I will sing.' By contrast, no empire had ever occupied the entire Sanskrit cosmopolis. Its spread was an instance of the pure and superior attraction of Sanskrit culture.[39] But here analysis seems almost to have collapsed into prejudice. One does not have to have spent many hours with Vergil's *Aeneid* to realize that it is anything but a blanket celebration of militaristic bravado. Aeneas, the title character, is the reluctantly 'pious' hero who takes his burden and duty upon him. Self-constraint and a sorrow over the destructiveness of war are a central concern of the epic, recalling the high point of the *Mahabharata*, the so-called *Bhagavad Gita*, where the hero Arjuna reflects on the futility of killing just before the grand decisive battle.[40] Still, in both cases, the war had to be fought.

Instead of insisting on crude cultural incongruity and irreconcilable contrast, more may be learned from keeping the dialogue open and pursuing a more sensitive parallelism. The Sanskrit world, after all, knew no shortage of powerful and expansive militaristic dynasties that availed

---

[37] Johanning forthcoming for an attempt to explore the parallels.   [38] Stroh 2007.
[39] Pollock 2006: 279 and chapter 7.
[40] Johnson 1994 (the Bhagavad Gita); on Aeneas, the reluctant hero, see for example Otis 1964: 279–282, 293–304, 316–317, 330–331 and 379–382, and most recently, with slight differences in nuance, Zanker 2023, chapter 4.

themselves of the sophisticated literary language to publicize the splendour of their court and impress it on rival rulers. The Kushanas, the Guptas and the Khmers all projected mighty empires and promoted the culture of Sanskrit.[41] In that respect, the Sanskrit cosmopolis was not fundamentally different from the Hellenistic world before the imposition of Roman rule. Political rivalry on the battlefield was combined with a cultural agon between the different courts that saw Hellenism expand its reach.[42] Later, historians of India see a similar cosmopolis take shape from the thirteenth century onwards, now based on the Persian language and culminating with the imposition of empire from Afghanistan to the south of India by the Mughals.[43]

Whether one empire actually managed to conquer most of its competitors or not, a 'cosmopolis' might still spread. This was because the expansion of the cosmopolitan language and culture was never a question of simple top-down imposition; it was a result of active appropriation and emulation by elite groups of the predominant idioms at the time. Rival monarchs, subject nobilities, local elites, all might adopt elements of the most successful images of power available to substantiate their own claims to pre-eminence. The imperial cosmopolis can be described, to borrow a notion once coined by the anthropologist Tambiah, as a galactic universe: at the centre perhaps there glows a particularly strong star, but there are also plenty of lesser centres exercising their own pull and emitting their own light dispersed across the system.[44]

Literature became an important arena of elite sociability, next to military prowess, sumptuous building or forms of athletic training, where members of the upper classes competed for distinction. As the leaders of aristocratic society, emperors and kings would patronize poets and other men of letters at court, while often joining in the activities themselves. Several Hindu monarchs became famed authors of Sanskrit in their own right. Many more tried their hand at writing, and not just in the Sanskrit cosmopolis. Of the Mughals, for instance, both Babur (r. 1526–1530), the dynastic founder, and Jahangir (r. 1605–1627) are remembered for the extensive memoires they wrote containing striking observations about life. Darah Shukoh (1615–1659), the ill-fated crown prince of Shahjahan who employed the Orpheus in the Delhi Audience Hall, composed complex philosophical and theological treatises.[45] In eighteenth-century China,

---

[41] Ali 2004: 19 on the centrality of the Guptas in establishing the Sanskrit model emulated by other courts over the following centuries; Coe 2021 on the Khmeers.
[42] Bang 2012.   [43] Eaton 2019: 10–18.   [44] Tambiah 1976.
[45] Gandhi 2020, chapter 7 and 8; Thackston 1999 (Jahangirnama) and 2002 (Barburnama).

the Qianlong emperor is proverbial for the profusion of poetic compositions that he would never miss an opportunity to bestow on the world.[46] At a closer look, many a Roman emperor turns out also to have dabbled in literature, not just the three famous and well-preserved instances of Julius Caesar, Marcus Aurelius and Julian.[47] Rulers, however, were only the tip of a much larger iceberg of writers active in aristocratic society. They would recite at dinners, visit each other for readings and sprinkle their works with dedications reflecting their circle of friends and allies. Apart from the ever-popular epics, this literature spawned a steady stream of short, elegant poems, speeches, letter collections and compendious prose works. In general, the practice of writing put a premium on playful intertextuality and took nourishment from an encyclopedic impulse.[48]

The learned, allegorical, florid and not seldom effusive style of much of this writing has not fared well among critics weaned on modernist precepts. Their aim was to strip literature of the very artifice, representational performativity and ceremony, its expressive dimension as Pollock calls it, that lay at the heart of the old cosmopolitan literary cultures. Yet ornate language was key to the rituals of status recognition and civility that were such a strong preoccupation of aristocratic society. In Persian, one speaks of Adab with a concept not much different from Greek *paideia* or Latin *humanitas*. These concepts signified the possession of a mixture of philosophical, rhetorical and poetical education that invested the person with the qualities of a gentleman, a person distinguished by his refined manners. A recurrent topic in one of the most central texts in the Latin tradition, Cicero's *On the Duties*, was *decorum*, the proper, the tasteful.[49]

It is not difficult to see how such an ethos is almost destined to clash with the aesthetic preferences of our age that ostensibly celebrates both the sublime and the transgressive in art. But to aristocratic society, command

---

[46] Elliott 2009: 107–113. See also the glimpse of an emperor's literary production offered by Spence 1974, including poems and a final reflection on his reign by Kangxi (1661–1722); further, Pu Yi 1987: 21 on the preparation of calligraphy in the palatial workshops, to which members of the late Qing dynasty would then apply the finishing touches.

[47] For example, Augustus (Suetonius *Augustus* 84–89, in Greek); Hadrian (*Historia Augusta*, Hadrianus 14, 8–16; 25, 8–10) or the client king Juba II of Mauretania (Roller 2003). See further Netz 2020: 615–616.

[48] König & Woolf 2013, in general, and chapter 2 on Rome in particular; Jonston 2012 on Roman literary culture. Kinra 2015, especially chapters 4–5, and Fleischer 1986 for respectively a Mughal and an Ottoman example of literary courtiers. See further on intertextuality, Johanning forthcoming, chapters 4–6 especially.

[49] Cicero, *On the Duties* (e.g., I, 93–105 and 126).

of *decorum* and dignified manners was the entry ticket to what we would now call polite society, not merely at court, but also in distant provincial cities or among the leaders of rural communities.⁵⁰ The fortuitous survival of the papers of a certain Dioscorus, from the village of Aphrodito in sixth-century CE Egypt, provides the classicist with a rare window onto the routine operation of lettered elites. If his poems and addresses fall far short of the literary brilliance achieved by the star practitioners at court, the limping metres and clumsy prose metaphors of this village leader are all the better testimony to the significance of literary culture. Normally composed for a specific occasion (e.g., to court the favour of a person in power, rather than for any artistic need), the texts of Dioscorus had to be written because literature served as an indispensable currency in the networks of power and patronage.⁵¹

Pollock's analysis of Sanskrit turns our attention to the question of language domains. The Sanskrit cosmopolis was focused on the expressive and ceremonial side of elite literary culture. Among the cosmopolitan languages, however, Sanskrit may have been relatively unique in maintaining a distance from more practical and administrative matters as it spread beyond the realms of North India.⁵² Fixity also made writing ideal for record-keeping, a crucial tool of elites that needed to extract resources from the agricultural and urban economy. Large armies, with contingents of diverse geographical backgrounds, equally needed a shared medium of communication and administration. In both cases, something less than the most elaborate versions of the literary languages would normally suffice. Even so, the military and administrative function was often instrumental in widening the reach of the language cosmopolis beyond the rarefied circles of court and elite society. The decision of the Mughal emperors to insist on Persian for all matters of administration across their vast Indian realm saw provincial elites and scribes turn to the courtly idiom as never before.⁵³

Similar processes were at work in the ancient Mediterranean. Egypt, thanks to its extraordinarily well-preserved cache of documentary papyri, allows us to observe close-up two radical changes in language use.

---

⁵⁰ Busch 2011: 65–68 (on courtly Hindi literature, but her observations can be extended to serve for all our cosmopolitan languages). On the civility of Adab, see briefly Kinra 2015: 90–91 and more extensively Metcalf 1984; Lefèbvre 2019 and Pomeranz, Bellino, Mayeur-Jaouen & Patrizi 2018. On *humanitas*, see Woolf 1998, chapter 3; on Paideia, Swain 1996.
⁵¹ Fournet 1999 is a fundamental study and edition. Ruffini 2018, chapters 4 and 10, for a micro-historical discussion.
⁵² Pollock 2006: 128–134.   ⁵³ Alam 2003: 162–167.

Consolidation of Greco-Macedonian conquest and rule, under the Ptolemaic dynasty, not only established the capital, court and Museum at Alexandria, but also brought a transition to Greek as the main administrative language throughout the Nile Valley. If anything, Roman conquest, as in the rest of the Eastern Mediterranean, strengthened the position of Greek as the elite language of the province, and at first, the Muslim takeover of Egypt in the mid seventh century brought little change. But when the Umayyad caliphs began to consolidate their conquests, a decision was made to favour Arabic as the language of imperial administration. During the eighth century, the papyri record registers a steady rise in the use of Arabic in the paper trail left by the taxation process.[54]

Meanwhile, in the western parts of the Roman Empire, both the introduction of Roman taxation and the stationing of the legions in camps around the provinces strengthened the foundations for the emergence of a Latin cosmopolis. In some provincial cities, small schools were set up by ambitious local elites for the education of their children. Next to these establishments, however, the military and administrative institutions of imperial statehood generated a social infrastructure that facilitated the spread and dissemination of a language cosmopolis. The expressive modes of literary production presided, so to speak, over a broader base of far more utilitarian notarial and record-keeping usages.[55]

4.3 Context: The Cosmopolitan Sociology of Integration

But how should one characterize the cultural integration fostered within the imperial cosmopolis? Benedict Anderson, one of the most influential cultural theorists of the last generation, used the notion of truth languages to capture the package of wide geographical reach, timeless literary idiom and hegemonic exclusivity that produced the world of imperial cosmopolitan integration. Yet the concept of the truth language has been somewhat neglected and put in the shade of its more famous twin, 'the imagined community'. To the extent that classicists have engaged with Anderson's thought, they too have rather been drawn to the notion of an 'imagined community'. The concept, after all, seems to offer a ready-made framework for understanding how people, otherwise unrelated, came to think of

---

[54] Sijpesteijn 2013, chapters 2 and 3. See further Borrut, Ceballos and Vacca 2024 about the development of an Arabic cosmopolis and its coexistence with multiple regional languages.
[55] Mullen 2024 surveys the many different record-keeping functions that facilitated the dissemination of Latin in the Western provinces and offers useful discussion in the introduction.

themselves across large swaths of territory as members of the same community. For what were the translocal identities forged by the cosmopolitan imperial cultures, if not 'imagined'?[56] Irrespective of whether one looks to the literati of the Han dynasty, the Perso-Indian cosmopolis or the Roman Empire's Second Sophistic, the leading practitioners all take pride in their capacity to move from location to location. Everywhere, so the boast went, their brand of culture was revered and respected by people in power, and everywhere they could expect to interact with persons of their own quality who identified with the same cultural standards. In the cosmopolis, transregional integration was conjured into existence through a shared community of reading.[57]

Nevertheless, to Anderson, the cosmopolis of the truth language differed fundamentally from the world of imagined communities. Dwelling a little on the contrast will help sharpen our sociological and world-historical profile of the imperial cosmopolis. Crucially, the imagined community had emerged only between the eighteenth and twentieth centuries, the era of modern globalization. Compared to the truth languages of the pre-industrial age, the imagined community represented a far more intensive and deeper kind of integration. While the truth languages had been cosmically anchored to project a universal set of truths, the imagined community developed by carving out regional blocks of more intensive communication from the old extensive spheres of cosmopolitan culture. Instead of a universal community, imagined communities claimed to represent a particular nation, each occupying its own niche within a wider international web of rivalling states.[58] The imagined community was a national construct, not an imperial cosmopolis. Whereas these had been aristocratic and hierarchical, the nation was bourgeois and egalitarian, ideally comprising everyone within its territory. At the most fundamental level, the imagined community had risen on the basis of the printing press and the market for books that it had generated from the late fifteenth century onwards in Europe. The number of books had exploded, and so had the number of authors and book owners. Reading publics became much bigger and deeper, and could thus form the basis of a broad national community. The imperial cosmopoleis preceded this development and relied

---

[56] Two examples from ancient history are Richter 2011 and, with more historical sensitivity, Johnston 2017: 6, 13 and 60.
[57] See Alam & Subrahmanyam 2007, for examples, in the Indo-Persian ecumene; Philostratus *Lives of the Sophists* illustrates the phenomenon extremely well in his portraits of the Greek intellectuals of the second century CE; Sima Qian, *Shiji* chapter 67 (the ability of the disciples of Confucius to move from court to court and offer useful precepts of state craft).
[58] Anderson 1991, chapter 2.

mostly on the manuscript. The number of books circulating was simply much smaller than the world made possible by printing.[59]

However, that does not mean that total volumes were trifling in the cosmopolis. A recent attempt to quantify the 'size' of ancient Greek literary culture estimates that there were perhaps about a thousand publishing authors at any point during the second century CE. The literary output of most of these would have enjoyed a dissemination of perhaps a few hundred or few thousand copies. In total, including authors surviving back from the fifth century BCE onwards, there might have been as many as 10,000 authors in circulation. Even relatively big libraries, though, would probably have held less than a thousand works. In effect, outside the biggest centres of learning in the Roman Empire, Athens, Alexandria and Rome itself, most of this literature would simply not have been available. The same study estimates that between 1.5 and 4 per cent of households in the Nile Valley owned a least a few book scrolls, with the Homeric *Iliad* responsible for perhaps a fifth of the total.

By contrast, most households in seventeenth-century England would have owned a printed bible, not in the Latin and Greek of antiquity, but translated into the vernacular.[60] This was key. The 'imagined communities' of Anderson depended on a development that brought writing closer to the spoken dialects of the majority. Eventually, general schooling was introduced to make people within the territory of a state conversant with the version of the vernacular that the mass production of books and other printed materials had made standard. The language was to be the same for every member of the nation, high or low. In practice, results have always fallen short of the promise. Linguistic sociologists will easily point to lingering hierarchies in language use. Region, class, race, age group and gender all continue to inflect the way people speak. Much language remains a sociolect. But think, then, how it would have been in a world where not even the attempt was made to create a standardized language encompassing the whole population?[61]

---

[59] Anderson 1991, chapter 3.
[60] Netz 2020, chapter 5, especially pp. 535–544 and 607–619. Netz estimates that a big library would have contained perhaps up to a thousand book scrolls. But most prose works and longer pieces of poetry comprised several scrolls; hence a big library would normally have contained fewer, even considerably fewer, than 1,000 works. The same logic applies to the number of copies circulating of an author at any one time. For most authors, the estimate is between 2,500 and 5,000 scrolls in circulation. Even at a low average of five scrolls per work, far fewer than 1,000 copies would have been in circulation at any given time in the Roman world.
[61] Adams 2003 is fundamental on the many contexts where Latin coexisted with local dialects and languages.

In fact, in the world of the imperial cosmopolis, not only was the attempt never made, but the wide spread of hegemonic languages depended actively on distancing the literary idiom from the manifold oral dialects of the peasant population. With a firm backbone in the (artificial idiolect of the) Homeric *Iliad*, the culture of Greek pursued a linguistic expression almost as far removed in place and time as possible: a poetic construct hailing from many centuries ago and a faraway region, mastered only by a tiny minority. As a result, we should always remember that neither Greek nor Latin was ever spoken by a majority of the population in the Roman Empire. Writing and schooling were mostly prerogatives of the socially eminent and were sustained by a narrow leisure class. Literacy extended beyond this very narrow segment to include lower gentry, some servants, urbanites and people in trusted administrative positions. But much of this literacy would have been functional and would not have entailed full command of the literary language. The person would have been familiar with the conventions of, for instance, registering accounts, issuing receipts or putting one's signature on a document or some other restricted need. For the Greco-Roman world, the suggestion of Harris that perhaps up to some 10 per cent of the population had acquired some degree of literacy has provoked much debate. However, for a preprint society of continental size, this is certainly not an ungenerous guestimate.[62]

In this linguistic environment, where most people spoke a dialect unregimented by schooling and grammar, the elites cultivated the cosmopolitan idioms actively to distinguish themselves from the broader population. Think of the Greek and Latin pejorative terms used of the illiterate majority, the *hoi polloi* or the *vulgus*; the cultured elite was everything they were not and mercilessly exposed their shortcomings in the mastery of the correct forms of the high language. The emphasis on the social distance between polished speech and uncouth talk that classicists will find in the portrait of *nouveaux riches* freedmen given by the Neronian courtier Petronius in his novel *Satyricon* has no shortage of parallels in the other cosmopolitan languages. In one of Sanskrit's classic texts, the *Sakuntala*, as I have been taught by Karsten Johanning, people from lower down the social hierarchy speak in their own sociolect, while the dignity of Sanskrit is reserved for royalty and aristocracy.[63]

---

[62] So Netz 2020: 609, fn. 118. Harris 1989.
[63] Johanning forthcoming, chapter 4. Thapar 1999 offers an instructive translation of the *Sakuntala*. See Boyce 1991 on the language of the freedmen in Petronius.

The imagined community of the nation also demanded the exclusive loyalty of its members. By contrast, the cosmopolitan court cultures were generally ecumenical; often they had to accommodate several versions of high culture at the same time and coexist with numerous local and regional traditions. Beyond the Great Wall, at their summer residence in Chengde, the Qing dynasty emperors would put up inscriptions in four languages – Manchu, Chinese, Mongolian and Tibetan – and thereby publicize the wide embrace of their power.[64] The multilingual proclamations at the palace read almost as a distant echo of some of the most famous inscriptions from 'classical antiquity'. The Rosetta Stone, for instance, records praise given by the temple priesthood of Thebes to Ptolemy V in Greek, Egyptian Hieroglyphs and Demotic script. Facing the rock-cut graves of the Achaemenid emperors at Naqsh-e Rostam in Iran, the inscription of the Sasanian ruler Shapur I, who we saw in Chapter 3 boasting of his grand triumphs between the 240s and 260s CE against the Romans, was composed in Middle Persian, Parthian and Greek.[65]

However, these spectacular inscriptions were only the tip of the much bigger iceberg of imperial normality. Everywhere the rulers had to appeal to different constituencies. That one could change under Roman influence and still stay Greek, as Greg Woolf once observed, was very much the norm.[66] While the Roman emperors promoted both a Latin and a Greek version of aristocratic culture, the Muslim Mughals struck a crucial alliance with the Hindu warrior aristocracy of Rajasthan. Their Persianized court patronized translation of some of the Sanskrit classics and attracted writers of both Sanskrit and Hindi.[67] Such diversity was only, to paraphrase the modern constitution of the Roman Catholic Church, splendid proof of the universality of the ruler.[68] The imperial monarchies handled their various elite constituencies by a combination of assimilation and co-optation through hierarchical subjection.[69]

If the imagined community of the ancient cosmopolitan languages and cultures was aristocratic and ecumenical, rather than egalitarian and exclusive, it finally also lacked the clearly circumscribed boundaries of the

---

[64] Zarrow 2004; Forêt 2000.
[65] Pfeiffer & Klinkott 2021 (on the Rosetta stone in the context of the Ptolemaic and Seleucid monarchy and their relationship with Egyptian and Babylonian priesthoods); Huyse 1999 (Shapur's trilingual inscription). Versluys 2017, chapter 3, for a recent discussion of eclectic symbolism in the Hellenistic and Roman imperial world.
[66] Woolf 1994.   [67] Busch 2011; Truschke 2016.
[68] Bang & Bayly 2011: 1–5, reflecting on, among other texts, *Lumen Gentium* section 23, 'splendid evidence of the catholicity of the undivided Church'.
[69] Lavan, Payne & Weisweiler 2016, chapter 1.

modern nation. Each of the cosmopoleis was conceived of as almost unbounded. There might be far distant territories beyond its reach, but the world that really mattered was defined by the cosmopolis; it constituted the civilized world and always cut across numerous peoples and regions. A ruler such as Ashoka might picture how his mode of civilized conduct, his *dhamma*, spread to all corners of the earth, but the horizons of most members that participated in the cosmopolitan culture were dominated by local concerns. Few were able or even aspired to gain office or a position high at court. Most had their ambitions firmly directed towards their local community or region.[70]

Operating within the frame of postcolonial theory, Homi Bhabha has coined the notion of mimicry. Under European rule, ambitious colonial elites adapted the new modernizing ideologies and cultures of the metropole. Yet their efforts never bought them real membership in the ruling society. However hard they tried, they could never be fully admitted to the dominant nation. Their efforts, in short, were constantly frustrated and resulted, as Frantz Fanon objected, in a state of enduring lack, of 'almost, but not quite'.[71] Something similar might be thought to have characterized the cosmopolitan cultures of pre-colonial society. Disparaging remarks about the uncouth or deficient nature of this or that group from the metropolitan perspective are anything but few and far between. But such views never hardened into the cultural barriers familiar from European colonialism. Even as the Mughal Empire was beginning to fragment, more Hindus rose to high rank under their Muslim overlords than ever before.[72] Greek and Latin histories may occasionally shower contemptuous remarks on the Syrian or Balkan backgrounds of the emperors of the third century CE, but it is precisely a critique of provincial dynasties that had successfully taken over power, not families that were left outside knocking on the door of high society and refused entry in spite of their accomplishments. Cosmopolitan cultures of truth languages expanded through what Anderson described as 'alchemical absorption'.[73] Emulation normally worked its transformative magic and never became mimicry, but served the interests of local elites quite well. This gave them a handle to position their society in a wider order and fortify their own status.

---

[70] Jonston 2017; Ashoka, Thirteenth Major Rock Edict ('victory by dhamma'; Thapar 1997: 256).
[71] Bhabha 1993, chapter 3 and especially chapter 4, with Bang 2021a: 40.
[72] Eaton 2019: 331; Kinra 2015: 52–59 and 82–85.
[73] Anderson 1991: 15. Examples of comments on the deficient or lacklustre Syrian and Balkan backgrounds of emperors: Herodian V, 5.2–8.10 (Elagabalus); *Historia Augusta* Maximini Duo 1, 4–6; Aurelianus 3.

4.4 Truth Languages and Monotheism

Cosmopolitan languages, however, did not just confer distinction; they also provided their practitioners with a sense of cosmic belonging and moral worth. As Anderson pointed out, they were not relativistic, each tied like nationalisms to their own people but cosmically centred, and became truth languages. Epics like those of Homer and Vergil, for instance, were read as repositories of transcultural ethical standards and moral guidance. The thickening networks of translocal communication paved the way for more universalized notions of truth, severed from their local origin. In the Hellenistic and Roman worlds, for instance, philosophers increasingly began to think of the divine as transcendent and unitary. They were soon joined by a host of religious cults that used the cosmopolitan community of language to widen their constituency and geographical reach.[74] In time, the most important would be the Christians. Originating as a small Jewish sect, the followers of Jesus left the local Aramaic-speaking environment of their founder behind to opt into the wider world of the imperial languages. The truths of Jesus were to be for everyone and made accessible in a stable form through the written Greek of the Testaments. Especially with the defeat of the Jewish rebellion and destruction of the temple in Jerusalem by Titus in 70 CE, Judaism had lost its traditional geographical anchor, and the ex-Jewish Christians become free to go their own way. They deftly opted to use the Greek-speaking Jewish diaspora that had developed in the service of empire since the famed Babylonian exile as a stepping stone and began distancing themselves from the Jewish community. Instead, they made their faith portable; its truths were not for one people alone, but for everyone and universal.[75]

However, the rise of Christianity was, as brilliantly realized by Garth Fowden, part of a general world-historical trend. Not merely in the Mediterranean but across the Afro-Eurasian arena, the various imperial cosmopoleis served as incubators of intensified religious rivalry and dialogue. Anchored in the written word, monotheist, universalist and transcendentalist forms of thought and organization proliferated, clashed and learned from each other. The result was the handful of great communities of faith that we often refer to as the world religions: Christianity, Islam, Buddhism, Hinduism and, to some extent, Confucianism.[76]

A star witness to this process would be Mani. This prophet hailing from the Sassanian empire in the third century CE carefully inserted himself in

---

[74] Mitchell & Van Nuffelen 2010. [75] Goodman 2007. [76] Stroumsa 2015; Fowden 1993.

a long succession of divine messengers right from 'Sethel the first-born son of Adam' all the way to Jesus, including Zoroaster and the Indian Buddha. In the Mediterranean, Manichean texts clearly bounce off from Christian and Jewish scripture, but within the Persian area the Zoroastrian emphasis is more pronounced. The Buddha, on the other hand, remains peripheral, but not more than a few centuries later Manichean writings made their way through central Asia to China, where at the monasteries of Dunhuang, Mani could be referred to as 'the Buddha of light'.[77] Much in the same vein, but with far greater long-term success, Muhammad joined the fray in the early seventh century to claim his place as the last in a long line of prophets from Abraham and Moses to, pointedly, Jesus. The latter could not, as the Christians held, have been the son of God. There was only one God, and Jesus would consequently have to be ranked among the prophets of whom Muhammad now had the final revelation from above.[78]

The monotheist strictures voiced by the founder of the faith that, with the Arab conquest from the 630s to the early 700s of much of the Roman and all of the Sasanian Empire, established itself as Islam, read as a strong but distant echo of objections already voiced by the Roman apostate emperor Julian in the mid fourth century. If the Christians thought of themselves as heirs to the Ten Commandments given by God to Moses on Mount Sinai, they were clearly wrong to elevate Jesus to divine status. The law of Moses explicitly outlawed the worship of anyone but Yahweh, the emperor objected. However, to Julian, the solution to the logical problems of Christianity and Judaism seemed the opposite of what the solution looked like to Muhammad. Whereas the latter had reinforced the exclusivity of God, Julian advocated the seemingly more reasonable view that the recognition of one overarching supreme God did not rule out the existence of many lesser gods connected with the different peoples, cultures and communities of the world. That was simply how things were in the empire.[79]

Yet, as it happened, Julian had not so much proposed a viable alternative to the jealous monotheisms developing in his times as identified a constraint on universal religious integration. Although the Enlightenment is today

---

[77] Gardner & Lieu, *Manichaean Texts from the Roman Empire*, 2004: 263, and for background, see chapters 1–2. More generally, see Fowden 1993: 72–76 and Folz 2010, chapter 4. Haloun & Henning 1952 for the Buddha of light text, and Mikkelsen 2003 on the Dunhuang manuscripts.

[78] The Quran 2, 83–260; 4, 170–172; 5, 40–83; 21; 9, 31–33. In addition to Fowden and Stroumsa and more specifically, see Neuwirth 2014 for the late antique context of the Quran.

[79] Julian, *Against the Gallileans* 677B, 728B–C, 885B–945C. Discussion in Elm 2012: 300–327 and Fowden 1993: 71–72.

often taken to task for its rationalism, it is still clear that the Scottish philosopher David Hume (1711–1776), when he observed that their dynamics were ruled by a flux and reflux between universal and local, had understood something very fundamental about the great religious traditions. Worship tended to gradually elevate a god until it was the only one remaining and its truths therefore had become universal. Yet, most people did not require answers to the problem of human existence in abstract or general terms; they needed answers to their particular situation and therefore required specific counsel and help. Abstract principle and distant divine force had to be made immanent, pulled down from upon high and put to work as actively present in the life of people and their most immediate communities. No sooner had a god had been elevated into solitary majesty, Hume therefore continued, than alternative, lesser divinities and cults began to proliferate to answer the need of humans and their communities for direct and special protection.[80]

In the study of religion, it is easy to focus too much on high scriptural theology. Art history, Jas Elsner and Stephanie Lenk have recently observed, constitutes virtually an alternative language showcasing an inexhaustible reservoir of material objects used to conjure divine presence whose power came to life only in the rituals of physically participating, and therefore locally gathering, people. Many of these objects reveal an intense dialogue between and across cults and religious communities. Bones, fabrics or other materials believed to have been in contact with sacred persons were venerated everywhere. Images of divinity were borrowed from cult to cult. One of the conventions for depicting the Caliph harnessed an image first connected with Isis and then taken over by the Christians for Jesus.[81] Islam grew out of the pre-existing religious landscape and, as it became the doctrine of successful imperial conquerors, it had to reach an accommodation with pre-established alternatives. It took a long time, centuries in fact, before this monotheism became the faith of the majority of the population in the conquered areas, and in some it never even reached that point.[82] The consolidation of the monotheist and

---

[80] Hume, *The Natural History of Religion* chapter VIII; see further chapter II on the specificity of human cultic needs and chapters VI–VII on the 'rise' into (mono)theism (1993: 138–140, 153–160). On the centrality of Hume's insight, see Strathern 2019: 81–92 and Gellner 1981, chapter 1. Against these, see Brown 1982: 10–21 and 1981: 12–22. For a counter to Brown, see Bang 2015b: 57–58 and duBois 2014: 87 and 110–113. The central point is hardly that the rationalist Hume denigrates the cult of saints, but that he identifies the need for concrete, localized rituals in spite of the monotheist theologies of the book.

[81] Elsner, Lenk & Parpulov 2017; Elsner 2020: 6–12.   [82] Bulliet 1979.

other universalist doctrines clearly depended on much more than imperial command and imposition.

Over the long run, the prestige and privileges attached to the faith of the rulers were undoubtedly conducive to attracting converts. However, usually to get it going, the process needed local mediators that could serve as ritual rallying points for devotees. The growth of Islam in India from the eleventh to eighteenth century was fostered by the patronage of Muslim ruling elites, but in combination with the proselytizing activities of holy men and saints. Commonly inspired by mystic doctrines of the unity of being and the omnipresence of the divine, these so-called Sufi saints were able to bridge the gap between local ritual communities and high religious doctrine. However insistently monotheist, the spread of Islam generated a sacred geography of saints, holy men and the shrines, graves and relics affiliated with their names, not just in India but across the Muslim world. This was how the generalized truths of a religion of the book could find practical implementation in the specific conditions of largely illiterate populations and enable local communities to find both a place and status within the wider cosmopolis.[83]

In the student of late antique Christianity, this should evoke a feeling of déjà vu. The saint and the holy man are not phenomena restricted to Islam. On the contrary, the rise of the holy man has been one of the most intensely studied topics in classics since Peter Brown, inspired by the work of prominent anthropologists, placed it at the centre of the evolution of the late antique Christian empire.[84] The Mediterranean had been and still was in the fourth century, as we saw the emperor Julian insist, a polytheist universe – a world full of local gods whose cults stood at the centre of the myriad small communities that lined the sea. Even so, as Julian also conceded, the imperial monarchy needed to align itself with and tap into the energy of the rising transcendentalist and universalist religious currents generated by the empire.[85]

In this, Julian was no exception among many of the third- and early-fourth-century emperors. They had all experimented with various universalizing religious formulae. His uncle, the emperor Constantine, had opted for the most radical and, as it turned out, lasting solution. When he became a convert to Catholic Orthodox Christianity and managed to unify the empire under his rule, he had suddenly paved the way for Christianity to become the sole faith of the Roman world. If their claim that God and

---

[83] Gellner 1969; duBois 2014: 116–123; Eaton 1993, in particular 207–219 and 255–257; Alam 2021.
[84] Brown 1971a.   [85] Elm 2012; Hopkins 1999.

truth was only one represented a radical break with the polytheistic order of the empire; it all the more fitted the fearsome and desperate ambitions of the late antique emperors to reinforce the unity of their realm. The government on earth ought to mirror the rule of God in the heavens. Both were to be elevated high, distant and almighty. With the sole and brief exception of Julian, the succeeding emperors all threw themselves behind Christianity, lavished patronage on its churches, granted privileges to its clerics and also began to withdraw funding from the old cults combined with the banning of some of their activities.[86]

Nevertheless, the Roman world did not turn Christian by mere imperial fiat. It took at least a century, or perhaps two, for the process to run its course. While human and divine authority feigned to recede from everyday interaction and become more elevated and secluded, Brown observed, people still needed to identify persons with privileged access to the secret realm of power, in heaven or on earth, who could intercede for them and provide patronage.[87] A niche had emerged into which the Christian holy man, martyr and saint could step, just as Hume had predicted and as the experience of Islam has prepared us to expect. As local elites began to respond to the change of heart at court, withdraw funding from the old city cults and channel their means into the erection of churches, cathedrals and monasteries, the cult of saints and martyrs helped focus local communities and carved out a clearer position for them within the new imperial dispensation.[88] Sometimes the qualities of a local god were simply more or less transferred to a newly proclaimed saint. At other times, the process was more complex. Yet the overall point reiterated by Page duBois a few years ago remains valid. The pagan world of local gods and cultic communities did not simply disappear; it was absorbed within Christianity.[89] Some historians have objected to the focus on holy men and saints that followed in the wake of Brown's work that the geography of power was still dominated by local landowners, magnates and imperial officials.[90] But that is exactly the point. The cult of saints, martyrs and holy men reflected the agency of such, often local elites in the Christianization of the empire and their cosmopolitan dialogue with the imperial court.

Here it is worth recalling the insight of Ernest Gellner that Hume's observation of the flux and reflux between transcendental god and local immanent cult might productively be combined with the sociology of

---

[86] Fowden 1993, chapter 4; Van Dam 2007.   [87] Brown 1981; 1982, in addition to 1971.
[88] Lenski 2016, chapters 8–12.   [89] duBois 2014, chapter 3. See further Lane Fox 1986, chapter 13.
[90] Nuanced discussion in Sarris 2011: 210–215.

conquest proposed by the Arab thinker Ibn Khaldun, whom we met in Chapter 3.[91] Conquerors generally saw their power dissipate over time. In the consolidation of rule, they inevitably had to forge links with the conquered population and gradually find that their group had been absorbed by the subjects. Eventually, they would lose power and see it taken over by the provincials. From one perspective, the Late Roman Empire gives the impression of a much-strengthened central government. However, the vastly expanded state apparatus which came out of this was manned by provincial elites able as never before to claim imperial rank.[92] The rise of the holy man mirrored the rise of local elites in the empire. And just as the seeming expansion of the number of state offices was unable to stem the forces of imperial regionalization and fragmentation, so the turn to a monotheist god was unable to prevent local and regional religious rivalry and strife.

As soon as the government sought to harness the church to the cause of imperial unity, it found itself embroiled in power struggles among the bishops and theologians that often eluded its control. At a series of dogma-deciding councils, starting with Nicaea in 325 CE, the emperors sought to make the numerous local bishops of the empire agree to a common theological framework. But definitions of doctrinal unity immediately provoked reaction and opposition. The outcome was invariably strife, division and eventual break-up into splinter churches or communions. Schism has even established itself in our English vocabulary as a concept to denote the dogged and uncompromising dissension among avowed monotheist communities. Most of the theological contents of the controversies of the early church were based on a hairsplitting exercise so fine that it is difficult to ignore the problem of social power. At least to us distant outsiders, it is obvious that such minute differences of belief acquired deadly importance only in struggles over office and control of institutions.[93] Repeatedly regional networks of power asserted themselves. The formation of the Christian ecumene, or cosmopolis, spawned the development of more regional churches from the word *go*. While the church of the Latin Western and the Greek Eastern part of the empire constituted a house torn by constant strife, Armenian, Syriac and Coptic churches gradually spiralled off – and this is to name only some in a development that was not simply defined by Christianity.[94]

---

[91] Gellner 1981, chapter 1. [92] Bang 2021a. [93] See also Elm 2012: 480–483.
[94] Woolf 2012: 263–268 on schismatic Christianity.

118   4 *The Imperial Cosmopolis*

The formation of universal empires in a band from East to West had seen the growth and thickening of cosmopolitan literary cultures. Full membership might have been reserved for a small elite that was generally keen to distance itself from the common majority. Yet it would be a mistake to see these cultures as forming only a narrow stratum which left the rest of society untouched. As the imperial courts learned to harness 'the language of the gods' and bring it into 'the world of men', they were able to touch far more people. The majority still lived lives focused on the local community but existed in a dialogue with the wider cosmopolitan culture dominated by the aristocracy. In the study of Sanskrit culture, the conceptual pair of the great and the little tradition has become part of the established analytical repertoire. Hinduism knew myriad local and regional cults. But through a process of Sanskritization, local village elites attempted to align some of these with the great festivals of the epic tradition of the literary language. In this process, however, local customs and legends also made it back into the 'high' tradition.[95] Great literary and little oral tradition existed in a dynamic dialogue.

To conclude/sum up, the monotheisms of especially Christianity and Islam that have normally been seen as the particular outcome of the late antique Romano-Persian world can from a world history perspective be more fruitfully recontextualized as part of an even wider development. The vast empires of the Afro-Eurasian world had served as incubators for scriptural and universalist or, as historians of comparative religion would prefer, transcendental forms of thought. In addition to the Western Eurasian monotheisms, Brahmanical Hinduism, Buddhism and various forms of Chinese thought, of which the most familiar is Confucianism, all had developed a high literary expression.[96] But none of these had really eradicated the local ritual attachments of previous ages. What they had done to a large extent was absorb the cults of local communities within wider translocal frameworks.[97] This is the context through which we should approach the study of Greek and Latin language and book culture.

---

[95] Marriott 1955, followed by Christensen 2025 and Frankfurter 1998 on Roman provincial society.
[96] Larsen 2018 and Letteney 2023 for two recent studies of how Christianity's truths slowly took on the contours of a formal literary canon and then, in turn, reformatted the literary culture of the late empire.
[97] Moin & Strathern 2022, chapter 1.

CHAPTER 5

Premodern Globalization?
Transcontinental Trade and the Rituals of Consumption in the Afro-Eurasian Arena

> Now when, on a previous occasion, the Son of Heaven had opened the *Book of Changes*, the text had read: 'The supernatural horses are due to come from the north-west.' When he obtained horses from Wu-sun, he liked them and named them 'The horses of Heaven'; but when he came to acquire the horses from Yüan who sweated blood, they were even finer. So he changed the name of the horses of Wu-sun, calling them 'The horses of the extreme west' and he called the horses of Yüan 'The horses of Heaven'.
>
> Ban Gu and Ban Zhao, *Han Shu (Book of Han)*[1]

The blood-sweating horses in which the seventh emperor of the Han dynasty, Wudi (r. 141–87 BCE), took such delight had come from the Ferghana valley in Central Asia. Nowadays divided between the former Soviet Republics of Uzbekistan, Tajikistan and Kyrgyzstan, the territory represented the westernmost reach of Chinese imperial arms in antiquity. In fact, the valley was practically out of reach for the Han empire. A first expedition had ended in absolute disaster. As the military force had struggled its way west round the Tarim Basin, hunger, local resistance and desertion soon saw its numbers dwindle to nothing. But with stubborn determination, the emperor launched a second expedition. This time the army made it through to descend on the Ferghana valley (Fig. 5.1). Soon, the local ruler found himself besieged in his capital by the forces of Han. Yet once the local nobility decided to gang up on their leader, kill him and hand over his head to the invaders, an accommodation was quickly found.

According to *The Book of Han*, the late first-century CE dynastic history that contains our earliest extant account, the leaders of the Chinese

---

[1] Ban Gu & Ban Zhao, *Han Shu (Book of Han)*, chapter 61, 8B. Translation quoted from Hulsewé & Loewe 1979: 225–226. The chapter is often ascribed to Sima Qian, the founder of Chinese historiography, but as Hulsewé and Loewe have shown, the text in his history has been supplied from the *Han Shu* by a later editor to make up for the loss of chapter 123 in the transmission of the original. For the significance of this passage, see further discussions (e.g., Folz 1999: 3–4 and Hansen 2012: 14). The title of this chapter nods to Bayly 2002.

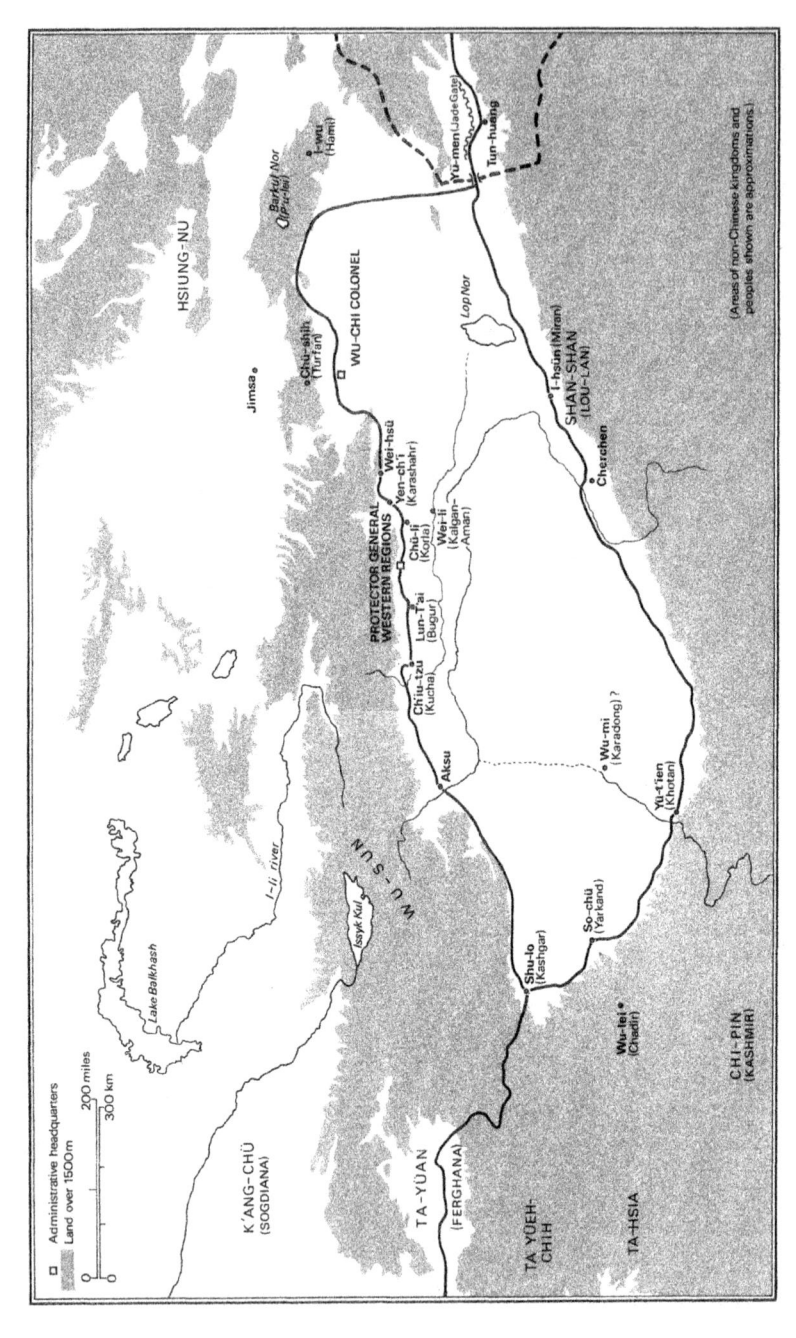

Figure 5.1 Map of Dunhuang, the Jade Gate, the Tarim Basin and the Ferghana Valley. Source: D. Twitchett & M. Loewe, eds., *The Cambridge History of China, Vol. 1: Ch'in and Han Empires* (1986), p. 406.

invasion decided to settle for the right to select a few choice exemplars of Ferghana's most famed horses and a sizeable contingent of more mediocre breeds. The imperial lines of supply and communication were stretched far beyond the breaking point, and the commanders were eager to return with a token victory before the entire force was cut off and trapped in a hostile territory without the possibility of relief.[2]

The opening of Chapter 2 already presented us with the elephants that the imperial campaigns of Alexander and his successors brought back from India and eventually Africa to employ in the wars of the Mediterranean. Ferghana's 'blood-sweating' horses are another example, this time from the opposite side of the Afro-Eurasian world, of how the widening range of imperial armies brought new 'discoveries' and enabled rulers to capture the resources of hitherto little known realms and regions in the centuries before and after the beginning of the common era. Elephants and fabulous horses were, of course, prized as marvellous engines of military power. Their attraction, however, went far beyond narrow military utility. After all, neither would prove decisive in battle. These creatures were even more cherished for their exoticism. Kept in menageries or put on display in public pageantry, they served to celebrate the unrivalled range of imperial power, omens that rule was blessed by the powers of the cosmos and able to tap every part of the reservoir of nature's forces.

The venture of the Han dynasty into Central Asia, as observed in the *Book of Han*, unleashed a torrent of adventurers. People of ambition and daring, with a good number of charlatans interspersed, came to court with tales of fabulous things and marvellous products from far-away countries.[3] Similar developments occurred in the Hellenistic and Roman courts. The demands of elites for exotic rarities across the expanding world of Eurasian empire spawned long-distance trade. Rome, for instance, enjoyed copious imports of Indian pepper and revelled in fine Chinese silks, to single out the two most conspicuous elements of a trade which would have included plenty of ivory, pearls and gemstones, as well as a sundry array of other spices, unguents, aromatic resins and some enslaved people from distant ethnicities.[4]

In the eyes of the traditional world history, a product of the nineteenth century and European colonial empires, world trade was perceived as the main engine of economic and historical development. When scholars,

---

[2] Ban Gu & Ban Zhao, *Han Shu*, chapter 61, 8B–11B (Hulsewé & Loewe 1979: 225–233).
[3] Ban Gu & Ban Zhao, *Han Shu* 6B–8A (Hulsewé & Loewe 1979: 221–225).
[4] De Romanis 2020 for a monograph dedicated to a discussion, if occasionally speculative, of the contents of a single cargo brought back to Roman Egypt from India. Petronius, *Satyricon* 34.4 includes two Ethiopian slaves in its description of a rich man's household.

therefore, found a number of oblique references in the dynastic records of the later Han to embassies from a ruler named Andun that had arrived at the Chinese imperial court from a far western realm called Da-Qin in 166 CE, they were quick to speculate. Might this 'Andun' not be one of the Antonine emperors, Antoninus Pius or Marcus Aurelius? The story of early-modern European commercial hegemony was dotted with accounts of similar embassies, sent by the East India companies, to distant and fabled imperial courts like that of the Great Mughal or the Qing emperor during the seventeenth and eighteenth centuries.[5] It was tempting to see here in the Han accounts a precursor of the world trade of the early-modern era.[6]

Still, there are obvious limits to the parallel. Whoever they were that appeared at the Han court, they could hardly have been a delegation sent officially by a Roman emperor, since the Romans had no concrete knowledge of the Chinese court and its empire. And even if this had been an official embassy, it is clear that it did not establish a permanent, routinized set of contacts between Rome and China. There was no organization able to spin the world into a unified set of routes such as followed in the wake of the circumnavigation of the globe by the Iberian powers of the late fifteenth and sixteenth centuries. Whatever links existed between the realms of the Roman Caesars and the Han dynasty, they were indirect in nature. Goods would have passed through many stations and intermediaries on the way. No one could navigate the meandering network from beginning to end, let alone control it through a centralized organization or even set out with a goal of reaching the other end. It was still far out in the future before the intercontinental trade routes became strong enough to reshape the course of world history by the creation of a commercial global hierarchy of markets.[7]

Even so, it is hardly a trivial thing that silks or pepper found their way to Rome in quantities big enough to scandalize moralists or for pepper pots made of silver to become part of the dinner service of the most affluent aristocratic households. But how to conceptualize this transcontinental world trade before the rise of global capitalism? What context can be identified to explain the forces that fuelled it? One way to tackle the problem of globalization before modern globalization would be to look

---

[5] For some more recent discussions of European embassies to the courts of Asian emperors, see, for example, Van Meersbergen 2019; Chida-Razvi 2014; Wills 2011; Hevia 1995; and Wills 1984.

[6] Raschke 1979: 645, with footnotes 848–850, demolished this theory beyond rescue but, going back presumably to McNeill 1976: 128, it is still mentioned favourably in world history accounts (e.g., Seland 2022: 1 and Lim 2018: 72). Nevertheless, the identification is highly speculative and the Chinese account also suspected the veracity of the report; see Hirth 1885: 42 for a translation of the passage in the *Hou Han Shu* (a fifth-century CE text).

[7] Hansen 2012: 8–9; Chaudhuri 1985; Gruzinski 2012; Abulafia 2019.

for comparable episodes in the history of cultural and economic integration over longer distances. Archaeologists have identified a considerable number of such cases, ranging from the Cahokia 'horizon' along the Mississippi to the ancient Mediterranean and the Roman Empire.[8] While these all exemplify processes of widening and intensifying contacts, they also fall far short of the geographical reach and thickening web of what is normally perceived as globalization.

Instead, the experience of modern globalization is distilled into a set of abstract principles – theories that are then employed to analyze these other more geographically circumscribed cases of societal integration.[9] Much can be learned from this exercise. However, crucially for our purposes, it has little to say about the trans-continental trade that emerged in the Afro-Eurasian arena between the separate 'globalizing' clusters of what we in this book have come to know as universal empires and language cosmopoleis. Approaching the question in abstract rather than historical terms has one main limitation: it overlooks the single most important characteristic of modern globalization. Modern globalization did not merely vastly extend the reach of integration; it was a process that linked up these separate worlds and rose on the back of their achievement.

One of these achievements was the development of a transcontinental trade in what people commonly refer to as luxuries. Yet, as C. A. Bayly observed, there was nothing superfluous about this trade. It might have been low in bulk and constituted only a small part of the trade that went on in these regions. But what it lacked in volume, it made up for in both value and cultural significance. Only a high mark-up per unit of weight would have been able to bear the enormous costs of transport. The worth of this intercontinental commerce was so substantial, in fact, that it was to capture this trade that the pioneers of modern globalization set out from Europe to circumnavigate Africa and inadvertently stumble on the Americas. Moreover, this trade was not simply a thin version of what was to come; it was shaped by its own, separate mechanisms.

Bayly described this premodern world trade under the label of 'archaic globalization'.[10] Of course, to the ancient historian, 'archaic' might give the wrong impression. The point, though, was not to suggest that this trade represented a sort of primitive, very early stage in the history of world trade. Quite the reverse; it was to insist on the strength and sophistication of its

---

[8] Hodos 2020; Pitts & Versluys 2015; Jennings 2011.
[9] Perhaps best illustrated by Jennings 2011, chapter 2.
[10] Bayly 2002; 2005. See further discussion, on the basis of Bayly, by Grewe & Hofmeester 2016.

driving logic. If that logic did not perhaps quite add up to a world economic system, it was better understood through the cultures of elite-dominated consumption in the complex societies of the Afro-Eurasian arena. Bayly's analysis had developed out of his studies of the sophisticated and far-flung trading world of pre- and early-colonial India. It was a universe where British 'free trade' had not yet come to dominate and reorient the flow of goods. Demand was still shaped by Indian imperial rulers and aristocrats, but their cultural preferences also inspired emulation in wider urban and rural elite circles. Thus, if the standards were set by aristocratic society, consumption even of intercontinental goods did not remain completely confined within its rarefied circles of power.[11]

In effect, the model of 'archaic globalization' throws a very illuminating light, as realized by a growing number of historians of premodern societies, on how the cultures of consumption in the universal empires and cosmopolitan communities of language and religion, discussed in the preceding chapters, generated a world trade ranging across the Afro-Eurasian arena.[12] What the culture of consumption of 'archaic' or premodern globalization looked like will be the topic of the next section. But we also need to move beyond 'archaic' globalization as a static ideal type and give it a history. The following section will develop a chronology and show how the Roman empire occupies a central place in the development of world trade before globalization. Finally, the last section will discuss alternatives to the model of 'archaic' globalization and characterize the pattern of world trade that emerged when universal empires expanded across the Afro-Eurasian arena.

5.1 'Archaic' Globalization and the Culture of Consumption

The wonder and celebration caused by the arrival of exotic animals has become something of trope in global history. Every period, court and imperial capital can tell its tale of fabled animals from faraway places being sent as gifts to the ruler and paraded in front of a curious and awe-inspired crowd. Charlemagne famously received an elephant from the caliph Harun Al Rashid (r. 786–809). Later, again, Pope Leo X (r. 1513–1521) was sent a white elephant for his coronation by the king of Portugal. Imported from the East Indies, this giant wonder would be immortalized in a drawing by Raphael, a star of Renaissance painting. Meanwhile, the Portuguese king could glory in

---

[11] Bayly 1986.
[12] Brown 2018; Yarrow 2018; Zinkina 2019. See also several contributions to Hopkins 2002.

even greater wonders, such as the rhinoceros that the German wood engraver Albrecht Dürer commemorated in a mass-produced print.[13]

At the other extreme of the Afro-Eurasian world, the rulers of the Ming dynasty already had the pleasure of witnessing African giraffes arriving from distant shores at the court in Beijing. The tall-necked animal was proclaimed to be a *qilin*, a mythological creature that was supposed to appear when the world was at peace and in harmony under the virtuous rule of the Confucian sage king.[14] In that regard, the Ming emperor much resembled the East Roman emperors. On the rare occasions when giraffes were sent from the Christian kings of the Sudan and Ethiopia to the court in Constantinople, as pointed out in a recent study, the emperors would include this wondrous combination of nature, the camelopard, in their menagerie. There the august world rulers ritually fed the graceful beasts by their own hands as proof of 'a peaceable kingdom where all animals, and all peoples, even those from the imagined edges of the earth – were rendered tame by the gentle hand of a Christian emperor'[15] (Fig. 5.2).

Jorge Luis Borges (1899–1986), the Argentinian author and worldwide favourite of literature departments, has perhaps more than anyone else rekindled our interest in marvellous and mythical beings. In his writings, unicorns, lamed wufniks, mermecolions and a myriad other fabulous creatures of nature flock to carve out a realm for the exercise of freedom and the human imagination.[16] Cultural historians have not been slow to pick up the inspiration; they have set out to excavate the exotic and fabulous creatures that before the scientific revolution used to inhabit our enchanted past. What they have uncovered, however, is an age-old language of ritual and power. When the giraffe showed up in fifth-century Constantinople, for instance, it was already a long and well-established participant in the Roman choreography of imperial might.[17] According to Pliny the Elder, it was Caesar the dictator who had been the first to exhibit giraffes in Rome. By then, others had already treated the population of the imperial capital to shows of crocodiles, hippopotamus and much else.[18] In the arenas of the imperial monarchy, the Caesars staged a pageant of the marvellous. Boars, lions, bulls,

---

[13] McKitterick 2008: 51 and 286–287; Gschwend 2010; Kinoshita 2012.
[14] Dreyer 2007: 89–90 (on qilin giraffes); Hulsewé & Loewe 1979:114, fn. 262, for ancient examples of the celebration of the appearance of the mythological qilin. Sen 2003: 216 more generally on exotic animals as prized diplomatic gifts in the history of the Chinese empire.
[15] Brown 2018: 96.   [16] Borges 2002.
[17] On the giraffe in the Greco-Roman world, see Gatier 1996.
[18] Pliny, *Natural History* VIII, xxvii, 69, and XL, 96.

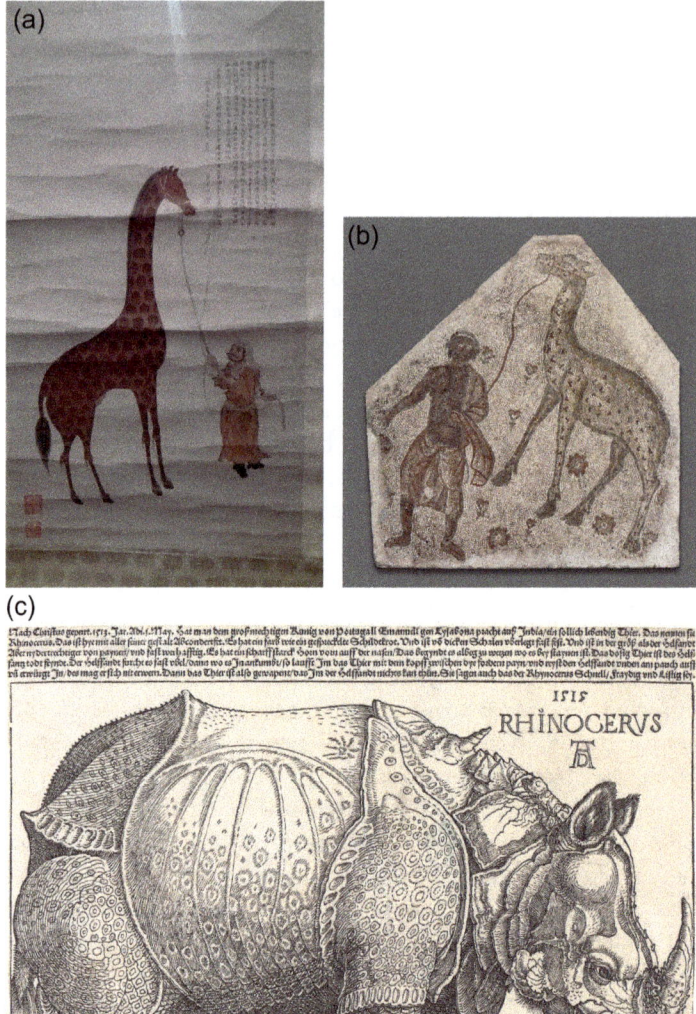

Figure 5.2 Celebration of exotic animals as providential omens of universal empire and benign rule.
a. *Qilin in Beijing* (painting by Chen Zhang, Qing dynasty version of a Ming painting). Photo: Peter Fibiger Bang during the 'Sharing a Common Future: Exhibition of Treasures from the National Museums along the Silk Road' exhibition at the National Museum, Beijing, 2019.
b. Mosaic of a camelopard in Roman Syria. Photo: Chicago Art Institute, CC0 Public Domain Designation.
c. Dürer's *Rhinoceros* (woodcarving), published in Nüremberg, prompted by the arrival of a rhinoceros to the court of King Manuel I of Portugal in 1515. Photo: Getty Images.

tigers, ostriches, rhinoceros, you name it, were brought in from the most distant corners of the earth and arranged in mythological displays and hunts. The Colosseum where much of this took place, was not only, according to the poet Martial, the biggest wonder among all the buildings of the world; it also counted people of every ethnicity in its audience and on a memorable occasion even saw a fierce elephant meekly kneel in front of the Roman Caesar. Everything was available to Rome and her ruler, a divine power in front of whom even the strongest forces of non-human nature would bow.[19]

The reach of imperial power was made manifest in its capacity to bring distant wonders to court. Whether in Rome or elsewhere, rulers and aristocratic elites took pride in the range of rare and sensational products and beings at their command. Persepolis, the palace built at the turn of the sixth century BCE by the Achaemenid emperors, contains perhaps *the* emblematic expression of this ideology. Its ceremonial staircase leading to the gigantic multi-columned throne hall is decorated by reliefs parading the tribute bearers that each year would assemble for new year celebrations. Here everyone from Ionian Greeks to Indians and Ethiopians, twenty-three peoples in all, from near and far, are lined up. Each ethnic group has its own distinct style of dress and offers the particular products of its region in service and submission. This could be everything from objects of exquisite craftsmanship to particularly treasured products or animals.[20]

Across the length and breadth of the Afro-Eurasian world of empire, monarchs endlessly replicated the Achaemenid boast and celebrated their own capacity to draw exotic tributes from numerous and far-away peoples. Whether one looks to the famous Barberini Diptych of the Late Roman court, now in the Louvre, miniature paintings in the Persian manuscripts of the Great Mughals or the ethnographic scrolls of tributary peoples produced for the eighteenth-century Qing dynasty, the basic idea and message remained the same (Fig. 5.3).[21]

Vast numbers of exotic tributaries were manifest proofs of a great power. How, for instance, does the Gospel of Matthew convey the significance of the birth of Jesus to its readers? It does so through the exotic tale of the three magi who came from their distant eastern homelands to render obeisance to

---

[19] Martial, *Book of Spectacles* 1 (the colosseum, a marvel of marvels), 3 (extraordinary ethnic diversity of the audience), 20 (elephant kneeling to the god Caesar), 9 (boar), 12 (lion), 18 (bull), 21 (tiger), 24 (bear), 26 (rhinoceros) and so on. Numbering follows the edition of Shackleton Bailey (Loeb 1993).
[20] Shabahzi 2014: 26–99 and Walter 1966 for pictures and description.
[21] https://collections.louvre.fr/en/ark:/53355/cl010114082 (Barberini Diptych); Beach & Koch 1997, pl. 19 (Mughal emperor receiving gifts from Europeans in subjection); Hostetler & Xuemei 2022 (tributary ethnography of the Qianlong emperor).

128   5 Premodern Globalization?

(a)

Figure 5.3 Imperial tributes: the celebration of tributes offered by subject peoples, from late Roman Constantinople, Mughal Shahjahanabad (Delhi) and Qing Beijing.

a. The so-called *Barberini Diptych*, ivory carving, showing a late Roman emperor protecting his subjects and receiving tributes from the most distant and exotic corners of the world, exemplified by tigers, elephants and people in 'barbarian' garments. Source: The Louvre (https://collections.louvre.fr/en/ark:/53355/cl010114082). Photo: Peter Fibiger Bang.

b. Mughal Emperor Shahjahan at his court, receiving Europeans bearing gifts or tributes. Persian miniature painting from the Padshahname (Beach & Koch 1997), the royal collection at Windsor. Source: Image courtesy of the Royal Trust of King Charles.

c–e. Images of Chinese tributary peoples, book scroll produced for the Qianlong emperor by Xie Sui, second half of eighteenth century CE (Hostetler & Wu 2022: 44–45, 62–63 and 116–117).

c. Official and lady of the people of Siam.

d. People from Poland.

e. The Gurkhas (headman and servant). Source (c–e): Images provided by the National Palace Museum, Taipei.

5.1 *'Archaic' Globalization and the Culture of Consumption* 129

(b)

Figure 5.3 (cont.)

Figure 5.3 (cont.)

the newborn baby. Here was a new monarch, far greater than the ordinary rulers of this world. A baffled and worried king Herod, whom the story has residing in Jerusalem at the time, even had to suffer the affront of being asked by the magi where that royal child might have been born. An event of such magnitude, it could readily be assumed, would not have taken place without clear cosmic signalling. In the narrative, even a star had to emerge on the sky to lead the worshippers to Bethlehem. On arrival, the three travellers throw themselves at the child's feet and hand over their rare and precious gifts of gold, frankincense and myrrh, an act of submission performed only for a (divine) world ruler. Exotic and precious materials from far-away countries had become the accoutrements of imperial and religious power.[22]

The desire of the powerful for distant marvels became a crucial spur to the emergence of long-distance trade in complex agricultural societies, both in the Afro-Eurasian arena and in the Americas. The Aztecs, for instance, cherished the import of exotic bird feathers from distant jungles to be worn by the political elite during their imperial ceremonies.[23] The command of such distant and exotic rarities served as an emblem for elites of their capacity to partake in the rituals of universal kingship and its quest for tribute. It was a crucial driver behind 'archaic' globalization, as noted previously, but the celebration of universal kingship was joined by two other key ideological formations shaping the demand of premodern world trade. The first was the cultic competition that we encountered at

---

[22] Matthew 2:1–12; Schneider 2006. [23] Olko 2012.

the end of Chapter 4 and the eventual emergence of cosmic and monotheist religions. The second were widespread and broadly shared 'humoral or biomoral understandings of bodily health' that prized access to exotic materials and substances in seeking to heal, strengthen and cultivate the personality of individuals.[24]

It was, after all, not just the earthly power of an emperor which could seek embellishment from foreign tribute. The dignity of the gods, as we just saw, did not have much lower pretensions. And if people generally ascribed authority to the gods, it was not simply as repositories of abstract beliefs but as active forces healing and saving human lives. From priest to doctor was but a short step. The efficacy of a prophet, martyr or holy man or woman knew few if any better tests than their healing power. Relics employed in religious ritual, just like the imageries that we encountered in Chapter 4, would often travel over vast distances and include a sundry array of marvellous materials.[25] Exotic goods, therefore, were prized as much for their aesthetic as for their therapeutic, physically transformative effects. Medicine, it should be remembered, was generally based on various notions of rebalancing the humours of the body, of combining sympathetic and antipathetic matters with each other. Hot substances against cool and vice versa. Human character was to be brought into balance with nature and, if possible, enhanced by tapping especially desirable properties thought to reside in a particular animal, plant, stone or other element of nature. Wudi, the Chinese emperor who so desired the 'heavenly horses', also dreamt of finding the recipe of immortality. People were sent out by the emperor, east and west, in search for its secret and sacred ingredients.[26] Perhaps surprisingly from a modern perspective, much of what we know of the use of spices and other exotic goods in the past comes from medicinal and religious tracts.[27]

Intercontinental trade came to comprise a range of numinous products sought by courts, priests and aristocratic elites to embellish and enchant the complex rituals through which their special position in society was articulated, and soon enough, they were followed by the ambitious segments of urban and agricultural society wishing, in their own necessarily more modest way, to claim honour and recognition for themselves. This was not the middle-class consumption that underwrites modern globalization, but it was nevertheless

---

[24] Bayly 2005: 15. [25] See the collection of Elsner, Lenk & Parpulov 2017.
[26] Sima Qian, *Shiji*, chapter 12, 'The Basic Annals of Han China' (Nienhauser, ed., *The Grand Scribe's Records*, Vol. 2, especially pp. 242–244 and 247); Marsili 2003.
[27] As is clear from the pages of Miller 1969.

substantial. However, the long-distance trade that emerged to serve these demands differed, and here we best return to the phrasing of Bayly:

> From modern capitalist consumption in that they emphasized the special products and qualities of distant realms. Whereas modern complexity demands the uniformity of Levis and trainers, the archaic simplicity of everyday life demanded that great men prized difference in goods, learned servants, woman and animals and sought to capture their qualities. Modern 'positional' goods are self-referential to themselves and the markets that create demand for them.

As modern globalization gathered strength between the seventeenth and nineteenth century, international corporations reshaped both markets and production. Products formerly specific to particular regions, the phenomenon celebrated in the rituals of tribute of grand empires, were lifted out of their original ecologies and put into production where it was economically profitable in factories and plantations across the planet. The famous cotton textiles of Bengal, for instance, were overtaken by the industrial mills of British Lancashire supplied by cotton plantations in the American South and in Egypt, among other places. While the global landscape of production was thus flattened, standardized and made less regionally specific, the same corporate forces slowly reshaped demand by active price policies and extensive advertising to generalized publics of consumers. The markets of 'archaic' globalization neither aimed for nor had the capacity to mould tastes and steer consumers to a generalized product.

In that respect, the goods brought from afar remained subservient to the values and demands of the social rituals and ceremonies of the worlds of universal empire. As Bayly continued,

> The charismatic goods of archaic globalization were embedded in ideologies which transcended them. In one sense archaic lords and rural leaders were collectors, rather than consumers. What they did, however, was more than merely to collect because the people, objects, foods, garments and styles of comportment thus assembled changed the substance of the collector.[28]

If difference from the mundane everyday existence was a key characteristic of these goods, it was in the sense of ritual distinction, granting those that could command these products access to a rarefied sphere of society. For 'the logic of such consumption was strategically to consume diversity'.[29]

---

[28] Bayly 2002: 52, with further explanation on pp. 60, 64–65. See further Bayly 1986.
[29] Bayly 2005: 17. For discussion of these passages and Bayly, see Bang 2008, epilogue, and Brown 2018, though the emphasis of the latter is more on difference than ecumenic and imperial consumption of diversity.

5.1 'Archaic' Globalization and the Culture of Consumption 133

A prime example of the strategic consumption of diversity can be found in the so-called Begram hoard. This find from Afghanistan has come to occupy a central position within debates about ancient world trade. Stored in two rooms in a building dating to the time of the Kushan empire, archaeologists have recovered a remarkable treasure. Bowls of Chinese lacquer-ware mingle with carved Indian ivories, painted Roman glass and plaster casts in Greco-Roman style. Some have seen in this assortment a motley batch of the international trade goods of which the Kushans are supposed have been the brokers. But that misses the character of the find. The objects constitute a carefully curated assemblage of precious and distant imports acquired to enhance the claim to power and prestige of a member of the Kushan aristocracy. Rare and rich materials are combined with exquisite craftsmanship and the allure of distant courts. No one could doubt the splendour and centrality of the owner.[30]

Similar principles can easily be identified at work in the culture of consumption that Mediterranean elites developed in the wake of empire and royal courts. On a closer look, the *Natural History* of Pliny, so often treated as a go-to quarry for quaint antiquarian learning, turns out to read almost as a manual for the avid collector of diversity. A notion of universal empire, a religio-cosmic philosophy of nature and medicinal observation permeate the pages of the encyclopedia. In its quest to record the life-world of Roman power, the zealous inclusion even of the most distant and exotic marvels served as tokens of Pliny's capacity to capture the universe in all its wonderful variety.[31] Category after category, from exotic animals to precious stones, masterful works of art and everything in between, are surveyed. The properties of every specimen are related, exceptional examples identified and the first to bring a particular rarity or marvellous thing into use noted. Of wheat, for instance, we are told that the imperial archive contained several letters sent to the emperors by the procurators in the province of Africa reporting some exceptionally, not to say incredibly, fertile seeds.[32]

Scattered across the work, one will also find mentions of Marcus Aemilius Scaurus. Belonging to the very cream of the late Republican nobility, his public spending and private collection became legendary. In addition to the hippopotamus and crocodile, already mentioned, his aedileship saw the construction of a marvellous theatre combining all sorts of wonderful materials and

---

[30] See Morris in von Reden, Fabian, Weaverdyck et al. 2022: 720–729, and at much greater length and depth, Morris 2021.
[31] Carey 2003: 84–85 makes the connection between diversity and marvels explicit. See further Murphy 2004 and Naas 2011.
[32] Pliny, *Natural History* XVIII, xxi, 94–95. See also Dio Cassius LXXVIII, 17.1 and 18.1 (on Caracalla).

products. He is also reported to have been the first to have owned a collection of gemstones in Rome and one whose quality the other grandees found it hard to match. When his countryside villa burnt down, Pliny then remarks, such a collection of objects, amassed and inherited through several generations of world conquest, went up in flames so that no Roman would ever be able to match him again.[33] This was, of course, rhetorical hyperbole, intended to voice the displeasure of Pliny with what he perceived as immoderate luxury. But what attracted Pliny's critique of Scaurus was what he praised in Rome: its capacity to bring all the choicest and rarest things together from everywhere. The city represented such an accumulation of materials and marvels, as if 'another whole world' had been concentrated in just this one place.[34]

Here, the model of collecting ascribed to Augustus by his biographer might help us to illuminate Pliny's misgivings. As Suetonius observed, the first emperor made sure to display to the public all the most remarkable things brought to him from the empire and beyond. Much was invested in the construction of temples, sacred groves and public parks, 'greening Rome'.[35] In Augustus' private collection, however, he took care to cultivate a moderate figure, relatively speaking. Instead of lavishly cramming his private homes with precious statues and paintings, for instance, he tried to stand out through possessing and displaying things notable mostly for 'their antiquity and rarity', focusing especially on 'bones of the giants and the weapons of heroes'.[36] Discernment and selection, focused on natural wonder and archaic heroism, took precedence over the mere accumulation of wealth. Greatness was measured not only in the scale of consumption but also in its style.

Through the art of collecting and amassing precious goods, elites entered into what has been described as tournaments of value.[37] It was especially the founders of cultural and social anthropology that have taught us to understand this phenomenon. Malinowski famously studied the so-called Kula Ring among the Trobriand Islanders. Here great men garnered prestige by accumulating and distributing ritual necklaces and wristbands made of

---

[33] Pliny, *Natural History* XXXVII, v, 11; XXXVI, xxiv, 113–116.
[34] Pliny, *Natural History* XXXVI.32: 'quam si mundus alius quidam in uno loco'. For a discussion of Scaurus, the collection of marvels and the unresolved tension in Pliny between celebration of imperial bounty and the condemnation of luxurious excess, see Carey 2003, chapter 4, especially pp. 96–97. See also Josephus, *The Jewish War* VII, 5, for an instructive link between imperial triumph and the collection of 'all the world'. See Filser and Close 2024 for an excavated example of a Roman villa that seems destined for such a collector of marvellous diversity.
[35] Hallet 2021.
[36] Suetonius, *Augustus* 72, 3 and 43, 4 ('si quando quid invisitatum dignumque cognitu advectum esset, id extra ordinem quolibet loco publicare').
[37] Appadurai 1986: 3–63.

seashells. The larger the number of ceremonial exchange partners, the greater the social standing.[38] However, ingrained in such contests is also a potentially self-destructive drive. This was revealed by the studies of Franz Boas and Ruth Benedict among the Kwakiutl on Vancouver Island of the American North-West Coast. The most prominent members of these societies had on occasion to defend and assert their status in grand events of gift distribution, the potlach. In the most extreme situations, the protagonist would claim superiority in massive gestures of feigned indifference. Vast accumulated stores of wealth would simply be thrown to the flames, seeking to put the opponent to shame by demonstrating that he would not be able to match this level of sacrifice.[39] To be sure, these societies were both non-state and were emphatically studied by Malinowski, Boas and Benedict as alternatives to a market economy. But as states emerged, ritual and gift-giving, public rank and sacred authority continued to shape value and demand, even as this sphere began to be served by extensive markets. Elite spending was still under the obligation of being conspicuous.[40]

It is not difficult to see how strong rivalries in such contests of conspicuous display could push the contestants into almost self-destructive expenditure in their bids to make or break each other's reputation. Elites in pre-industrial societies have therefore often tried to curb the competitive urge among its members. Moral condemnation of excessive expenditure, as in Pliny's remarks about Aemilius Scaurus, was one method. The Augustan principate was keen to promote sobriety and self-discipline among an aristocracy that had torn itself to pieces in the struggles for power of the civil war period. Private ambition had to be contained and channelled into societal service. In his public conduct, Augustus made a point of allowing the people to share in his resources, a phenomenon that the French historian Paul Veyne termed *euergetism*, while conspicuously leading a much more modest private life.[41] Social norms were often supplemented with sumptuary laws that sought to restrict the right to certain prestige goods to the highest ranks of society. In the Roman case, the right to wear golden rings became a prerogative of the equestrian and senatorial orders while the emperors did their best to keep the stone of red porphyry for themselves.[42]

---

[38] Malinowski 1922, especially chaps. 3, 11, 12 and 14.
[39] Benedict 1934, chapter 6. Tsing 2015 for a recent and very influential anthropological discussion of numinous and ritual goods.
[40] Veblen 1899; Bayly 1986: 285–286 and 298–300, especially.   [41] Veyne 1976.
[42] Pliny, *Natural History* XXXIII, viii, 32–34 (on the order of the knights and golden rings); Maxfield & Peacock 2001–2007 (on Porphyry).

Law and morals, however, were feeble regulators. Spearheaded by the imperial courts and powerful religious institutions, aristocracies, priests and urban populations nourished cultures of ceremonial and prestige goods consumption across the societies of the Afro-Eurasian world. Diversity was necessary to uphold the splendour of a royal and aristocratic lifestyle. Sima Qian, the founder of Chinese historiography whom we have already encountered more than once, offered illustration in a telling passage. Confronted with claims that the Qin ruler should not take men from beyond his kingdom into service, the first minister is made to object by using the following simile:

> At present Your Majesty has jade from the Kun Mountains brought to him and possesses the treasure of Sui and He. From your girdle hang pearls as bright as the moon, and you wear the Taia sword. You drive horses like Xianli, put up banners adorned with green phoenixes, and set up drums made from the hide of the divine alligator. Qin does not produce one among these various treasures, so why does your Majesty take pleasure in them?[43]

The question was rhetorical. Autarky would have reduced the capacity and stature of the Qin monarchy. People and objects had to be sought from beyond its frontiers.

The careful reader will notice that most of the things and materials mentioned hailed from within the extensive imperial sphere that the Qin dynasty went on to conquer. That was no different from the Roman world. The major part of the trade spawned by the demand of rulers and elites originated from inside their empires. The great realms were, after all, in themselves vast worlds. Yet, just as imperial rulers cherished ambitions of unlimited conquests, so the 'consumption of diversity' knew no bounds, and a small but immensely valuable trade from beyond the realms developed.[44]

Each state-world and empire normally developed its own particular combination of valued, distant products. However, among the regionally diverging cultures of consumption, some goods rose to cross-continental significance. Precious metals, gold and silver especially, were highly valued everywhere; so were gems, pearls and ivory. Fine textiles might also acquire 'global' status. Chinese silks early became prized among Afro-Eurasian elites. Spices and aromatic resins, harvested from the far-flung regions of the Indian Ocean, became another stable of ancient world trade. The list is far from exhaustive, but spicy tastes and fragrant scents encapsulate the work performed by the goods of archaic globalization. The odours of daily life were

---

[43] Translation by R. Dawson in *First Emperor: Selections from the Historical Records* (Oxford, 2007): 26. Passage from *Shiji*, chapter 87 ('Biography of Li Si'), discussed by Bang & Turner 2016.
[44] Schafer 1963 remains a valuable discussion of this phenomenon.

those of an organic world. The stench of animal and human excrement, the smoke of fireplaces and the smell of rot would have been everywhere. Life depended on the presence of work animals and sweaty manual labour. Much urban manufacture saw the processing, often odorous, of animal products. Think of ancient fullers using urine to clean the woollen fabrics or the notoriously foul smells associated with the activity of tanners turning animal hides into leather. Perfumes, incense and spices were employed by the elites to 'purify' the atmosphere in which they walked.[45] Exotic scents and tastes helped people of power and substance to distance and cushion themselves from what Cicero famously perceived as the slavish world of toil and necessity.[46] Their life was, literally, to unfold within circles charmed by the spirit of the holiday. It was not by coincidence that the Roman Caesars on occasion would spray saffron water over the audience in the theatre.[47] The lavish and generous gesture made clear what it meant to share in the ruler's bounty. Rituals and ceremonies of courtly, sacred and aristocratic power required a rarefied and elevated atmosphere.[48]

5.2 Does 'Archaic Globalization' Have a History? The Pattern of World Trade

So far, then, the notion of 'archaic' globalization and its focus on the demand fostered by premodern cultures of consumption and their imperial, religious and medicinal theories, have turned out to provide an illuminating context for the transcontinental trade that developed under the Romans. However, the concept was developed to account for the early modern period. 'Archaic' globalization was that of the pre-capitalist world trade, mostly of the Indian Ocean, that the European circumnavigators of the planet 'cannibalized', conquered and reoriented into a global system centred on Atlantic Europe. Yet Afghan lapis lazuli and Indian pepper have been found in the graves of the pharaohs.[49] Did nothing change in the three millennia between the Egyptian Bronze Age

---

[45] Freeman 2008; Keay 2006 on premodern spices. Elliott 2024, part 1, and Bradley 2015 on Roman smells and senses; Peacock & Williams 2007 on the ancient incense trade.
[46] Cicero, *On Duties* I, 150–151, with Finley 1985, chapter 2.
[47] On this practice, see Pliny, *Natural History* XXI, xvii, 33, with the explanatory note ad loc of Bostock & Riley (*The Natural History*, London, 1855), gathering other references (e.g., Seneca, *Letters to Lucilius* 90, 15, and Lucretius, *De Rerum Natura* II, 414–417; the latter develops an explicit contrast between the foul smell of rotten carcasses being burnt and saffron sprayed in the theatres or incense burnt on altars).
[48] Rowlands & Fuller 2018: 189. Instructive is Herodian IV, 8.8 & 11.2 (on the emperor's 'progress').
[49] Rowlands & Fuller 2018: 187–191.

138   5 Premodern Globalization?

and the sixteenth-century CE? Identifying a history for 'archaic globalization' is clearly one of the tasks that now confronts ancient history.

This, of course, goes way beyond the scope of this book. But, for now, at least the contours of a few broad phases can be sketched out and the place of Rome be located within this chronological scheme (guidance in Fig. 5.4). By the thirteenth century, Venice had risen to dominate the trade across the Mediterranean in Oriental spices and textiles intended for consumption in Europe. Every year convoys would set out from the Adriatic to bring back the treasured products from Alexandria in Egypt and ports of the Levant. At the other extreme of Eurasia, the southern Song dynasty resided in Lin'an, or modern Hangzhou. Perhaps the biggest city in the world, with easy access to sea, Lin'an possessed a harbour that drew countless merchant vessels from the coastal regions of South-East Asia and even from beyond the Bay of Bengal. Even the Venetian merchant, Marco Polo, who is supposed to have visited the city after it fell under Mongol rule, marvelled at the far-flung commercial pull of the former Song capital. No other harbour, including his beloved Venice, could match its range of visitors and goods. In between these two poles lay the Indian Ocean. Tropical spices and products that were craved by the ruling elites across Afro-Eurasia were shipped from southern India and islands of today's Indonesia in almost all directions.[50]

But when did that trading world emerge? The long-distance trade of the Bronze Age was less far-flung and organized around slightly different principles. 'Archaic' globalization in its first phase was based on a more extreme articulation of its underlying mechanisms. The two Bronze Age centres that we know best, the Nile Valley and especially the Mesopotamian floodplain, were relatively uniform environments. To break the uniformity, elites resorted to imports of a small range of prized products from afar. The expeditions of the Egyptian pharaohs to the mythical land of Punt for gold have become legend. So has the acquisition of tall cedars from Lebanon to serve as columns in the buildings of Mesopotamian kings. Even more important was the availability of bronze. However, bronze alloy required both copper and tin. Copper was far from universally available, but tin was even rarer, a metal which could be obtained only from very few, often distant locations. A central element in the organization of long-distance trade became the procurement of bronze or copper and especially tin. Assur, which centuries later would rise to the status of an imperial conqueror, had a prehistory as a centre of an extensive commercial network that in the early second millennium BCE sent woollen

---

[50] Hansen 2020, chapter 8; Pezzolo 2021; Moule & Pelliott 1938: 326–342 (Marco Polo on Hangzhou). Vogel 2013 argues for the basic authenticity of Polo's claim that he had travelled China.

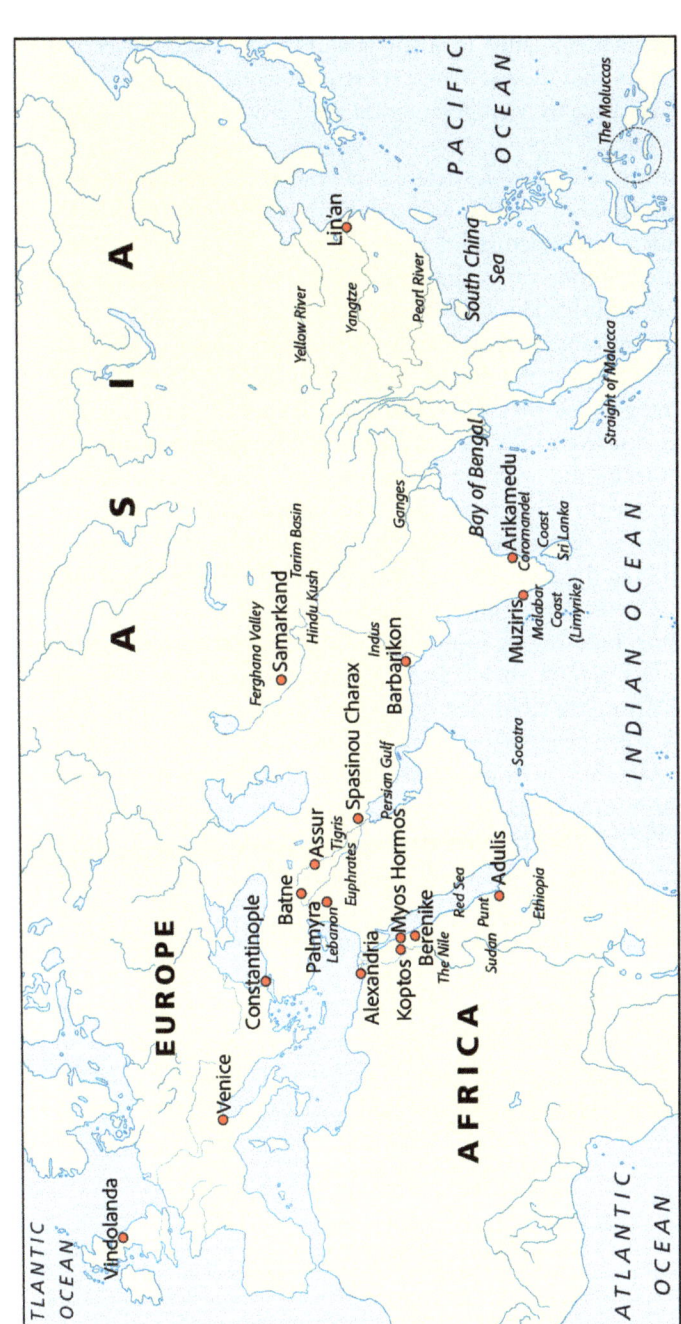

Figure 5.4 Some important locations in the history of premodern world trade. The map does not purport to be a full map of ancient world trade, but offers a guide to the places mentioned in this chapter. Map by Peter Fibiger Bang and Wolfgang Filser.

textiles and tin from Mesopotamia to Anatolia and brought back silver and gold in return. The tin that the Assyrians exported likely had a central Asian origin and may have come to Mesopotamia via the Persian Gulf or through overland caravan routes.[51]

With the transition to iron as the default material of edged implements, the strategic importance of bronze was reduced and the shape of long-distance trade radically restructured.[52] Both the range of material culture diversified and, most importantly, the core regions of state-forming societies expanded enormously. The small scale of the Bronze Age gave way to the far more populous and geographically extended societies of the first millennium BCE. This was the period when the pattern of world trade slowly began to take shape that the traders and sailors of the European Atlantic would set out to capture by the turn of the fifteenth century CE. In the Mediterranean, the westward expansion of Phoenician trading stations was an early sign.[53] But it was really the formation of vast empires across Afro-Eurasia that saw things fall into place.

As the Qin and Han dynasties clashed with the people of the steppe and pushed into the Tarim Basin, silks reached Central Asia in far-greater quantities than ever before. No sooner had Augustus conquered Egypt than Roman traders joined their Greco-Egyptian colleagues to boost commercial links from the Red Sea coast into the Indian Ocean. On arrival, the goods were brought to Coptos in the Nile Valley and then boated down to Alexandria, from where they were sold on to markets across the Mediterranean. India, however, could also be reached through the Persian Gulf. From Palmyra in the Syrian Desert, caravans soon began to set out for the Euphrates and then travel downriver to either make contact with merchants from India at the bottom or mouth of the Persian Gulf or go all the way themselves. A copious archaeological cache of Chinese silks from the graves of the Palmyrene merchants or peppercorns from Berenice on the Red Sea coast bespeak the substance of this trade. The values involved were enormous. Palmyra's mesmerizing ruins are in no way inferior to the opulence of medieval and early modern Venice. A single papyrus reveals that the richest cargoes brought back to the Roman world

---

[51] Barjamovic 2018 (but this was still a world of very small numbers); p. 120 estimates 1,500 donkey loads going annually from Assur to Anatolia. At 65 kilograms per donkey, this is just short of 100 tonnes: one or two medium-sized shiploads, in short. See Larsen 2015; Steinkeller 2021: 50 and 61 (on the need of Babylonia to fetch key materials beyond the flood plain) and Moreno García 2021: 16–17 (on the similar needs of Egypt). More generally, see Barjamovic forthcoming and Zinkina 2019: 41.
[52] Kristiansen 2018a: 10.   [53] Monroe 2018; Sherratt 2016.

were capable of matching the fortunes of some of the most powerful people in the empire.⁵⁴

The Red Sea and Persian Gulf routes remained the most important arteries of the westward trade in exotic textiles, aromatics and spices from Roman times up until the early seventeenth century.⁵⁵ The fate of individual cities and harbours waxed and waned, but the structure remained the same. When the Portuguese succeeded in circumnavigating Africa and entering the Indian Ocean in 1498, they set out with aggressive determination to capture and monopolize this trade, especially in pepper from the Malabar Coast of South India. However, much to the surprise of the historians of European world trade, control escaped the Portuguese. The old Levantine routes proved resilient. Centuries of accumulated experience and commercial networks kept the current of spices flowing. Rather than undermining the old channels of trade by dumping the price, the Portuguese adopted a different strategy. To recoup the enormous outlay in establishing forts along the route and building canon-armed merchantmen, they opted to keep the price of their pepper high in Europe. While the coffers of the Portuguese king profited, this strategy also had to accept the continuous commercial viability of the Levantine routes. Only when the Dutch and English East India Companies joined the fray and embarked on vigorous competition, more than doubling total pepper imports over the seventeenth century, did prices fall to a level where the old Roman routes were undermined and the spices of the Indian Ocean began to be supplied to the Mediterranean by the merchants plying the Atlantic.⁵⁶

If the Portuguese set out to supplant the old Levantine routes, established in Roman times, they still aimed for many of the same kind of commodities. It has become increasingly clear that pepper, the backbone of their trade, first became an item of massive import from the Malabar Coast in Southern India to the Mediterranean under the Roman Empire. Pepper, to be sure, was certainly known in the region, long before. Nevertheless, demand and import rose to another level under the Romans. Just how much is impossible to say. Statistics are simply out of reach. The recent spate of excavations at the Red Sea harbours of Berenike and Myos Hormos, as well as on the island of Socotra at the entrance to the Gulf of Aden, have brought the ancient pepper trade to the top of the agenda.⁵⁷ A few figures have also survived the destruction of time, but do not lend themselves easily as a basis for calculating totals. The numbers are simply too isolated, lacunose and scattered in time to be

---

⁵⁴ De Romanis 2020; Rathbone 2001; Schmidt-Colinet, Stauffer & Al-Asad 2000; Will 1992.
⁵⁵ Seeland 2011.   ⁵⁶ Steensgaard 1974.
⁵⁷ Brun, Faucher, Redon et al. 2018; Sidebotham 2011; Peacock & Blue 2006–2011; Strauch 2012.

combined with any certainty. Nevertheless, the figures leave little doubt that pepper imports reached substantial levels. Prices fell to a point where it was not only the very richest in society that would have been able to afford the sharp, dried fruits from South Indian hillside forests.[58]

People of moderate affluence, especially in the cities of the empire, did their best to emulate the standards set by the top of society in order to stake out their own claims to respectability or at least get a whiff of the opulence enjoyed at the tables and ceremonials of the rich. This is a process which can be followed very clearly in the spread of painted decoration in the ruins of Pompeii and Herculaneum. Found at first only in the largest and richest houses, people of more middling wealth began to pick up on the fashion and have their houses decorated with wall paintings in the current style. However, their paintings were fewer and usually more modest in execution compared to the elaborate schemes found in the houses at the top of the social hierarchy.[59] Something similar should be imagined with the spread of pepper consumption, and probably a few other products brought back from the Indian Ocean, especially the aromatic resins of the Arabian peninsula.

Like pepper, incense also saw the volumes imported to the Mediterranean increase and, just as with pepper, might also have found users outside the highest circles of society.[60] In response, the political and religious elites would have distinguished themselves through more lavish use in their social rituals. The emperor Elagabalus, in seeking to enhance the standing of the cult of which he was the main priest, is told to have 'heaped every kind of spice' on the altars receiving his copious animal sacrifices.[61] Among the inscriptions from Parentium, on the Northern Adriatic coast, one reports the award of a public funeral to a young member of the local city council where three pounds of incense were to be burned on the funeral pyre.[62]

By far the biggest archaeological find of pepper from the Roman world consists in a storage jar, of South Indian fabric, containing some 7.5 kilograms

---

[58] Cobb 2018; Mayer 2018; Evers 2018, for this argument and up-to-date gathering of the textual as well as archaeological evidence.
[59] Wallace-Hadrill 1994, chapter 7.
[60] Caseau 2024 for a trans-epochal discussion of incense and not least the frequent substitution of more easily available, less expensive fragrant substances for the Arabian product.
[61] Herodian, *History* V, 5, 8. See Price 1987: 95 for the ritual significance of such lavishness.
[62] CIL (*Corpus Inscriptionum Latinarum*) Vol. V, Reg. Ital. X, Parentium no. 337. While I share the broader point of Salmeri 1997 about the widening social penetration of incense, I differ on the interpretation of this particular inscription. Compared to emperors or senators, a decurion may look modest, but they counted among the top 1–2 per cent of the population, and three pounds of incense to be burned in one ritual would have been unaffordable to all but this stratum of people.

of black pepper. Found in a courtyard in direct proximity to the Great Temple of Berenike on the Red Sea coast, its contents were presumably stored to be employed and burned in religious rituals, as testified by numerous finds of charred peppercorns on the site.[63] There is a wide gap between such ceremonial and copious piety and the couple of denarii recorded as spent by a Roman soldier at the fortress of Vindolanda in the early second century on a little pepper. This, we can imagine, would have been used sparingly on special days to enliven his dinner.[64] In a more affluent person, such behaviour might be derided as petty and miserly. To the philosophical satirist, Persius, this could simply serve as the character trait of the excessively tight-fisted.[65] Modest consumption among middling people may not have impressed the rich and lettered elite, but its effect was anything but trivial. The accumulated weight of a class of mostly urbanite and military consumers, which would have to be counted in the hundreds of thousands, added a noticeable boost to the scale of the trade.[66] A few relatively big sea-going ships began every year to set out from Egypt and go directly across the Indian Ocean to South India, instead of, as most did, hugging the coastline, from harbour to harbour, in a circular movement. It is very likely that this trade began to approach the levels of the medieval spice trade that the Portuguese set out to capture.[67]

However, the Roman pepper trade stands only at the beginning of the development of the Afro-Eurasian spice trade. It has often been assumed that the pepper trade declined sharply as the empire went into its third-century crisis and civil wars. But there is barely any evidential basis for this belief. Our sources for the trade in Oriental goods are as patchy before as after. Nor is there much reason to suppose that consumption would have been so neatly tied to the political vicissitudes of the empire. As the Roman world moved into late antiquity, urbanism remained strong and vigorous in many regions of the empire. Some argue that reduced imports are reflected in a rise in prices. Pepper had become in shorter supply compared to the first century. Yet, if the prices went up, it must reflect persistent demand, and it then becomes difficult to understand what would have prevented traders setting out from Egypt to buy up supplies in India and bring them back to the empire. The Red Sea or the Indian Ocean did not experience any significant disruption by war. Far from it, the archaeology of its coastal regions bespeak

---

[63] Tomber 2008: 76. Hense 2018 on the great temple, section 50 on the find of pepper. Cappers 2006, chapter 4, provides a survey of the archaeobotanical evidence recovered in the excavations at Berenike; see pp. 112–119 on pepper at Berenike and across the Roman Empire.
[64] Tabulae Vindolandenses (*The Vindolanda Writing Tablets*), ed. Bowman, Thomas & Adams (London, 1994), II, 184, I, 3–4: Tagarminis piper (denarius) ii.
[65] Persius, *Satire* VI, 19–21.   [66] Friesen & Scheidel 2009; Mayer 2012.   [67] De Romanis 2015.

a thriving and continuously evolving world of harbours, trade routes and commercial communities all through the Roman period.[68]

The belief, however, that prices rose is derived mainly from a comparison of the average level reported by Pliny in his *Natural History*, with the prices stated for pepper in Diocletian's famous edict on 'Maximum Prices'.[69] *Maximum* may well be of the essence here. Like is not being compared with like. The edict was promulgated to curb sharp spikes in prices when marching armies suddenly boosted local demand in seeking to procure provisions. What relation most prices stated in the edict as the legal maximum bore to daily reality is well-neigh impossible to fathom, not to speak of their relation to the presumed but vaguely known normal rate of the preceding centuries.[70] A wider background of the edict is the fiscal collapse of the imperial silver coinage that saw the denarius virtually transformed into a token. With barely any silver content left, the buying power of the coins collapsed and prices began to rise across the board. The combination of a monetary system in the midst of radical transformation and a maximum price with an uncertain connection to what was charged in the marketplaces hardly provides a firm foundation for comparison with the prices of prior centuries and most of all makes clear just how desperate the plight of the ancient economic historian is. There are so many things we cannot know with any degree of precision. In that case, it may be better, as is attempted more generally in this book, to tie our image of Roman developments into wider historical contexts.

Of course, it would be implausible to assume that the levels of intercontinental trade had not fluctuated over the centuries. But just how much is something that is now mostly beyond recovery. Yet whatever the periodic ups and downs, in the long run the late antique spice trade clearly remained vigorous and continued to develop. When Palmyra was sacked by Aurelian in his struggle with Queen Zenobia, the trade moved further north up along the Euphrates. Less than a century later, the town of Batne crops up in our records as the centre of an annual fair where 'opulent merchants' would flock to deal in the goods brought from India and China. The fair of Batne was far from a trifling commercial gathering, but represented a concentration of wealth large enough to attract the attention of a Persian general who, according to the historian Ammianus Marcellinus, for a time had his hungry eyes fixed on the

---

[68] Seland 2014a; Tomber 2008.   [69] Argued most systematically by Cobb 2018.
[70] The preamble expects that in many places the prices would be well below the maximum defined in the edict. The maximum is introduced to curb the demands of those that seek to profit from the sudden rise in demand by the expenditure of imperial soldiers. For a new and excellent English translation, see Kropff 2016 (http://kark.uib.no/antikk/dias/priceedict.pdf). For the original text, see Lauffer 1971 and Crawford & Reynolds 1977–1979.

site that so temptingly offered itself for plunder.[71] Berenike, one of the main harbours of the Red Sea route, experienced its urban culmination only in the fourth and fifth centuries, after a second-century slump during which rival Myos Hormos presumably had been more important.[72] Among the imperial possessions donated by Constantine to the Church of St. Peter in Rome was an Egyptian estate expected to deliver some 50 medimnoi or more than 2,600 litres of pepper, not to mention a sizable cash yield and plenty other aromatic substances, including 150 pounds of cloves.[73] Clearly, the flow of spices into the Roman world had anything but dwindled into a thin trickle. In the so-called *Cookbook of Apicius*, a late antique Latin text, four out of five recipes make copious use of pepper. The availability of the little black corns could obviously be taken for granted.[74]

Not only did pepper remain a sizable import to the Mediterranean, but the range of spices and density of networks increased.[75] On the island of Socotra, graffiti scribbled on the walls of a holy cave by foreign visitors over the first half millennium CE, document the emergence of a strong contingent of Indian merchants crossing the ocean to the Persian Gulf, the southern shores of Arabia and the entry to the Red Sea.[76] Meanwhile the eccentric cosmography of Cosmas, a sixth-century work written by an Egyptian monk, leaves little doubt that the routes connecting Rome's most important African province with Ethiopia and India remained vigorous. Amid the text's rampant jumble of theological argument mustered against Greek astronomy, suddenly the eleventh book turns into an account, apparently based on personal experience, of harbours and markets in India

---

[71] Ammianus Marcellinus, *History* XIV, 3, 3, discussed by Seland 2014b.
[72] Basic up-to-date overviews of the archaeological evidence are provided by Sidebotham and Blue in Brun 2018. It is noticeable that the largest urban remains of Berenike date from the fourth and fifth centuries (when Myos Hormos had ceased its activities). Sidebotham 2011: 68 still prefers to think of first-century Berenike as having reached its population maximum. However, that chimes badly with his observation that the population of the early period seemed more temporary, maintaining close ties to the Nile Valley, while the population of the late city treated it as a permanent home (2011: 78, 264, 278). At any rate, all agree that the city, with ups and downs, or it seems to me sometimes just gaps in the archaeological record, continued well into late antiquity as a vibrant commercial emporium.
[73] *Liber Pontificalis* chapter XXXIV (on Pope Sylvester) lists among the imperial gifts to St. Peter's in Rome an Egyptian estate that would deliver fifty medimnoi of pepper (among other unguents and spices), analyzed most recently by Seland 2012.
[74] Apicius, *De Re Coqinaria*, edition by André 1974. On my own rough and ready recount, at least 356 out of 460, basically 4 out of 5, recipes prescribe the use of pepper. Strangely, Apicius is often cited for the ubiquity of pepper in Roman cooking before the alleged decline in late antiquity. It confirms rather the opposite conclusion.
[75] A point already made by Miller 1969, chapter 1.
[76] Strauch 2012: 541. The vast majority of texts were written in the Indian Kharosthi script – an impression confirmed by Procopius, *The Wars* I, xx, 9–12, which report on Indian silk merchants sailing to Persia.

and Sri Lanka, before hinting at the existence of routes farther east to 'the clove country' and 'Tzinista which produces the silk'.[77]

By the sixth century, activity was growing significantly in the eastern parts of the Indian Ocean. As peasantries made inroads into the jungles of Southern China, Indo-China and the Indonesian islands, state formation followed suit. To strengthen their authority, kings and big men in the region sought to import the complex Sanskritized ceremonial of Indian courts and religious institutions. Across East and South-East Asia, Indian forms of kingship and religion began to spread. But with this development came also a bigger demand for ritual goods. Already a source of several prized exotic materials, the region saw the trade in spices, fragrant types of wood and rare animal products increase enormously. A further boost was given by the rising demand of Chinese elites and urban populations. Under the Tang and Song dynasties, the demographic weight of the Middle Kingdom was shifting from the grain-growing plains of the centre to the expanding rice paddies of the south. Cities on the coast rose in importance and developed into some of the most commercially vibrant markets in the world at the time. A rare occurrence at the beginning of the first millennium, ships plying the waters of the South China Sea regularly made it to the Strait of Malacca and even across the Bay of Bengal by 1000 CE.[78]

The global volume of trade in the Indian Ocean increased, and so did the assortment of available goods circulating. In western Afro-Eurasia, cinnamon and ginger joined pepper in the standard repertoire of exotic spices. Cloves, nutmeg and mace, three spices that grew only on the Moluccas, a small set of islands in the Indonesian archipelago, now rose to an established position at the top of the hierarchy. They had been known and craved long before, but it is only during this period that even these exclusive tropical substances became regularly available to elites in Europe.[79] Next to pepper, the coveted Moluccan

---

[77] Cosmas Indicopleustes, *Cosmography*, book 11, trans. McCrindle (Cambridge, 2010 [1897]: 367). Andrade 2018, chapter 3, takes the evidence of Cosmas as a sign that the routes from Roman Egypt had begun to pick up again, after a third- to fourth-century slump. But the Persian presence on which Andrade focuses did not begin only in the supposed interim period and therefore did not necessarily cause a Roman contraction. Tomber 2008 shows a world of vigorous commercial ties with participants from Egypt, Persia and India. See further Evers 2018, for the previous centuries, stressing the commercial strength of participants from outside the empire.

[78] Hansen 2020, chapters 7 and 8, on the thickening networks of state formation and trade in Indonesia and Southern China by the year 1000 and the rest of the book, more generally across the Afro-Eurasian world. See further Miksic 2021; Sen 2003; Gungwu 1958.

[79] Freedman 2008: 21–22 on the profile of the spice spectrum of medieval Europe. Key 2006, an unusually well-researched popular history, instructively connects the increasing role of Moluccan spices with the evolving commerce of Indonesia and the South China Sea from the sixth to seventh century onwards (pp. 76–104).

triad eventually became a key target of European commercial enterprise. The Dutch East India Company, arguably the world's first full-blown capitalist corporation, built its business around the conquest and vigorous control of the small spice islands. Contrary to pepper, the geography of production and supply of these fine spices was so restricted that an actual global monopoly was achievable.

Roughly speaking then, the history of the post–Bronze Age intercontinental trade can be sketched as the result of two developmental waves. The first was based on the expansion of the trade in pepper (and silk), westwards across the Indian Ocean. This is where Rome takes its place. The second wave, beginning in late antiquity, added to the range of goods, rising in part from the intensification of commercial exchanges in the eastern parts of the Indian Ocean. Merchants from Islamic lands now came to play a key role as connectors. Whereas the merchants of Roman Egypt had normally not ventured further than the Malabar and Coromandel Coasts of Southern India and the island of Sri Lanka, networks of Muslim merchants extended their reach all the way to the Strait of Malacca and beyond.[80]

Archaeologists working at sites on the Red Sea that were active in the Indian Ocean trade both during the Roman and the Islamic periods confirm this image. Both the number and quantity of imported spices grew between the two periods.[81] The long-distance trade of the Roman Empire, in short, did not constitute a high point that the European merchants of the early modern period somehow reached again after a long medieval lull. It achieved something far more significant: it laid a very important foundation stone for the premodern world trade of the Afro-Eurasian arena.[82]

5.3 Alternatives? World Systems and Silk Roads

It is now time to look at the alternatives to the notion of 'archaic' globalization. Two are especially prominent: so-called world systems theory and the idea of the Silk Roads. First, world systems. Not only but especially archaeologists have debated intensively whether one can understand the Afro-Eurasian long-distance trade in terms of a world system. The theoretical

---

[80] Palombo 2021 on the strength of the many intersecting networks of traders in the Islamic world.
[81] Van der Veen & Morales 2015. See further Peterson 1980 on the significance for medieval Europe of the expanding range of spices developing under the Arab caliphate.
[82] Pace Sidebotham 1996: 288 ('Roman interest broader and longer than any other') who, in spite of his unquestionable merit in cultivating the study of the Indian Ocean trade, nevertheless manages to overlook the centrality of the spice trade for the Mamluk rulers of medieval Egypt, the significance of the Muslim pilgrimage to Mecca or the expansion of the East African slave trade to the Middle East.

concept was originally developed by Immanuel Wallerstein as a corrective to textbook economics. International trade, he objected, was not the imagined level playing field where participants met freely in exchange for mutual benefit. Capitalism was, to be sure, based on international trade, but that trade served to organize participants into a hierarchical division of labour. At the periphery were producers of raw materials, at the centre capital and technology. Capital and technology, though, were not 'innocent' factors of production. They were tools of control that invested the central core of the system with the power to dominate and exploit the periphery. The gains of trade were not divided equally but claimed disproportionately by the hegemonic core.[83]

Centred in Western Europe, the capitalist world system, in Wallerstein's book, rose to global dominance with the plantation economies of the Caribbean and East India Companies of the early-modern era. Outside the Caribbean (and the North American colonies), as historians have pointed out, domination had to wait until the long nineteenth century. Before that, the gravitational pull of the European core was not strong enough to reorganize and subject local economies to the needs of a global economic system. Railroads and steamships, and the enormous increase in transport capacity that they brought about, were crucial in 'opening up' the vast land-mass of Africa and Asia to European economic penetration. Without these, it is difficult to see how the ancient Afro-Eurasian world could have been pressed into a shared economic system where financial decisions made in a central core somehow dictated the periphery. Could we, for instance, describe the pepper-producing Malabar and Coromandel coasts of India as somehow subjected to Rome and dominated by its financiers? That would hardly be reasonable. The south of India was not in any meaningful way controlled by distant imperial capital.

Several systems of core-periphery relations can, on the other hand, easily be identified: the big empires of the age. Whether China, Persia or Rome, the vast bulk of their economic activity was located inside each of these realms. In the Wallersteinian terminology, they are called 'world empires'. Tributary empires is another label which could usefully be applied because taxation and tribute would often have been more important than trade in articulating hierarchies; it was control of military power rather than capital and technological advantage that shaped the transfer of resources.[84] The

---

[83] Wallerstein 1974.
[84] Bang 2008; Hopkins 2018, chapter 6. Friedman 2018 for a reassertion of more traditional core-periphery models in the study of ancient societies.

5.3 Alternatives? World Systems and Silk Roads

Roman submission of Egypt, the most productive region of the Mediterranean, primarily came to expression in the payment of a copious grain tribute. Every year, a large fleet departed from Alexandria to deliver tax wheat to feed the population of Rome.[85]

While it is possible to locate a centre inside the universal empires, from the Mediterranean to China, it is more difficult to identify a core controlling the transcontinental flow of goods. As Bayly remarked, it was not obvious what was core and what was periphery.[86] 'Archaic' globalization developed 'before hegemony'; its articulation was more diffuse.[87] It is then, perhaps, not surprising that the notion of the Silk Roads, with all its romantic allure of caravans and desert trails, has gained traction as the main alternative to world-system analysis.[88] However, the Silk Road carries problems of its own, two especially. First, there was no Silk Road in the sense of a direct established route running across Afro-Eurasia, in spite of what the many maps produced in books and museums might indicate (Fig. 5.5). No one would ever have set out with goods from China with the Roman Empire as the intended destination or vice versa. Secondly, it was not the overland routes of Eurasia but the Indian Ocean that was the main conveyer of goods traded long-distance. What existed was a vast range of local and regional trading circuits that intersected and overlapped.[89]

Take the bales of Chinese silk that ended up in the Roman Empire. They would have started their journey as diplomatic gifts or payment for supplies and horses given by the Han dynasty to the elites of the oasis communities lining the Taklamakan Desert in the Tarim Basin or to nomadic groups on the imperial steppe frontier. Here they would have served as objects of prestige consumption. Archaeologists find them in substantial quantities in elite burials of the region, but some of the silks also made their way into central Asian commercial networks as payment for Indian ritual goods. Having crossed the Hindu Kush, the silks would then travel down the Indus, some ending up with the Kushan and other ruling elites, some in markets of cities such as Barbarikon.[90] It is only at this point that silks began to be directed towards consumption in the Roman Empire. Some were brought to the Persian Gulf,

---

[85] Garnsey 1988, chapters 14–15, a classic and expert discussion of Rome's control of food grains.
[86] Bayly 2002: 50.
[87] The term of Abu-Lughod 1989. Beaujard 2018 claims a Trans-Afro-Eurasian world system unified in a single hierarchy, yet sees multiple cores: a contradiction in terms.
[88] The most high-profile intervention is that of Peter Frankopan (2015).
[89] Hansen 2012: 8–9; Rezakhani 2010.
[90] Hansen 2012 repeatedly emphasizes the significance of imperial expenditure and diplomacy for 'Silk Road' trade, rather than big commercial ventures (p. 112); see further Yü 1967. Contrast Whitfield 2018: trade is presumed to be the driver of development, but the mechanism is never made explicit.

Figure 5.5 Picture of a Silk Road map in the Archaeological Museum of Lanzhou, Gansu Province, China. Note the absence of the all-important routes from Palmyra/ The Persian Gulf and the Red Sea harbours to North, West and even South India. Photo: Peter Fibiger Bang, March 2024.

where Palmyrene merchants bought up part of the supply to bring it to markets in the Roman world, while others would have served the demand of aristocracies in the Parthian and Sassanian Empire.

The meandering course taken by silk and other such goods across the Afro-Eurasian arena would almost seem to be a perfect example of the self-organizing wizardry expected of Adam Smith's 'invisible hand'. But exchange happened on a field which was far from unified and even; it had to traverse something better described as a broken landscape, fractured by nature, divided by communities.[91] At the start of the chapter, we saw how an ambitious Han emperor sought to circumvent the immediate neighbours on the imperial frontier to gain direct access to the coveted 'blood-sweating' horses of Ferghana. The goal was reached, but only just and temporarily. More often than not, the transfer of goods had to pass through the control of intermediary hands. Sixth-century Roman historians writing in Greek report

---

[91] See also Purcell 2015.

5.3 Alternatives? World Systems and Silk Roads

two plans to circumvent the Persians in the silk trade. The Sogdian merchants of Bactria had at the time established a network dominating the silk trade through the Tarim Basin, but had become dissatisfied with the conditions offered by the Persians at the receiving end. Therefore the Sogdians joined the Türks, a nomadic warrior coalition of Central Asia, on an embassy to seek alliance with Constantinople, in the rear of the Sassanian Empire, against their mutual enemy. By then, Constantinople had already for a time toyed with the idea whether the merchants of the East African kingdom of Adulis could intercept the silks, going from Northeast India via the Persian Gulf, and redirect them through the Red Sea. In both cases, nothing came of these ambitions. The Persians were too close to India, the Sogdians too far from the Roman world.[92]

Regional compartmentalization of commercial networks was reinforced by logistical constraints and nature's rhythms. The monsoon, for instance, imposed a seasonal pattern on travel across the Indian Ocean. Trips had to be timed to fit in with its alternating direction of winds: south-westerlies in the summer; in the winter, they would be blowing the opposite way, from the north-east. If delayed on the outbound voyage, a ship might have to wait another season before returning. Often the availability of materials was intimately tied up with the seasonal movements of migratory groups. The famous pepper of South India was gathered by so-called forest people as they moved through the hilly woodlands.[93]

The trade of 'archaic' globalization cut across one frontier of ecologies and modes of living after the other. Too many zones were crossed for full knowledge of the whole trajectory of a good to be generally available or even possible. After several centuries of copious imports to the Roman world, the Severan courtier Philostratus could still imagine that peppercorns were miraculously picked by monkeys in the Indian forest. What took place in the world of Chinese silk producers simply remained beyond the pale. Merchants, with a stranglehold on information about the distant origins of goods, no doubt did their bit to preserve and exaggerate the exotic legend of their valuable wares.[94] The distances were simply too long, with travel times easily running into several years, so a unified picture could

---

[92] *History of Menander the Guardsman*, ed. and trans. Blockley (1985), chapter 10; Procopius *Wars* I, 20; Feltham 2009; Bang 2018a; Whittow 2018.
[93] Weaverdyck, Fabian, Morris et al. 2022; Morrison 2002.
[94] Philostratos, *Life of Apollonius of Tyana* III, 4, 2–3. De Romanis 2015: 149–150 finds a remnant of local folklore in this passage. More generally, see Freedman 2008: 133–137.

not be produced. Goods may have moved between regions, but the conditions were skewed in favour of regional fragmentation.[95]

Even so, if goods often circulated within regional networks governed by their own logics, it still is possible to discern some general principles that shaped the selection of materials capable of 'spilling over' from one circuit to the next. These types of goods crossed either one of two frontiers. The first type consisted in products manufactured within a core sedentary zone that somehow became treasured as especially refined among elites of the other sedentary core regions. The other kind of good straddled the frontier between the sedentary societies and the more mobile populations on the margins of the sown, whether steppe, desert, hilly uplands or (tropical) forest. Cultivated over generations, these peoples of 'the margins' had a deep knowledge of the natural properties of their habitat. Some of the products they had learned to lure out of nature's hand, for nourishment, medicine and magic, also came to double as treasured markers of mysteriously exotic contrast in the rituals of power and healing among the sedentary elites of cities, temples and courts.[96]

'Archaic' globalization, therefore, was shaped around the big imperial worlds that we saw dominating the sedentary peasantries of Afro-Eurasia in Chapters 3 and 4. Each of these represented a concentration of wealth and consumption that exercised a pull, not merely on their own core territories but like giant whirlpools also managed to draw in materials from distant margins. The intercontinental trade grew out of the frontier zones where these forces intersected and made some materials jump from one sphere to the other.[97] In that way, 'archaic' or premodern globalization, as we have seen in the sections of this chapter, developed out of the cultures of elite consumption that prized the capture of exotic diversity. These had begun to develop from the Bronze Age and the beginning of state formation. A second phase began after the Bronze Age, and it is in this context that Roman commerce with the Indian Ocean belongs, where the world of empire expanded across the continents of Europe, North Africa and Asia to create the polycentric pattern of long-distance trade that the early-modern merchants of the Atlantic would set out in a third and final phase to conquer, reshape and centre on Europe between the sixteenth and eighteenth centuries.

---

[95] An assessment confirmed by Andrade 2015. Schulz 2024 is a little more upbeat about the success of ancient explorers but still also reveals how their activity never resulted in a set of routinized contacts that broke the pattern of regional overlap.
[96] Fuller & Rowlands 2018.
[97] Von Reden, Dwivedi, Fabian, et al. 2023 on the significance of frontier zones for the Afro-Eurasian economic history; Oka 2018 on the intersecting core areas.

CHAPTER 6

Resistance, Rebellion and Renewal

For the time has come to begin judgment from the house of God.
1 Peter 4:17 (my translation)

6.1 Apocalyptic and Millenarian Uprisings

The idea that the time is nigh, that a day of judgment is imminent and awaiting a sinful humanity, has resonated powerfully throughout Afro-Eurasian history. This passage, hailing from inside the Roman world and ascribed in the New Testament to Peter, the Apostle, perhaps found its most dramatically fateful reception in nineteenth-century China. In *Good Words to Admonish the Age*, the biblical line inspired a lengthy entry on the ills of Chinese society. China had reached a moral nadir, the reader was told, had cultivated idols and could now expect divine retribution in the form of disasters and foreign invasion. The exegetical work was penned and published in 1832 by Liang A-Fa, a Chinese convert of the Protestant missionaries who had followed in the wake of the growing British–China trade to Guangzhou. In the analysis of Liang, old notions that an imperial dynasty would govern by virtue of the 'mandate of heaven' until moral corruption rendered its scions unworthy of rule blended seamlessly with the apocalyptic and eschatological expectations of Christian theology.

During the 1840s, this text helped produce one of the most eventful examples of cultural connection in the age when modern globalization took shape.[1] A villager, Hong Xiuquan, became convinced by the text that he was a conduit of divine revelation and the brother of Jesus. For years he had studied the Confucian classics and made several attempts to pass the imperial civil service examinations. An imperial degree would have won him status as a venerable member in the lettered cosmopolis of

[1] Bayly 2004: 151–158.

the gentry. Instead, repeated failure brought deep personal crisis and eventually extravagant salvationist visions. None of this would have mattered much if the new self-proclaimed prophet had not found a fertile preaching ground among the Hakka population living on the upland frontier of Southern Chinese agricultural society. Marginalized and engaged in prolonged feuding with rival agricultural groups, the Hakkas saw meaning in Hong's apocalyptic visions. They were a chosen people, destined under the leadership of their prophet to fight and pave the way for the arrival of a righteous society, 'the heavenly kingdom'.[2]

Once the Taiping movement got under way, it quickly gathered momentum. The late Chinese imperial countryside suffered under severe strains. Population growth was enormous and competition for land intense among the ever-increasing number of peasant cultivators. In that situation, the Taiping became the rallying force for much of the struggling peasantry, and by 1850 rebellion was full blown. Its armies marched up the Yangtze Valley, until the unthinkable happened and Nanjing, one of the old capital cities of the empire, was taken in 1853. The Heavenly Kingdom had arrived on earth, and there it stayed till the forces of a badly shaken Qing dynasty finally managed to obliterate its challenger more than a decade on. Many millions of lives had been consumed in the mayhem, which ranks among the bloodiest wars in human history.[3]

The striking but still light entanglement of local socio-political currents with the advancing representatives of global capitalism and European colonial enterprise that became visible in the Taiping Rebellion would only intensify over the next generations. The growing global network of colonial power, transport and communication also harboured its own resistance. If capitalist entrepreneurs and colonial administrators travelled and communicated faster and further, so did their critics and opponents. For the first time in history, a global movement of anti-imperialism formed. Across colonies, metropoles and empires, the critics of capitalism and colonialism made use of the global colonial infrastructure of steamships, rail, mass printing and telegraphs to network and engage in debate over aims and strategy as never before. The old order and traditions had to be brought down. Revolution was the battle cry, either of the workers or through national independence.[4]

However, if the Taiping Rebellion in some respects pointed forward towards this world of global entangled revolutionary politics, it also in

---

[2] Kuhn 1977, with the Petrine passage discussed on pp. 354–357.
[3] Spence 1999 & Kuhn 1978 for extensive accounts and analyses of the rebellion.
[4] Ballantyne & Burton 2012, introduction and chapter 3 especially.

6.1 *Apocalyptic and Millenarian Uprisings*

a very significant manner pointed backwards. There was, after all, both an ancient Chinese and a Roman layer sedimented in the thinking of the rebel movement. As early as the second century CE, apocalyptic and millenarian rebellion had fomented against the Eastern Han dynasty under the banner of Taiping, the Great Peace.[5] Where the language of the late nineteenth- and twentieth-century global revolutionaries was secular, international and anti-imperial, the Taiping movement was religious, restorationist and 'confined' to China. Moral renovation was to regenerate a just order for the imperial 'all under heaven'. In that respect, the Taiping Rebellion, in spite of its gigantic scale, had much in common with many other peasant rebellions in Afro-Eurasian history.[6]

International revolutionaries of the twentieth century certainly celebrated the example set by the rebels of the agrarian world. Mao's Communists, for instance, hailed the efforts of the Taiping, as any visitor to the museum inside the compound of the former presidential palace in Nanjing can confirm. Spartacus, the leader of the most famous Roman slave rebellion, thus became a firmly established symbol of resistance to oppression, from Soviet communism to liberal America.[7] Yet in the new critical discourse, the aims, ambitions and attempts of the old rebels of agrarian society soon began to seem antiquated and inadequate. Lacking in the eyes of the new critical avant-garde both articulated theory and a clear programme of action, they were saddled with the label of 'pre-political'. It was simply too difficult to make sense of past resistance in the secular language of revolutionary politics. As recently remarked by Lisa Eberle about the Roman Empire, there may have been plenty of apocalyptic prophecy and critique of the established order going around, but it was hard to pin any of this onto an actual rebellion.[8] However, if we keep the experience of the Taiping in mind, that may not be decisive. It was far from preordained that Hong's apocalyptic visions would have found a group of rebels ready to listen and bring them into action.

More important, academically, is that a vast comparative literature has developed, exploring the mechanisms of resistance in the agrarian world before modern secular politics.[9] Resistance here is not to be understood as just any kind of rebellion or insurgent activity. The history of Rome and other

---

[5] Puett 2015: 243–255. (The early Taiping was not alone; another millenarian movement developed under the name of the celestial masters.)
[6] In brief, see Crone 1989: 74–77.   [7] Malamud 2009, chapter 8.
[8] Eberle 2018: 194; Hobsbawm 1959, struggling to overcome the limitations of the notion of a pre-political peasantry.
[9] Wagner 2021 for an introduction to this literature.

agrarian empires is crammed with attempts by rival members of the governing class to usurp power, turn the imperial army against the reigning monarch or comment subversively in literary writings on the tyrannical nature of rule. All these phenomena belong almost solely to the internal politics of the ruling class.[10] What the comparative literature has opened a window onto are the strategies and capacity of peasantries, enslaved populations and local societies to resist or rebel against their imperial overlords.

The Roman experience should find its place within this wider and deeper world history, as Stephen Dyson once remarked in what remains perhaps the single most important study dedicated to the phenomenon. Our record is in fact teeming with notices of rebellion, from the slave revolts on Sicily and in Italy during the era of the Republic to the Jewish uprisings under Nero, Trajan and Hadrian and that of the Bagaudae of late antique Gaul, to name just a few.[11] However, only against the backdrop of a general history of empire and colonialism would it really be possible to illuminate the meagre titbits of information that our sources, invariably penned by members of the elite, normally deign to convey about most rebellions under Roman rule.[12] Received wisdom has it that a global approach is bound to reify the perspective of the powerful and repeat the official, codified version of events. Quite the contrary, once we turn to world history: then a set of concepts, tools and parallels becomes available, the better to tap the information on resistance left in our sources.

This literature will point to the significance of charismatic leadership provided by prophetic figures, bandits and aristocrats pressed to the margins of society and other liminal individuals. Lined up next to each other, the rebel leaders of the agrarian world constitute a gaudy spectacle that makes the claim of Hong Xiuquang to be the brother of Jesus anything but exceptional. Nothing less than the extraordinary was needed to stand up to the forces of established rule and inspire followers with the courage to rise up.[13]

The literature on peasant resistance will also tend to see imperial power as defined by its frontiers. Imperial government was confronted by

---

[10] The limitation of the classic study of MacMullen 1966 (neatly summed up on p. 242) or, most recently, Jolowicz & Elsner 2023, where upper-class discourse, usurpation and the activities of marginalized groups are all bundled together. On usurpation, Flaig 1992 is fundamental.

[11] In addition to Dyson 1975, Goodman 2015 and Eberle 2018 provide up-to-date discussion. Pekáry 1987 compiled an impressively long list of known incidents from Augustus to Severus.

[12] Lavan 2017 for a discussion of the literary ruling-class discourse on rebellion in the Roman world.

[13] See Adas 1979, chapter 4 in particular, and Hobsbawm 1969, for two classic studies.

stark limitations, both along external as well as internal frontiers, cultural, religious, social and ecological.[14] However, the power of the universal empires of Eurasia, as pointed out in Chapter 3, was anything but homogeneous; they were massive conglomerates extending their sway over a great variety of different ecologies and communities. These could not be governed uniformly; that was implicit in the claim to universal monarchy. The level of control and reach of rule varied enormously across the geographical expanse claimed by a world emperor. Reservoirs of resistance and quasi-independence, against both imperial and local lords, persisted everywhere. Vast forested regions and hillsides, often one and the same thing, always remained difficult to access for the representatives of courts and centralized government. Unable to support the same density of population, such thinly populated areas resembled the external frontiers of the realms and were, just like these, much harder to control than the densely settled agricultural plains that provided the basis of state power. Subversion often came from the frontier.[15] Finally, the literature will also point out that most rebellions were unsuccessful and that small-scale resistance was more significant. Accordingly, this chapter will start with everyday resistance, then move on to larger rebellions and their charismatic leaders before finally addressing the significance of the external frontier in overturning empire.

6.2 Everyday Resistance

Most acts of resistance in the Afro-Eurasian arena of universal empires would have been small-scale and represented forms of protest against local grievances; they harboured few, if any, grand ideas about a general liberation from the current order of things, but must be seen as part of the general struggle between social groups about the distribution of wealth, burdens and privileges. If people on the lower rungs of the social hierarchy often suffered brutal exploitation, they were still not powerless and unable to assert their interests. The peasantry and enslaved workers might, for instance, try to resist the harshest claims from big landowners and lords by various forms of collective action. Campaigns of working slowly or sabotaging activity were one method. A grasping tax collector could see the peasants team up against him and physically drive him off the land or ally with some local strongman to the same effect. Agricultural communities might also try to petition the rulers to alleviate their burdens and protect them against excessive claims. Weapons of the weak, as these

---

[14] A point made forcefully by Dench 2018.   [15] Dyson 1975: 172.

strategies have aptly been called, are everywhere on record in the agricultural communities of the pre-industrial world and have also been studied for the Roman Empire.[16]

So, too, has what must to many have been the last recourse, flight from the land. Every time the Roman historical record yields detailed information on rural relations, the abandonment of land by the peasants is an issue. The Late Roman law codes harp on so-called *agri deserti*, and the Egyptian papyri confront us with the phenomenon of *anachoresis*, withdrawal from the cultivated fields.[17] At all times, some peasants would fall too heavily into debt or be pressed too hard by the demands of rulers and landlords. Some of these chose to give up, move out of reach and establish an existence away from the landlords in more outlying areas, just as some slaves decided to risk flight rather than suffer further abuse. Here they might be joined by military deserters who had become disenchanted with army life. In short, there was always a pool of mobile and dispossessed people on the margins of agricultural society. In the historiography of new-world slavery, these are studied under the name of *maroon communities*.[18]

A great deal of romantic hope has sometimes, in the anthropological and historical literature, been pinned on these groups. Some have found in them the establishment of a utopian counter-state living according to an 'art of not being governed'.[19] But this is probably making too much of these. Many groups living on the frontier of agricultural society had not chosen to move away but simply developed a way of life adapted to the ecological potential. They had not been shaped primarily in reaction against the state makers and often also depended on exchanging some of their products or labour with the population living on the cultivated plain. In that sense, they were integrated, often to a surprising degree, with the more regulated world of the sedentary farmer.[20]

---

[16] Bradley 1994 emphasizes the strategies of everyday resistance available to the enslaved population in the Roman world, rather than open rebellion. See Hauken 1998 for a study of the petitions of agricultural communities in third-century Anatolia. On the 'weapons of the weak', see Scott 1985.
[17] Jones 1964: 812–819 collects the evidence for *agri deserti*, but it should now be read less within a general perspective of decline.
[18] Florentino & Amantino 2011; Price 1996.
[19] Scott 2009. Eberle 2018 places the emphasis squarely on these strategies in her analysis of Roman resistance.
[20] Lieberman 2010 and Subrahmanyam 2022, chapter 10, for critiques of Scott. Blouin 2014, chapter 7, emphasizes the economic integration of the area beyond the sown with the population of the fields in Roman Egypt.

6.2 Everyday Resistance

Paradoxically, this also goes for those who turned to banditry. They have been portrayed as figures who in the style of a Robin Hood would take from the rich and give to the poor. Both feared and vilified by sedentary elites and rulers, bandits could serve as a receptacle for the grievances and hopes of retribution of the less privileged and oppressed.[21] Such myths tell a lot about the level of quiet suffering and frustration in agricultural society. But reality normally proved more prosaic. To avoid capture, bandits were dependent on a support base and protection in local society. More often than not, protection was provided by local landowners who found it useful to take a group of strongmen under their wings to help them maintain power in their communities. To take a famous example, we might compare the much-publicized Thuggees of early British India. Colonial fears were at first projected onto these bandits to represent them dramatically as a group of horrifying 'religious stranglers'. In calmer postcolonial times, they have been seen as representatives of a Hindu reaction against Mughal and later British imperial rule, or a form of social banditry. In reality, the 'thugs' seem to have been 'the bandit retainers of local Indian landlords', who occasionally went on expeditions to plunder travellers and on their return would share the spoils with their master. Much the same can and has been said forcefully about the Roman empire. In regions such as Rough Cilicia, which had a reputation for banditry, the gangs were closely allied with local landowners and big men.[22]

The low-level violence of bandits and everyday resistance of the peasantry did not normally constitute a fundamental threat to imperial order, but rather demarcated the limits of its reach. A part of agricultural life always escaped close control by distant rulers. Local societies were able to preserve a degree of autonomy because government depended on prominent members to provide it with information about their communities. These people had their own channels of information and communication. Regional networks of markets, cycles of religious festivals, communal associations, webs of marriage, kin and patronage all brought people together and transmitted news, gossip and personal intelligence. Local knowledge, the intimate familiarity with a place and its people, was crucial for operating in daily life but accessible, only indirectly and in part, to the representatives of distant courts.[23]

---

[21] Hobsbawm 1969.
[22] Wagner 2021: 421–422; Wagner 2007. On Roman banditry, see Shaw 1984 and Hopwood 1989.
[23] Geertz 1983.

What really was stirring in subject societies was a question, the answer to which often eluded rulers as they responded with a solid dose of suspicion or even paranoia and panic. A thick undergrowth of rumours and prophecies constituted a powerful sounding board for putative rebels.[24] One of the most notable books on Eurasian empires of the last generation was Philip Kuhn's *Soulstealers*. It called attention to the fears of the mighty Qing emperor in the mid eighteenth century about networks of rebellion fomenting inside his vast realm. Trifling incidents of conflict involving mobile people on the fringes of agricultural society were blown out of all proportion. In the imperial imagination, they grew into signs of sedition and a coming uprising. Officials were ordered to capture the members of the alleged conspiracy, without delay or excuse. But there was probably no such thing, and they simply responded by desperately seizing whoever came within reach.[25]

Intermittent bursts of panic were the flipside of a governing disposition commonly shaped by caution. A striking feature of the famous exchange of letters between the emperor Trajan and his special proconsular emissary to the province of Bithynia-Pontus, Pliny the Younger, is the reluctance of the Roman authority to get dragged into the rivalries and feuds of local communities. Christians, even though their loyalty to the empire was in doubt because of their refusal to participate in the cult of the Caesar Augustus, were not directly to be hunted down. Anonymous accusations were also generally to be ignored.[26] Roman officials had better avoid being manipulated into being an instrument of the personal hatreds and hopes of revenge circulating in local communities.

What Pliny and Trajan professed in letters, studies of Roman provincial legal practice confirm. The default position of officials higher up the hierarchy was to refer cases back on appeal to another treatment by local judges, rather than pass sentence in conflicts they had little chance fully to comprehend.[27] Cautious restraint or panicky clampdown: either way, the response by imperial authority was the result of its inability to penetrate the thickets of local communities. Again and again, the moment when the low-intensity strategies of resistance in communities erupted into full-scale rebellion came as a surprise to imperial rulers. But it did so often also to

---

[24] Wagner 2021 on the insurgent significance of rumours; Ripat 2011 for an instructive article on the prophecies of astrologers in Roman society. Astrologers were occasionally banned from the capital, but only when the authorities feared riots and unrest.
[25] Kuhn 1990; Bayly 1996 contains perhaps the best analysis and description of the 'informal' information networks of agrarian societies.
[26] Pliny, *Letters* X, 96, especially 4–5 and 97 with Bang 2011a: 186. [27] Kelly 2011.

the subjects. Frustrations might simply just linger. Revolts commonly snowballed from small beginnings until the fame of a leader suddenly spread through the countryside and attracted a steadily growing number of followers. Surprise is a recurrent theme in the literature on anti-imperial rebellion. Even the early colonial state, armed with a statistical mind and electric telegraphs, normally failed to predict major uprisings.[28]

6.3 Peasant Rebellion

Under the impression of the communist and national revolutions of the twentieth century, students of anti-imperial rebellion originally set out to identify similar struggles in the past.[29] But as they dug deeper, it became clear that this framework was misleading. Neither the postcolonial fight for national independence nor Marxist class struggle of an industrial proletariat found ready parallels in the agricultural past.[30] Peasants may have belonged to the labouring classes, but they were rarely informed by a revolutionary vision of an entirely new form of society. At most, their aspirations looked in carnival fashion to turn things upside down, making the masters serve and the servants do the bidding. It was, in the classic insight of Mikhail Bakhtin, a way of reminding the rulers of shared humanity and traditional ideals of society.[31]

The record left by Rome does little to contradict this image. Even the massive revolts of the enslaved population under the Republic, on Sicily in the 130s and in Italy in the 70s BCE, have left no trace of an alternative societal vision. This might, of course, be a product of the sources. We do not have the voices of the rebels – only the narrative of the victorious self-declared masters. Yet a desire to escape and win freedom from enslavement was in itself a radical goal.[32] The same goes for the occasional attempts of peasants to burn the records of their debts to break away from the control of their landlord. The ideologies of modernizing social transformation were a product of the late eighteenth and nineteenth centuries, the age of

---

[28] Wagner 2010; Goodman 2015.
[29] Thompson 1952 opened the quest in Roman studies (social rebellion). Another prominent example is Benabou 1976 (inspired by the independence struggles of the 1950s and 1960s to produce a postcolonial story, depicting the society of Roman Africa as shaped by Roman colonization and increasingly vigorous forces of Indigenous resistance) or the collection edited by Pippidi 1976.
[30] On the Greco-Roman world, see the despondent remarks of De Ste Croix 1981, chapter 7, v and p. 452, especially.
[31] Bakhtin 1984: 256 encapsulates the insight, more broadly developed in the introduction and chapter 3.
[32] Bradley 1994.

the enlightenment, liberalism and revolutions. As these ideas were publicized and debated in the ever-thickening and widening networks of global communication during the nineteenth century, they became increasingly influential and able to inspire social movements in societies in the midst of radical modernizing transformation. It would be misleading to force our image of ancient rebellions into such a historical context.

There is, in a similar vein, little evidence of nationalist independence struggles. How could there possibly have been? Nationalism, as we saw in Chapter 4, was a secular ideology, dependent on the cultural integration of the peasant majority forged by print publics and general schooling in the popular tongue. These phenomena were late developments everywhere in history, not a product of the ages of antiquity and premodernity. In Greco-Roman society, citizenship was tied to small, often face-to-face, local communities organized as city-states, not a wider ethnicity or nation.[33] The gradual extension of Roman citizenship until Caracalla in 212 CE, granted to all free males in the empire, did not alter this overall situation. By then, the Roman citizenship had been hollowed out to a cosmopolitan, legal status and did not in any meaningful sense create a single people out of the vast, widespread and heterogenous imperial population. People continued to think of the empire as consisting of different ethnic and linguistic groups.[34]

If neither nationalist nor social revolution has turned out as a useful analytical framework, world historians talk instead of nativist, revivalist or restorationist rebellions.[35] These were local or provincial uprisings where communities rose against the imposition of rule by a foreign conqueror. Conflicts over land and imperial taxes were often at the centre. Imperial claims put a strain on the social equilibrium and in the resulting disruption pushed groups to violent resistance. Peasants and landless labourers, however, were limited by village organization; they needed leaders who could bridge their many small communities. More often than not, the peasants turned to the privileged sections of agrarian society, especially the land-owning gentry, for leadership.[36] Regions as different as the late Roman West and the Mughal Empire have been described as falling to peasant uprisings. Upon closer look, however, these rebellions turn out to have been led by landowners, warlords and other prominent members of local society,

---

[33] Hansen 2006, chapter 4 (Greek ethnicity is cultural but divided on hundreds of city-states); Ma 2024 stresses the significance of the autonomy of individual poleis even more.
[34] Ammianus Marcellinus, for instance, could still in the fourth century describe the Gauls in terms of a foreign, exotic other (XV, 11–12).
[35] Crone 2012, especially chapter 8; Adas 1979, introduction.   [36] Whittaker 1994: 276.

6.3 Peasant Rebellion

asserting themselves and their communities against imperial demands.[37] It was far from uncommon that the rebel leaders had a prehistory of close involvement with the imperial order. In the Roman case, Arminius of the Cherusci most readily springs to mind. This Germanic warrior king has earned immortal fame from his defeat of the Roman governor Varus and his three legions in the battle of the Teutoburg Forest in 9 CE. But before that, Arminius had served as commander in the Roman army of a contingent recruited among his own people and even earned elevation into the aristocratic, equestrian order. But when the Romans under Varus began to reduce their territory into a tax-paying province, the proud Germanic warrior society rose under Arminius, turning his experience against the former ally, now oppressor.[38]

Strains, however, were not necessarily restricted to the early period of occupation. Chinese history is proverbial for its periodic uprisings. In Egypt, after two centuries of Roman rule, the peasantry rose in parts of the Delta. Named after the so-called *Boukoloi*, the herders, the rebellion originated in the marshlands on the margins of the cultivated areas. A surviving papyrus tax report from the Mendesian nome, as recently argued persuasively by Blouin, allows us a rare glimpse of the underlying social conditions. Changes in the course of the deltaic river branches diminished the amount of water available for irrigation. On top of this came the Antonine smallpox epidemic that claimed a large number of victims among the peasant families. Although less land and fewer people were available for cultivation in the district, the government still tried to avoid giving too many concessions, seeking to instead keep up its total tax demand. The grant of moratoria was, so to speak, outweighed by attempts to redistribute the burden among the remaining households. Faced with heavier demands, some cultivators gave up and abandoned their land. But, of course, this only made things worse for those left behind. The district was trapped in a downward spiral, with more and more families abandoning their fields to live in the marshlands.

At some point in the 160s CE, open conflict erupted between the authorities and the runaway peasantry. The dispossessed began raiding some of the remaining villages, and the officials responded by calling in the

---

[37] Van Dam 1985 (on the Bagaudae); Alam 1986 (on the zamindars); Habib 1999, readjusting his 1963. Rostovtzeff 1926: 442–448 for a classic statement, describing the third-century crisis as the war of peasant soldiers against urban, Roman civilization.

[38] Velleius Paterculus, *Roman History* II, 117–120 (comments how the Roman governor, Varus, had haplessly spent his time dispensing justice and hearing trials as if Germania had been securely pacified, rather than continuing to wage war).

army. Massacres of heavy-handed repression added fuel to the already burning fire. A priest, Isidorus (his given name meaning 'the gift of Isis'), emerged as the heroic leader of the protests and managed, as the historian Cassius Dio added in a crucial observation, to link the dispossessed groups of the wetlands with the other Egyptians. Soon large parts of the Delta were in open rebellion. Even Alexandria was threatened by the rebel host. The Roman governor of Syria had to be called in with military reinforcements and succeeded in quelling the uprising only after several years of a patient and methodical counter-insurgency operation.[39]

The student of anti-imperial rebellion will immediately be struck by the role played by the Egyptian priest here. In the accounts of pre-nationalist uprisings against the colonial authorities, religious figures, priests or prophets commonly had a leading role. They came with a message usually phrased in a language of apocalyptic prophecy of the end of times and the restoration of a new just kingdom. Often, it was not necessarily the absolute level of repression and exploitation that ignited protests, but rather infractions by the authorities of what was perceived as the just and moral order of society and the social status of communities. Here insurgents found common ground with the rulers. Tacitus, the consul and senator, normally in his histories ascribed the outbreak of rebellion to abuse and misconduct by individual representatives of Rome.[40]

Apocalyptic and prophetic language was also not the preserve only of rebels. It was too powerful a medium for rulers to ignore. In a world where gods were generally held to intervene in human life, signs of their approval or displeasure were sought everywhere. Rulers, therefore, had to claim that their power was written into the divine order of the universe and revealed in prophecy. Even the emblematic epic of empire, the *Aeneid*, had an entire song dedicated to the Cumaean Sibyl and her oracle, prophetically laying out a future for Rome culminating in the return of the golden age under the divinely ordained monarchy of Augustus.[41] World historians have elevated the contest between the Ottoman, Süleyman the Magnificent, and the Holy Roman Emperor, Charles V, into a juncture of millenarian prophecy especially characteristic of the early-modern period.[42]

The truth is that the rival claims of rulers to embody the final universal monarch of prophetic millenarian scripture echo across the arena of the Afro-Eurasian world down through the centuries from antiquity to the

---

[39] Blouin 2014, chapter 8 and 9. Cassius Dio, *Roman History* LXXII 4.1–2 (Loeb Classical Library, ed. by Cary).
[40] Woolf 2011.   [41] Vergil, *Aeneid* VI, 791–807; Potter 1994 and 1990.
[42] Green-Mercado 2018, with Subrahmanyam 2003, all of it built around Fleischer 2018.

early modern. In the history of great imperial confrontations in Western Eurasia, Odeanathus of Palmyra emerges in prophecies of the third century as 'the sun-sent ... lion' who would inflict defeat on the Persians and 'perfect, unblemished, and awe-some, he will rule the Romans and the Persians will be feeble'.[43] After victory in another round of Romano-Persian confrontation, the emperor Heraclius (r. 611–641) was hailed as the new Alexander, who had come as 'the saviour of the world' to inaugurate a new age for humanity.[44] Against this background, we are better prepared to appreciate the ambition of Akbar, the great sixteenth-century Mughal emperor, to pose in his newly built residential city, the fabled Fatehpur Sikri, as the instigator of a new millennium.[45] Millennial and apocalyptic prophecy was simply one of the favoured registers of power across premodern Afro-Eurasia, a key site of contestation for rulers and rebels alike that was governed by its own deep temporality.

In the case of the *Boukoloi*, it is of course difficult to know what exactly Isidorus preached. Egypt, however, had a long tradition of millenarian expectations. During the decades-long Theban rising against the Ptolemies (206–186 BCE), a counter-pharaoh had appeared, claiming to be a saviour sent against the foreign Macedonian dynasty to restore the righteous traditional order of the land. A prophecy, the so-called *Oracle of the Potter*, predicted the fall of Alexandria and its immoral Hellenistic dynasty and the return of power to the old Egyptian regal centre in Memphis. The text was penned during the late second century BCE but kept circulating under Roman rule. It is probably in such terms we should think of Isidorus.[46] If so, he would join the ranks of many other rebel leaders in world history. In the Roman Empire, the chaotic year following the fall and suicide of Nero and the fire of the temple of Jupiter on the Capitoline Hill, alone, saw the Druids come out to prophesy that power would now transfer to 'the transalpine peoples', while another rebel leader, Mariccus, offered himself up as 'the protector of Gaul and a god'. The Jews were by then already in rebellion in Judaea and animated by prophetic scripture foretelling that the time of the East had come and the rulers of the world

---

[43] *13th Sibylline Oracle*, vv. 164–165 and 170–171 in the edition of Potter 1990 (with translation p. 177 and commentary).
[44] Reinink 2002 (quotation from p. 83). [45] Moin 2012.
[46] On the Theban rebellion and other risings in Ptolemaic Egypt, see Veïsse 2022; McGing 2016; Ludlow & Manning 2016. On the continued life of *The Oracle of the Potter* and similar texts during Roman times, see Harker 2008: 120–124. Goodman 2015: 61 is right to stress that there is no direct link from these texts to an actual rebellion. But they are nevertheless suggestive. For a version copied in the third century CE, see *The Oxyrhynchus Papyri (P. Oxy)*, Vol. 22, 2332.

would march out of Judaea.[47] Two generations later, another Judaean rebel leader, Simon Bar Kochba, was believed, at least by some of his followers, to be the messiah.[48]

Representatives of the nineteenth-century colonial state branded forms of millenarian rebellion as an expression of superstition and fanaticism. Armed with the infamous Gatling machine gun and easily manoeuvrable field artillery, they looked with disbelief and condescension on rebel warriors who would charge at them with premodern weaponry. That these warriors often went forward to their predictable death, thinking themselves invulnerable, protected by charms and other forms of magic, only added to their sensational exoticism in the eyes of the Western public. Similar expressions of disdain for their rebellious subjects are not hard to come by among premodern rulers. The same Tacitus who reported on Mariccus in Gaul added that, when the leader was captured in battle and then thrown to the animals in the amphitheatre, 'the stupid crowd thought him invulnerable when the beasts did not attack him, until he was executed in front of Vitellius', the current but short-lived emperor.[49]

However, there is one important difference. While the European colonialists saw the conflict in terms of a clash between progress and rational science, on the one side, and superstition and stifling tradition, on the other, there was no such fundamental epistemological and technological chasm separating Tacitus, the member of the Roman ruling class, from the rebel subjects. Their superstition was not fundamental; they merely read the divine signs incorrectly. It was not wrong that a world ruler was destined to come out of Judea – only that he would hail from among the Jews. In fact, the prophecy was about the Roman general Vespasian and his son Titus, who had been sent to quell the uprising and then emerged victorious in the struggle for the imperial purple after the fall of Nero. It was the vanquisher of the Jews and new Roman imperial dynasty that had been predicted.[50]

Divine cult and religious truths might set people apart or at loggerheads, but religion was also one of the few languages that could reach across communities and different social groups. That was, we recall, the significant

---

[47] Tacitus, *Histories* II, 61 (Mariccus); IV, 54 (Druidic prophecies); V, 13 (Jewish expectations of world rule); 4 Ezra 11:1–12 surely, as Martin Goodman observes (2015: 60), echoes this apocalyptic and Messianic anti-Roman sentiment. More generally, see Momigliano 1987 and Bowersock 1987 on the interconnection of prophecies between the various religious communities of the Mediterranean and their politically shapeshifting character.
[48] On these various examples, see Dyson 1975: 158–160 and Potter 1994: 171, 49–54.
[49] Tacitus, *Histories* II, 61 (my translation).   [50] Tacitus, *Histories* V, 13.

achievement of Isidorus during the *Boukoloi* uprising in Egypt. To gather momentum, the runaway peasantry of the wetlands had to link up with other parts of provincial society. Social protests, therefore, rarely appeared in pure form, but were often mixed up with and even overshadowed by other elements. The Donatist Conflict among the Christians in Late Antique Roman North Africa is a good case in point. Many historians have seen the struggle between the followers of the Bishop Donatus and those supporting the emperor and the imperial Catholic Church in terms of a peasant uprising. The letters of St. Augustine, the Catholic bishop of Hippo Regius in Numidia, report with horror and indignation the so-called *circumcelliones*. Flocks of these seasonal farm labourers moved through the countryside, subjected Catholic landlords to violent humiliation, and destroyed or handed back records, so that slaves could walk away free and peasants could have proof of their debts owed to the landlord annulled. All such actions were taken right out of a textbook on peasant resistance and, in the eyes of the bishop, a scandal.[51]

Yet at the heart of the conflict – described so dramatically by Augustine in order to incriminate his rivals in the eyes of the imperial court – was a theological controversy over the succession of bishops in the many African congregations. Could a bishop be ordained by someone who had compromised with the Roman authorities during the persecution ordered by the emperor Diocletian? The Donatists said no; the Catholics said yes. What they both agreed upon, however, was that it was crucial for a priest to stand in the right line of succession. Over several generations, the two branches clashed over the control of churches, congregations and communities. It is hard to believe that the thriving countryside that archaeologists have uncovered in late Roman Africa was torn asunder by violent uprisings for all that time.

Still, there were local episodes where frustration erupted into open conflict. One had seen the imperial authorities clamp down on a group of migrant workers led by two 'Captains of the Saints'. Gathered around a radical cult of martyrdom, the workers had set about turning the tables on the masters and restoring justice. The landlords, terrified, had called in the army, and soon the restive labourers were put to the executioner's axe. Rebellion had been nipped in the bud, but discontent lived on. The rustic population turned the graves of the executed into altars and began worshipping the victims as saints. When two representatives of the imperial

---

[51] Augustine, *Letter* 185, chapter 4; Shaw 2011 for the most extensive examination of the Donatist issue, the evidence and the many facets of the struggle.

government, aiming among other things to restore the unity of the church, came to the district, the local Donatist bishop turned to these groups to recruit an armed band of supporters and resist the imperial visitors. And this was a strategy that the Donatist leaders would repeat. Often landowners themselves, they already had ties with the mobile segments of African agricultural society. They would hire them for harvests and other temporary jobs. But the *circumcelliones* also proved to be useful allies in the struggle for control of the churches.[52]

Does this mean the social content of the conflict was negligible? That this was purely a symbolic thing, as Shaw concluded? That would trivialize the conflict. The question, after all, was not simply one of empty theological squabbles, but about who would be the leaders of the African communities and congregations. Compare how Shi'a Islam simply evolved after civil wars over the rightful succession to the Caliphate during the seventh century CE. The Shi'a claimed that the right line of leadership went through Ali (app. 600–661), the cousin of Muhammad and fourth caliph, rather than Mu'awiya (620–680), the founder of the Umayyad dynasty accepted by the Sunnis. Such issues were evidently of the utmost importance. Likewise, when Macedonius, the bishop of Constantinople in the mid fourth century, managed to secure military support from the emperor to install a bishop of his line in the Paphlagonian city of Mantinium, the local population took to arms, 'sickles, axes and whatever else was to hand', and bloodily repelled the intruders.[53] A bishop was a key patron of a community and peasants needed, in their everyday existence, patrons that could shield them against the effects of a bad harvest or offer protection against outside demands.[54] This explains their willingness to stand up for their communal leader.

In fact, the majority of Christians in the African provinces seem to have belonged to Donatist congregations. As Christian preachers proselytized in the hinterland behind the coastline, rural cults were transformed into shrines for martyrs and saints. The strength of Donatism may well be a result of this process. Uncompromising, the message of the Donatist bishops resonated more strongly with the harsh notion of justice preached by lesser clergy in rural communities and the accompanying celebration of

---

[52] *Optatus* III, chapter 4. Discussed by Shaw 2011, chapter 4, although tending to exaggerate the cleft between this incident and the Donatist establishment.
[53] Sozomen, *Church History* IV, 21 (my translation), brilliantly analyzed by De Ste Croix 1981: 446–451 in a context of competition over rural patronage. The structural similarity to the Donatist struggle in Africa is hard to miss.
[54] Garnsey & Woolf 1989.

martyrdom. Here it was not so much a matter of high theological reflection as of ritual participation: the singing of chants and simple mottos, festivals commemorating a local saint, even intoxication. The vast majority of villagers knew little or no Latin, let alone Greek. Their language was not written but belonged to the local continuum of oral dialects that writers in imperial Latin banded together under the rubric of Punic. Catholic bishops also tried to mobilize rural networks and occasionally orchestrated their own circumcellions. Compared to their Donatist rivals, however, they tended to rely more on the imperial government. In their writings, they emphasize their dedication to the unity of the church across the empire while the Donatists are portrayed as isolated regional schismatics. Against the stronger local networks and anchorage in African provincial society of the Donatists, the Catholic bishops could muster the support of the imperial authorities and the wider church beyond the province.[55]

In that respect, the conflict was an almost ideal-typical expression of how power was structured and distributed in the historical empires of Eurasia. As long as the forces of localism did not break out into full-scale rebellion, the imperial rulers normally had to live with and tolerate a degree of local divergence. Much as they tried, in the current case, to promote the unity of the church with rulings, funds and personnel, the wider Christianity still spread in the provinces, and the emperors inevitably found themselves confronted with rival regional networks of clerical patronage and their ritual communities. Unity proved an elusive quest, constantly undermined by regional dissidence. An emperor and his representatives might try to strike down on a particularly querulous leader or visit retribution on small riotous groups, but even so dissidence endured. The courts had only limited staff available in provincial society. Most government was, as seen in Chapter 3, in the hands of locals. Short of engaging in all-out war, that set very clear limits on the capacity of the courts to act. Tacit acceptance was a necessity. With or without open approval, the dissident networks would go on. The Donatist conflict in the western parts of Roman North Africa never really found its resolution, but lasted for generations. That, of course, also left the Donatists free to attempt, although unsuccessfully, to have previous imperial judgments

---

[55] Dossey 2010, chapters 5, 6 and especially 7. Shaw 2011, chapters 9 and 10, on oral language, song and ritual, strangely though with several parallels to the religiosity and the dissemination of ideas during the Reformation where print had become so much more important. Instead of budding print publics, the proper comparative framework would be that developed for local saints and Islam in Morocco by Ernest Gellner (1969), on the dialogue between universal creed and local ritual (see Chapter 4).

170   6 Resistance, Rebellion and Renewal

reversed and gain the favour of the imperial court. Doctrinal homogeneity was impossible; in practice, the imperial rulers had to compromise and accommodate regional difference.

If the constellation of power left the forces of localism considerable room to ignore, deflect and resist the dictates of distant rulers and their officials, empire had one decisive advantage: it was transregional, cosmopolitan and transcended the many local, ritually defined communities of agrarian society. Confronted with full-scale rebellion, imperial authorities were usually able to counterbalance the stronger local or regional anchorage of the rebels by drawing on the resources from other regions of the empire.[56] The Egyptian *boukoloi* were defeated by troops pulled in from Syria. Perhaps the most famous of the uprisings under Rome, the Jewish rebellion under Nero, succumbed to an army gathered from Syria, Egypt and the various client kings of the Near East.[57] Again and again, rebels met defeat because they found themselves 'organizationally outflanked' by their imperial rulers. That did not necessarily mean that all insurgencies were futile. Sometimes rebellious communities and their leaders were able to wrest a more favourable deal from the imperial government as peace was restored. Once consolidated, however, imperial power was not easily unseated, unless its capacity to mobilize the resources of other regions to wear down a regional insurgency had been seriously weakened. That result was normally brought about only by a combination of internal division and external pressures.[58]

6.4 Overturning Empire or Renewal on the Frontiers?

For Rome, that situation arrived in the centuries of late antiquity, from the third to seventh century CE. As described in Chapter 3, this was a period that saw an increasing provincialization of imperial power, but it was also a period that saw pressure rise on the frontier. Again, we turn to comparison with the other universal empires of Eurasia for guidance and parallel experiences. As the Mughals, for instance, during the seventeenth century continued to push the frontier of their power further beyond the floodplains of Northern India,

---

[56] Mann 1986: 7, for the expression; Gellner 1983, the model in chapter 2; and Motyl 2001, chapter 1, for a sociological explanation of the structural advantage of empire.
[57] Josephus, *The Jewish War* III, 1, 3. Gambash 2015: 189–191 note that strategies of appeasement, normally followed a Roman defeat of subject rebellions.
[58] Mann 1986: 7. The discussion in Moore 1966: 201–227 is classic. Social revolution required the imperial super-structure to have been destroyed by external pressure. But in the absence of a modern revolutionary programme and party to take leadership of the peasantry, the outcome is more likely to be a change of rulers.

6.4 Overturning Empire or Renewal on the Frontiers?

they eventually confronted the Marathas in the South.[59] In spite of prolonged campaigning and the relocation of the court to the region, victory continued to elude the Mughal ruler. The hilly and forested country was impossible to control. No sooner was a Maratha princeling subjected than he or other members of his clan relocated and started over in a different inaccessible location. Worn out by the struggle, the emperor Aurangzeb died after several decades in the south. Never to return to the heartland of the empire and the magnificent palace in Delhi constructed by his father, he had so to speak been consumed by the conflict and found his final resting place in Khuldabad.[60]

The endless warfare had swallowed enormous resources and sparked more intensified competition among the Mughal governing class for the remaining revenue generated by the empire. Efforts were intensified to strengthen the extraction and control of tribute, but that required Mughal elites to dig themselves deeper down into provincial society. Just as the extended hold of Christianity on Roman provincial populations sparked the formation of rival regional networks, so the weakened Mughal court saw its authority drift away to increasingly powerful and independent governors that sat atop provincial networks of patronage. Meanwhile, the Mughal pressure on the society of its southern frontier had forced the Marathas to build up their military organization and fighting capacity. Soon they were able to reverse the military balance and begin to expand into Mughal territory. Within a few decades, the power of the central court had both been hollowed out from within and forced to retreat on its external frontier. Its days as the hegemon of the Indian world were quickly coming to an end.[61]

The parallels with the processes that saw Roman power unravel in the West in the fifth century and then collapse in the Middle East with the rise of Islam during the seventh century are hard to miss. All the ingredients are there: a weakened central court, regionalization of power and the rise of strong forces on the frontier. The fiscal crisis and return of civil war in the third century had caused Roman government to fragment. By the fourth century, however, power had been restabilized. The tax base had been rebuilt and the army brought under control. Yet the restoration of government and the drive to strengthen the hold on imperial resources led, just as the Mughal template suggests, to the consolidation of power onto

---

[59] See the basic analysis in Eaton 2019, chapters 7–8, and Richards 1993, chapters 10–11.
[60] Kinra 2021: 780–781 for a summary.
[61] Hintze 1997; Wink 1986; Alam 1986; Bayly 1983, introduction and chapter 1; Richards 1975.

a number of regional courts.⁶² None of this was immediately lethal, but division did come at a cost for the long-term stability of Mediterranean-wide empire. Much as the different courts tried to cooperate and help each other, they were also rivals.⁶³ No emperor could be sure that a colleague might not try to put him out of business, as in fact happened often enough, and no other emperor would put himself seriously at risk to save a colleague. The ability of imperial government to overcome problems in one part of the empire by calling in assistance from other areas had been reduced.

This became clear in the first half of the fifth century. Britain, Gaul, Spain and Africa, all provinces that had known stable imperial rule for centuries, fell out of the hands of the court, now relocated in Ravenna in Italy, within a few decades. The western court had been trapped in a downward spiral. As more and more territories and their revenues were lost, the court found it increasingly difficult to mobilize the resources necessary to stem the tide and reassert its control. Soon it had been reduced to irrelevance.⁶⁴ All this happened while the eastern court in Constantinople was able to weather the storms, hold onto its possessions and then launch an offensive in the sixth century to regain territories in Africa, Spain and Italy. By the early seventh century, however, problems came also to the eastern court. Locked into a decades-long existential struggle with the Sasanians of Persia, both powers wore themselves out. Cannibalizing each other in epic campaigns of conquest and reconquest, the two leading imperial monarchies of western Eurasia had become unstable, ripe for the taking. No sooner was a peace concluded between them than the Arabs, conveniently situated in the proverbial middle ground, swooped in and embarked on a set of whirlwind campaigns. In less than a decade, 634–642 CE, Palestine, Syria and Egypt had been wrested from the control of the Romans and Sasanian Persia had been dealt a devastating blow. Both established monarchies tried to strike back, but both clearly lacked the resources to mount a decisive and sustained counter-offensive. Their reserves had been exhausted in their struggle against each other. When the Arabs quickly took possession of the revenues of Syria, Egypt and Mesopotamia, some of the richest regions of western Eurasia, the means were lacking to rebuild their strength, and it proved impossible to turn things around.⁶⁵

---

⁶² Bang 2021a: 276–278.　⁶³ Shaw 1999.
⁶⁴ Wickham 2005, chapter 2, for a political survey of the late empire region by region, pp. 87–88: the final nail in the coffin was the loss of Africa to the Vandals.
⁶⁵ The observation in the mid seventh-century *Armenian History Attributed to Sebeos* (Thomson, Howard-Johnston & Greenwood, 1999) is suggestive: 'but the Greek king could raise no more

6.4 Overturning Empire or Renewal on the Frontiers?

The weakened position of the central courts, in short, had made established imperial rule vulnerable. However, it was not primarily the taxpaying peasantry that was able to bring it down. As the Mughal case teaches us, the decisive push often came from the frontiers of imperial society. No one has studied this problem more systematically than historians of imperial China. They have identified a particular dynamic for the frontier. Rather than a line, the frontier must be understood as a broad zone where populations of sedentary agriculturalists became scarcer and gradually gave way to more mobile populations of both agriculturalists and pastoral nomads. In Chinese history, focus has been on nomads to the north and west of settled agricultural society, but there was also a southern frontier, as we have just learned, of agriculturalists, hill and forest people.

In the Roman empire, nomads featured prominently on the southern frontier in North Africa and on the Arabian frontier of Syria. The Northern frontier along the big European rivers, on the other hand, had more agriculturalists, but living less densely and therefore also capable of more animal husbandry. What was characteristic of all these various groups was that they were more difficult to control for the sedentary rulers. Still the expansive movement of imperial power into the frontier zone did not leave the mobile groups untouched, even if they could often not be taxed. They were forced to develop their defensive capacities in response to imperial pressure and saw a military elite emerge from their midst to lead them into war. Whether one looks to China or Rome, as Dick Whittaker pointed out in a classic comparative study, the interaction of empire and frontier population spawned dynamic social development.[66] A good example would be the small Garamantean kingdom and city that archaeologists have found living around one of the oases far to the south of the advancing imperial frontier in Libya.[67]

Compared to the sedentary rulers, these frontier societies enjoyed one advantage: a high military participation rate. Mobility meant that a larger part of the population was available for warfare than in sedentary societies; its labour was not claimed by powerful, often urban landlords. As argued in Chapter 2, it was the development of a sedentary solution to this constraint

---

troops to oppose them' (chapter 136, p. 98). Howard-Johnston 2010: 444–445 insists that the damage to the two monarchies of decades of all-out war 'should not be exaggerated', an assessment which is difficult to reconcile with their abrupt collapse and the deep inroads each had been able to make into each other's possessions in the preceding years. Clearly, the two powers were standing on feet of clay, seriously weakened by each other; see Bowersock 2012, chapter 3.

[66] Whittaker 1994; Di Cosmo 2002. Classic is Lattimore 1940, while Dyson 1975 already alluded to this parallel.
[67] Mattingly 2013.

that had enabled the Roman Republic and the Qin dynasty to rise as great conquerors on the back of vast massed peasant armies. By the end of antiquity, those days were long gone, and recruitment patterns had changed.

On the frontier a balance had developed. Coalitions of warriors would occasionally form to embark on plundering raids of the sedentary areas. To keep the peace, imperial rulers might respond by simply paying off the raiders. Such payments of a reverse tribute, for instance, became an important source of the Chinese silks that we saw in Chapter 5, making their way to the Roman world. Another option was to ally with some of these groups and pay them to fight for the empire against their neighbours. Mobile populations on the frontier became a useful reservoir of manpower that empires attempted to tap. They were not always easy to manage. When the city of Oea, modern-day Tripoli in Libya, mobilized the Garamantes in their rivalry with bigger Lepcis Magna, the regular army had to come to the rescue and restore order.[68] However, it was only by the late fourth century that the situation began to slip out of hand for the Roman authorities.

The fiscally challenged court had resorted more and more to hiring contingents of soldiers drawn from the frontiers, especially along the Rhine and the Danube. This changed the balance fatally. Instead of being enrolled in the regular units of the army, these Germanic soldiers served in their own ethnic contingents under their own leaders. That was an attractively cheap solution to a cash-strapped court, and the Germanic troops repeatedly proved their mettle in battle.[69] But the enormous pull of the imperial army had the unintended consequence that the frontier was mobilized. A warrior society developed under the leadership of a multitude of warlords. Seeking positions in the imperial service, they also tried to secure a stable source of income for their military retinues in the quiet periods. It was as part of his struggle with the court in Ravenna to obtain funding for his soldiers that Alaric, the Goth, ended up plundering Rome in 410 CE. The top prize, however, was access to land or control of its revenues. No more steady source of income was available in pre-industrial societies. The western court saw the warlords chip away at its territory and tax base until its position had been taken over by a string of Germanic warrior-kingdoms, from the Franks on the lower Rhine to the Vandals in North Africa.[70]

---

[68] Tacitus, *Histories* IV, 50. [69] Lee 1997 (on the late Roman army).
[70] Whittaker 1994, chapter 6. For a recent magisterial account of this process, see Meier 2019, noting for instance that the Franks did not so much migrate as simply expand from their home base.

Later, in the seventh century, the Arab tribes on the frontier of Rome and Persia had similarly been mobilized in the struggle between the two realms. Under the impact of the two grand empires, processes of state formation were taking shape on the Arab peninsula, and the military capacity among the tribal coalitions was building up.[71] The influence of the imperial world is highly visible in the prophecies and revelations of the Quran that Muhammad started proclaiming in Mecca during the big confrontation of the Sasanian and Roman emperors: 'The Romans have been defeated in a nearby territory. But following their defeat, they will be victorious.'[72] The sermons that make up the Quran are fully conversant with the religious world of the empires. Both Christianity and Judaism had won adherents in Arab society, and the reader finds Muhammad engaging in an extended debate with members from both religions about how to worship the one and only God. They were all the children of Abraham and should now abandon their errors and join the new, perfected revelation of Muhammad. Tirelessly, the many different Arab communities are admonished to give up their special gods, abandon the worship of their local idols and unite in the one religion. Only thus could local division and sectarianism be overcome.[73]

In purveying this message, Muhammad was surprisingly successful. It is striking that one of the first contemporary accounts of the Arab conquerors, an Armenian history from the mid seventh century, especially took note that 'abandoning their vain cults ... they all gathered in unison'.[74] Just at the moment when the old empires were probably at their weakest, Muhammad had succeeded in forging the Arabs into a unified force. This was the stuff of which world-historical conjunctures are made. Divided, the Arabs had been easily managed by the imperial courts, even during the decades of their great confrontation, but now they had become invincible. To the Armenian Christian who penned the account, nothing less than eschatological prophecy would do to explain the events. Reaching for the Old Testament book of Daniel, he inserted the Arabs, or Ishmaelites as they had come to be called after the first son of Abraham, in a succession of powers. The Arabs signalled the arrival of the fourth beast and final kingdom that 'surpasses in evil all kingdoms', conquers everything and lays humanity waste before a god-hallowed order would then eventually materialize to bring release and

---

[71] Whittaker 1994, chapter 7.
[72] The Quran, 30, 2–3 (trans. Talai Itani; www.clearquran.com/030.html).
[73] The Quran, 30, 30–32. On the late antique context of the Quran and Arab state formation, see briefly Marsham 2021: 356–357. More extensively, Neuwirth 2014; Bowersock 2012; Fowden 1993.
[74] *Armenian History Attributed to Sebeos*, chapter 42, section 135, p. 96.

salvation.[75] These apocalyptic expectations would not have been foreign to the new Muslim conquerors. The day of judgment was indeed near, but to their mind they of course represented not the 'anti-Christ' but the final revelation.[76]

While we leave the believers to ponder who was right, from the perspective of this book the important thing to note is that millenarian mobilization on the frontier did not bring social revolution but imperial renewal. To approach the fall of the Roman Empire mainly as a Western European question of the fifth century renders our vision too narrow. The late antique world must be placed in its proper Afro-Eurasian context. While the fragmented character of the Germanic warrior groups brought political division to Western Europe, Arab organizational unity produced a result more indicative of the world-historical norm. At the time when the Muslim conquerors subjected most of the Roman and Sassanian empires to the Caliph, the Tang dynasty established imperial rule in East and Central Asia on a cosmopolitan scale that outdid even their Han dynasty predecessors. Meanwhile, the Germanic rulers had never sought so much to overturn the Western empire as capture a consolidated place within the Roman world. Eventually, one of them grew strong enough to lay claim to the imperial title himself: Charlemagne. The Afro-Eurasian world would continue to be dominated by universal monarchies.

---

[75] *Armenian History Attributed to Sebeos*, chapter 47, section 162, p. 133; Book of Daniel, chapter 7.
[76] Howard-Johnston 2010, chapters 14 and 15 on Rome, Persia, Muhammad and the Arabs, chapter 3, on the *Armenian History Attributed to Sebeos*. Fischer 2011 (on the Arabs before Muhammad).

CONCLUSION

Beyond Globalization – The World Histories for Rome

Finally, after some twenty years, in the time of my youth, a man of uncertain background emerged who claimed to be Nero. The name held such prestige among the Parthians that this man found vigorous support and was only with difficulty surrendered.

Suetonius, *Nero*[1]

Connections and Comparisons

The figure of the false Nero is one of the more exotic and curious phenomena that inhabit the quiet and rarely visited corners of Roman history. Yet Suetonius, the secretary of Hadrian and biographer of the Caesars, was far from alone in reporting on the remarkable returns of the last scion of the Julio-Claudian dynasty. The incidents appear on the pages of writers from the senator Tacitus to the sixth- to seventh-century John of Antioch.[2] Several impostors arose in the decades after Nero's suicide in 68 CE. All variously attempted to raise troops in the eastern parts of the Empire or sought the assistance of Parthian rulers eager to foment trouble in the camp of their archenemy. In the end, they all failed miserably in their rebellion. These occurrences might all easily be written off as an odd parenthesis, were it not for the fact both that their fame lived on as material for prophecy and that they seem to find many a parallel across the span of Afro-Eurasian history. Wherever one looks, Medieval Scandinavia, Tudor England or Czarist Russia, examples abound.[3]

---

[1] Suetonius, *Nero*, 57.2 (my translation).
[2] Tacitus, *Histories* II, 8–9 (on the first imposter); on John of Antioch, see *Ioannis Antiocheni fragmenta quae supersunt omnia*, ed. and trans. S. Mariev (Berlin, 2008), chapter 131. See Pappano 1937 and Gallivan 1973 for collection and basic discussion of the textual evidence.
[3] Potter 1994: 109 and 142 locates the returning Nero in the context of ancient prophecy and finds many parallel examples in Roman political culture. On the impostor who claimed to be the deceased son, King Olav, of Margrete I, the ruler of Denmark, Norway and Sweden, see Etting 2004, chapter 17. Longworth 1975 places the rising of the Cossack leader, Pugachev, who pretended to be Peter III,

177

Characteristic, and perhaps especially close, parallels can be found in the imposture stories that circulated after the ascension of the Mughal Emperor, Shah Jahan, in 1627. In the brief succession struggle which followed the death of his father Jahangir, a junior Mughal prince was used as a placeholder on the throne for a few months. When Shah Jahan arrived at the royal capital from the provinces, the young pawn was seized and mercilessly executed. Soon after, however, one or several persons popped up, claiming to be the deceased prince, the rightful ruler of the Mughal Empire. As in the Roman case, this did not escape the attention of rival courts and powers. Ever alert, just as the Parthian dynasts were, the neighbours sensed an opportunity for interfering in the affairs of their opponent. Fearful of Mughal expansion, the Portuguese in Goa quickly started contemplating whether they could use the man for their purposes but shelved these ideas once they began to doubt the authenticity of his claim. The Safavid rulers of Iran, on the other hand, had fewer misgivings and gave shelter to the impostor prince for decades. This was probably not because they were more credulous than the Portuguese but because it suited their interests. Another pretender to claim Mughal princely status was, after a short while, returned in 1636 as useless by the Ottoman emperor, Murad IV, to Shah Jahan for swift execution, just as our false Nero had eventually been given up by the Parthians and handed over to the Roman emperor.[4]

Marginal characters such as these occupy a central role on the pages of the new global history. They allow the historian to revel in the rich details of local life while engaging in traditional, archival work at the micro-level and still pursue global history. Crossing boundaries between empires and cultures, these characters are seen as emblems of marvellous cultural connection. Often they are taken as pregnant with the promise of globalization and identified as an especially early-modern phenomenon before European hegemony was securely established.[5] But world history should not be reduced primarily to a search for often feeble or isolated precursors of modern globalization. Even as we question some of the assumptions that separate Western civilization from the 'rest', we end up taking the architecture of European colonialism for granted. Connections between a perceived

---

the deceased husband of Catherine the Great, in the context of a long series of peasant risings and royal impostors in Russia. Meanwhile, the pretender Tudors have risen to become a stable of popular history (e.g., Amin 2021).

[4] Flores & Subrahmanyam 2004.

[5] For two examples, see Hunt 2014 and Subrahmanyam 2012. Ghobrial 2019 stresses the value of the 'archival' or micro-historical aspect of connected global histories.

West and what were to become colonized societies are always privileged over other arguably more important links and contexts. To take our current example, the royal and imperial impostor was not primarily a product of the age of the European circumnavigators of the globe and the connections they forged, but an age-old phenomenon. However, to discern this, we need to put micro-history aside for a moment and begin to question our macro-historical framework by turning to comparison.

At a closer look, not only do many similar examples populate the annals of Rome, but the phenomenon of the royal pretender even occupies a central position in the first surviving extensive work of history. In the pages of Herodotus, we find the story of the false Smerdis and his attempt to capture the Achaemenid throne during the campaign of Cambyses in Egypt in 525 BCE.[6] Suspecting treason, the Great King already had his younger brother Smerdis assassinated. Instead, two Zoroastrian priests had emerged, one of whom pretended to be the deceased prince and, in the absence of the ruler, had taken control of the palace and central government. In the account of Herodotus, Cambyses dies of an accident as he embarks on the return journey from his Egyptian campaign to deal with the rebellious impostor.

The path had thus been cleared for the Persian nobleman and future Achaemenid emperor, Dareios, to team up with a group of like-minded restorationist assassins and kill the pretender. Yet the story almost sounds too fantastical. Might we not here suspect a propaganda ploy of Dareios to justify his usurpation of power? Modern historians may well be right to doubt the veracity of this account and dismiss it as fable. But while assessing just how much of a tall story it is that Herodotus presents us with, it is not enough to look at the incident in isolation; it is necessary to widen the perspective and establish a comparative context.[7] Set against the background of Afro-Eurasian history, the Smerdis affair, fantastical as it sounds, turns out to reflect a far from uncommon situation in the politics of ancient societies.

What really animated Herodotus to write his history were the remarkable events that saw Athens and Sparta fend off two imperial Achaemenid invasions of the Greek mainland. However, to explain this unexpected and marvellous triumph, the old historian found that he had to lift his gaze from the immediate theatre of war. It would not do merely to look at

---

[6] Herodotus, *Histories* III, 61–79, narrates the Smerdis affair.
[7] Waters 2021: 118; Rollinger 2021; Briant 2006: 98–106; Wiesehöfer 1978 for various modern analyses and discussions.

Marathon, Thermopylae, Salamis or the Aegean world of the Hellenic city-states. He had to broaden his scope to encompass the entire Achaemenid empire and effectively develop a comparative account of power in most of the world known to him. This book has attempted to follow in the footsteps of 'the father of history'. It shares with him, and modern world history, a fascination with the marvellous. But our world is bigger than his and therefore we have to paint on a broader canvass.

The expanded world of the Achaemenid Empire was itself a reflection of much wider expansive processes occurring across Afro-Eurasia. Each of the last five chapters (Chapters 2–6) has set off from a curious and marvellous incident of historical connectivity: elephants in Italy of the third century BCE; the inter-imperial entanglements of claims to universal power in the third century CE; the fascinating career of Alexander and Orpheus as figures of literature and emblems of royalty from Hellenistic Alexandria to Mughal Delhi; the craze for exotic prestige goods, whether 'blood-sweating' horses or Chinese silks, cultivated by elites, East and West, from antiquity till the age of colonialism; and finally apocalyptic prophecy from Rome to China. But the matter was not left at that. Not satisfied merely to identify examples of proto-globalization, weaker and less wide-ranging than the real thing, the chapters then turned to comparative history. The aim was to 'liberate' our connective examples from the hegemonic theoretical narratives of our present and find stronger and more meaningful contexts. They were not simply examples of 'globalization' in the abstract but the result of historical developments that can be described in much more concrete terms.

The Roman Republic was seen as a response to the expansion and increasing density of sedentary peasantries and state-making elites across the continents in the last half of the first millennium BCE. The Mediterranean empire, conquered by the Republic, was then revealed to be part of a general Afro-Eurasian trend towards the formation of grand universal realms that bestrode the zones of sedentary agriculture from antiquity till the age of colonialism. The rise of Greek and Latin as transregional languages and eventually Christianity as a monotheistic, empire-wide religion was reformatted to fit into a history which contains both the cosmopolitan promotion of Sanskrit across and beyond India and the establishment of Islam as an ecumenic religion. Imports of pepper and other exotic goods from the Indian Ocean to the Roman Mediterranean were then placed in the context of a rising tide of Afro-Eurasian intercontinental trades.

Yet this ancient world trade ought not to be hailed simply as an early, albeit abortive attempt at modern globalization. Quite the contrary, it represented a foundational episode in the development of the 'archaic' long-distance trade that the early-modern Iberian and North-West European merchants set out to capture and break up in a process which reoriented global commercial flows to centre them on Atlantic Europe. Finally, the book turned to resistance and rebellion by those at the bottom of hierarchies and on the margins of sedentarized society. No story of the establishment of power, after all, can be complete without an understanding of the forces that would undermine it. World history, far from simply confirming the view from above, as the complaint so often goes, provides the Roman historian with a wider framework in which to make sense of the often brief notices and scanty records surviving of rebel activity.

In all of the preceding chapters, comparative history has served to complement and better contextualize the study of cultural connection. What might have been written off as merely marginal or ephemeral phenomena all of a sudden become emblems of crucial trends and developments. By widening our imaginative horizon and historical perspective, comparison has expanded the repertoire of illuminating parallels and interpretative models available to us as historians. Rome has been fitted into a whole range of new and more meaningful contexts than those traditionally used. Yet sometimes it is argued that comparison only serves falsely to reinforce distinctions between societies, confirming each as a self-contained unit. That conviction has fuelled the turn to the writing of connected histories by some within the field of global history, and that indeed is a risk of comparative history. Some popular comparisons have occasionally been a little too fast in confirming the fundamental differences between a modernizing West and a stagnant East. But this is far from the inevitable result of the method. In this book, comparison has been employed to the opposite effect. The Roman Empire has certainly not been confirmed as a closed container, fundamentally separate from 'the rest'.[8] If anything, its 'integrity' as a unit has been radically questioned and undermined, by identifying a whole series of central characteristics that overlap with the other great agrarian societies of Afro-Eurasia. Connection or comparison is a false dichotomy: to produce proper history, they need to be made to work together. Anything but singular, Rome fits into a wider world history – wider too than this relatively slim volume can comprehend.

---

[8] I say in friendly objection to Hoo 2022, especially p. 10.

Alternative Perspectives, Other Stories, the Way Forward

Located at the margins of Roman history, the story of the returning Nero also challenges us to reflect on what stories have not been included or perhaps rather neglected in this book. Agrarian state formation and the demographically expansive drift of peasant society, the universal empires of the Afro-Eurasian world, ecumenic literary cultures and religions, pre-capitalist world trade, peasant rebellions: in examining these, a lot of ground has been covered in order to recontextualize the Roman experience. But there are many other potential stories and perspectives that could also be explored. Cities, gender, household and family organization, for instance, are three themes that could easily be pursued to deepen the portrait of state-making, sedentary societies developed here.[9]

A particular subgenre of world history has been focused on oceans since the immortal book *The Mediterranean and the Mediterranean World in the Age of Philip I*, by Fernand Braudel (originally 1949).[10] Before the age of rail, not to mention airplanes and cars, water was crucial for large-scale, bulk transport. For all the fame of the imperial roads of Rome, it was the big rivers and oceans that constituted the highways of pre-industrial societies.[11] From a global perspective, however, oceanic history tends to be macro-regional history, all the while reminding us about how important local ecology was in shaping pre-industrial societies. *The Corrupting Sea*, by the medievalist Peregrine Horden and the classicist Nicholas Purcell, is a prime example, and so is the medievalist Chris Wickham's *The Donkey and the Boat*.[12] Other ecological zones that might warrant more attention would, for instance, be big forests or mountains.[13]

One of the ecological zones to have drawn most attention from world historians is the Central Asian steppe. Its seemingly endless grasslands, reaching from the doorstep of China to Hungary, are often presented as the pivot of pre-colonial world history. Home to sturdy transmigrant nomads and their flocks of sheep and, most importantly, swift horses, the steppe had both mobility and enormous military potential. Wielding their composite bows, groups of nomads could quickly assemble into a formidable cavalry force that, time and time again, would inflict punishing defeats on sedentary rulers. When we add to this a mobile lifestyle, it is easy to see how

---

[9] Woolf 2020; Bossler & Lal 2018; Goody 1990.
[10] Braudel 1972; Abulafia 2011; Beaujard 2019.   [11] Campbell 2012, for a Roman example.
[12] Horden & Purcell 2000.   [13] McNeill 1992.

the steppe might be thought to have provided the decisive connecting infrastructure of pre-industrial Eurasia.[14]

However, in Roman history, it is only during the fifth century CE that the steppe moves to the centre of affairs. The arrival of the Huns on the Hungarian plain and the rise of their king, Attila, to a fearsome and seemingly invincible warlord wreaking havoc on the Balkan provinces dealt a significant shock to the empire. Little is known about the origins of the Huns before they showed up on the pages of horrified contemporary Roman historians – leaving all the more room for speculation. One particularly fascinating theory is that the Huns were the descendants of the people known as Xiongnu (in Chinese).[15] This nomadic warrior people had been fearsome adversaries of the early Han dynasty in the second century BCE. But after their eventual defeat, one part of the Xiongnu is supposed to have migrated west. There are no real archaeological traces of this movement, either of where or how far it went.[16] The only thing to go by is later Chinese accounts of the peoples living on the edges of their empire.

Information available about conditions on the steppe beyond the imperial frontier was hazy, not to say speculative. Writers tended to invent origins within the orbit of Chinese civilization for the people they described.[17] It is difficult not to admire the learned antiquarian ingenuity behind the ambition to reconstruct the meandering route supposedly taken by the Xiongnu. But the evidential situation facing the ancient Chinese authors was really not very different from that confronting Tacitus when writing his *Germania* about the peoples living beyond the Rhine and the Danube. Most archaeologists and historians today would be hesitant, to say the least, to rely on Tacitus' identification of tribes and ethnicities in writing the history of the far-flung region, especially as the work ventured beyond the immediate confines of the Roman Empire.[18] The same caveat should go for world history.

Yet, even if the theory of East Asian origins – one that hangs by only the thinnest, most speculative thread – should turn out to be right, there are still several centuries separating the Hunnic adversaries of Rome and the Xiongnu. Clearly, the central Asian steppe was not simply a fast-flowing channel connecting East and West in unity, such that events at one end

---

[14] Golden 2011; Lattimore 1940 remains fundamental and classic. Kradin 2014 for the extensive Russian tradition of scholarship working on nomadic societies in Central Asia.
[15] Kim 2013, especially 26–31. For various discussions, see Meier 2019: 156–171 and the contributions of Geary, Kulikowski and Pohl in Di Cosmo & Maas 2018.
[16] Brosseder 2018 is fundamental.   [17] Hansen 2012: 32.   [18] Mattern 1999: 75–76.

had immediate repercussions at the other. If ever that situation had occurred, it would have been during the heyday of the Mongol conquests of the thirteenth century CE which saw their armies blazing a trail of victories from Hangzhou to Baghdad.[19] The Huns, on the other hand, belong in a different context. Their rise is part of a long story of the flexible formation of short-lived and fractious warrior groups on the steppe. That process left little room for the preservation of a cohesive and distinct ethnic group on the move for centuries. Feeding off the plunder of sedentary areas, fluid coalitions of nomads constantly formed, shedded parts of the membership and reformed in tandem with the military success of the leader.[20] Cyrus II the Great, the founder of the Achaemenid Empire, may well have died on a campaign pushing against the Massagetan nomads inhabiting the plains east of the Caspian Sea.[21]

In East Asia, the nomads had been an important, if fluctuating power from the end of the third century BCE. The foundation of the Chinese Empire had also seen the armies of the sedentary rulers push into steppe society and been forced to develop its military capacity. But in western and central Eurasia, the nomads rose as a strong power only in the fifth and sixth centuries CE. Arguably similar forces triggered the development as before in the East. The slow expansion of sedentary society combined with the military mobilization of imperial frontiers described in Chapter 6 drew nomadic warrior society into the orbit of imperial politics.[22] As a pioneer of late antique global history, the late Mark Whittow, so brilliantly demonstrated, from then on it became part of the geopolitical strategy of both the Romans and Persians to cultivate alliances with warrior coalitions on the steppe. Soon the Gok Turks and Avars had absorbed the fragments of the previous Hunnic coalition. The Avars, having gained control of the Hungarian plain, were presumably led by a few aristocratic warrior clans that had ventured west rather than submit to the control of the Gok Turks after their defeat of the Rouran coalition in Central Asia in the early 560s CE.[23]

---

[19] Abu-Lughod 1989.
[20] Meier 2019, 397–470 and 994–1019 (on the waxing and waning of the Hunnic and Avar warrior coalitions). Bartfield 1992: 1–8 and 2001 for the volatile character of nomadic warrior coalitions in general (subsisting, as a shadow empire, on plunder and booty from the sedentary regions).
[21] Herodotus, *Histories* I, 204–216. [22] Crossley 2019, chapter 3; Di Cosmo 2002.
[23] Genetic studies of the human remains in a number of graves, belonging to the very top of Avar society, suggest an East Central Asian origin; see Csáky, Gerber & Koncz 2020. But this is precisely not evidence of the movement of entire peoples, but of an aristocratic clan in search of opportunity and allies elsewhere (a feature, as we saw in Chapter 2, that is well-known in the history of 'colonization' in the ancient Mediterranean). I am much obliged to Ursula Brosseder for expert and patient guidance on this question.

Alternative Perspectives, Other Stories 185

The Turkic ruler, therefore, maintained a claim to be the rightful ruler of the Avars. Fragmentation, however, was almost inevitable. Nomad bands would each form to prey on one of the core sedentary regions that lay scattered and stretched out in an east–west band across Eurasia. The central Asian khagan of the Western Gok Turks proved an attractive ally for the Romans, happy to welcome a power that could threaten the back of their Sassanian archenemy. Likewise, the Avars, within striking distance of the Balkans and Constantinople, were useful to the Persians.[24] The steppe, in short, does have a role to play in a world history about Rome. But for most of the period of Roman history, its presence was marginal.

If then the Eurasian steppe was too peripheral and the Mediterranean too regional, the backbone for the Roman world history of this book was to be found elsewhere. Sandwiched between ocean and steppe, the main agricultural zones of the Afro-Eurasian world stretching in a band from East to West have provided the central arena. It was this complex of 'cited' agrarian societies that Marshall Hodgson, the visionary historian of Islam and the premodern, identified as the main stage of world history between the rise of Sumer in the Mesopotamian Bronze Age and the age of industrialization.[25] However, at the foundations of this story lay the vast majority of the world's population, the sedentary peasant families, men, woman and children, who cultivated the fields and tended the domesticated animals. These are mostly silent in our record, their voices muted by the deafening roar echoing down through history of the states, empires, literary cultures, ecumenic religions, exotic trade flows and even rebellions and frontier militaries that formed the substance of the preceding chapters. And yet the evolution of all these phenomena largely traces the slow expansion of more densely settled peasant populations. Their shape, so to speak, left a decisive mark on the overall contours of the world of cities and ruling elites. As the Indian school of subaltern studies have taught us, the records and institutions of the powerful formed an indirect imprint of the peasantry and enslaved people.[26]

Confirmation of this view may be sought from pre-colonial Meso- and South America. Here, too, cities, states and empires arose from the most productive agricultural regions. Occasionally, the analysis has gestured towards this parallel experience. But there is evidently much more to be learned from a sustained and systematic comparison. However, the focus of this book has been on identifying an interconnected story, not simply to

---

[24] Whittow 2018, based on a brilliant reading of *Menander the Guardsman*, chapter 10 (especially).
[25] Hodgson 1974, Vol. 1, 50 and 109–114. Geyer 2018: 64–70 for a discussion. [26] Guha 1983.

deliver an exercise in analytical comparison, valuable as that would be. The evolution of complex societies in the Americas, after all, took place separately and in isolation from the Afro-Eurasian world. Of course, that might enable the student of world history to observe 'the new world' as an independently run experiment, offering a testing ground for explanations developed on the basis of 'the old'. Much can be gained from this, but there are also limits. History, after all, is not a completely mechanical process. The timing, for instance, was obviously very different in Afro-Eurasia and the Americas.

Large empires, in the form of the Aztec Triple Alliance and the Incas, had begun to form 'only' in the century up to the arrival of the Spanish 'conquistadores' at the turn of the fifteenth century. So far, therefore, these parallels have been particularly illuminating to students of the early Bronze Age Near East.[27] The intensification, maturation and expansion generated by Iron Age societies resulted in a new wave of stronger and institutionally more diversified state formation. It is among the inheritors of this Afro-Eurasian development that the Roman historian should first seek for inspiration and our closest interlocutors. In these years, considerable efforts are made to create cross-disciplinary collaborations focused on Mediterranean or premodern Global Asian studies. Why not be a little more ambitious and try to cultivate conversations that cut across conventional regions? Students of complex pre-industrial societies, whether of South Asia, East Asia, Islam or the Mediterranean, have a lot to learn from each other, as I have tried to show in this book.[28] If we want rejuvenation, this is where we should look. What an exciting prospect – and the dialogue has only just begun.

---

[27] Feinman & Moreno Garcia 2022.
[28] A practical way of achieving the programme suggested by Scheidel 2025.

Bibliographical Essay

General World History

Good introductions to the field of global and world history are offered by Conrad (2017) and Crossley (2008). Illustration of the range of potential perspectives may be found in the collections of Hopkins (2002) and Belich, Darwin, Frenz and Wickham (2016). Pomeranz (2000) and Bayly (2004) brought world history to new prominence. A recurrent question has been the problem of the rise of the West. Elvin (1973), Braudel (1981–1984) and Goody (1996) are classic; Morris (2010), Scheidel (2019) and Quinn (2024) provide three notable interventions from ancient historians. The need to conceptualize a world history before the logic of modernity became predominant is argued with particular lucidity by Bin Wong (1997), Hodgson (1993) and Chaudhuri (1990).

Peasantries, Epidemics and State and Empire Formation

McNeill (1976) identified the link between sedentary agriculture, urbanization and epidemic disease as a crucial force shaping pre-industrial world history. Harper (2021) brings the story up to date, while Scheidel (2017) emphasizes the constraints and hierarchies of pre-industrial economic life, Scott (2017) the capacity of nomads to flourish and escape the plight of historic peasantries, and Belich (2022) the radical impact and repercussions of the Black Death for later European developments. While the book in hand was being written, a team led by ancient historian Sitta Von Reden (Freiburg) has published three large volumes surveying economic activity and state formation across the Afro-Eurasian arena in the centuries from Alexander to the third century CE (2020–2023). Hansen (2000), Yoffee (2015) and Woolf (2020) offer global surveys and analysis of ancient cities and city-states while Bang and Scheidel (2013) covers state formation in the ancient Near East and Mediterranean. On ancient slavery in world history,

Cameron and Lenski (2018) is now the place to start, followed by the four volumes of the *Cambridge World History of Slavery* (2011–2021).

On empire in world history, Lieven (2000), Kumar (2021) and Hall (2024) offer inspiring introductions. Bang, Bayly and Scheidel (2021) provides extensive theoretical discussion, comprehensive survey and global synthesis. On universal empires, the predominant form across the Afro-Eurasian world before European colonialism, see Bang and Kolodziejczyk (2012). For comparative explorations of the dynamics of these empires, sometimes also categorized as tributary, see the monograph of Bang (2008) and a host of comparative volumes: Alcock, Altroy, and Morrison et al. (2000); Mutschler and Mittag (2008); Scheidel (2009 & 2015a); Bang and Bayly (2011); van Berkel and Duindam (2018); Beck and Vankeerbergen (2021); Pines and Rüpke (2021). Burbank and Cooper (2010) distinguishes two main varieties of premodern empire, a Roman and a Mongol nomadic. Lieberman (2003–2009) emphasizes the nomadic, as does Crossley (2019).

Culture, World Trade and Resistance

On cultural connection rather than societal comparison in world history, see Subrahmanyam (e.g., 2003 & 2012). Ghobrial (2019) is a collected volume showcasing the significance of the approach for the writing of global history. See Stoneman, Erickson and Netton (2012) for the *Alexander Romance* as a site for such interconnectedness. Arnason, Eisenstadt and Wittrock (2005) is a good entry to the question of the Axial Age, while Pollock (2003) explored his model of the cosmopolitan languages on a range of South Asian cases, not least Persian. No classicist can fail to learn from Truschke (2016), Kinra (2015) and Busch (2011), a set of detailed studies of aspects of Mughal and Indian medieval literary culture. Comparisons of some of the cosmopolitan languages have been produced by Beecroft (2010) and Mallette (2021). Lloyd (1996) and Lloyd and Sivin (2002) compare ancient Greek and Chinese scientific cultures, an aspect neglected in the present volume. On monotheism in world history, Strathern (2019) must now be the starting point. On the interrelatedness of Christianity and Islam in late antiquity, see Fowden (1993 & 2014), Neuwirth (2014) and Stroumsa (2015).

On ancient world trade, Chaudhuri (1986) and Hansen (2020) provide a strong analytical overview of how the system had developed over the first millennium CE. Beaujard (2019) impressively collects much material on the Indian Ocean but is weaker analytically. Kristiansen, Lindkvist and Myrdal (2018) and Di Cosmo and Mass (2018) are two strong collections discussing the mechanisms, drives and available models of premodern world trade. On the issue of the Silk Road(s), Hansen (2012) is the best available discussion. Apparduai (1986) is fundamental on the culture of consumption. Tsing (2015) is a brilliant analysis of how the spirit of 'the gift' continues to cordon off even some modern goods from the wider spectrum of market consumption. Nabhan (2014) should be read for its evocative, sensory analysis, rather than its scholarly rigour. Fricke (2024) is a fascinating brand-new collection on incense and its allure in premodern societies and world trade.

On the question of rebellion and resistance, Scott (2009) is the best starting point. Adas (1979) and Guha (1983) are classic and still worth consulting. Bradley (1986) already taught us to incorporate the experience of slavery rebellion in the Americas into our understanding of the Greco-Roman world. Crone (2012) is never less than thought-provoking in her discussion of millenarian-inspired uprisings in early Islamic Iran.

Bibliography

Abulafia, D. 2011. *The Great Sea: A Human History of the Mediterranean*. London.
—— 2019. *The Boundless Sea: A Human History of the Oceans*. Oxford.
Abu-Lughod, J. L. 1989. *Before European Hegemony: The World System A.D. 1250–1350*. Oxford.
Acosta-Hughes, B., L. Lehnus & S. Stephens eds. 2011. *Brill's Companion to Callimachus*. Leiden.
Adams, J. N. 2003. *Bilingualism and the Latin Language*. Cambridge.
Adas, M. 1979. *Prophets of Rebellion: Millenarian Protest Movements against the European Colonial Order*. Chapel Hill.
Akin, E. & H. Crane. 2006. *Sinan's Autobiographies: Five Sixteenth-Century Texts*. Leiden.
Alam, M. 1986. *The Crisis of Empire in Mughal North India: Awadh and the Punjab 1707–1748*. Oxford.
—— 2003. 'The Culture and Politics of Persian in Precolonial Hindustan'. In Pollock, pp. 131–198.
—— 2021. *The Mughals and the Sufis: Islam and the Political Imagination in India 1500–1750*. Albany.
Alam, M. & S. Subrahmanyam eds. 1998. *The Mughal State 1526–1750*. Calcutta.
—— 2007. *Indo-Persian Travels in the Age of Discoveries, 1400–1800*. Cambridge.
Alcock, S., T. N. Altroy, K. D. Morrison et al. 2001. *Empires: Perspectives from Archaeology and History*. Cambridge.
Alcock, S., J. Bodel & R. Talbert eds. 2012. *Highways, Byways and Road Systems in the Pre-modern World*. Chichester.
Ali, D. 2004. *Courtly Culture and Political Life in Early Medieval India*. Cambridge.
Ameling, W. 2013. 'Carthage'. In Bang & Scheidel, pp. 361–382.
Amin, N. 2021. *Henry VII and the Tudor Pretenders: Simnel, Warbeck, and Warwick*. Stroud.
Anderson, B. 1991. *Imagined Communities: Reflections on the Origins and Spread of Nationalism*. Rev. ed. London.
Ando, C. & S. Richardson eds. 2017. *Ancient States and Infrastructural Power: Europe, Asia, America*. Philadelphia.

Andrade, N. 2015. 'The Voyage of Maes Titianos and the Dynamics of Social Connectivity between the Roman Levant and Central Asia/West China'. *Mediterraneo Antico*, Vol. 18, 1–2, pp. 41–74.

   2018. *The Journey of Christianity to India in Late Antiquity: Networks and the Movement of Culture*. Cambridge.

Anooshahr, A. 2018. *Turkestan and the Rise of Eurasian Empires: A Study of Politics and Invented Traditions*. Oxford.

Anthony, D. W. 2007. *The Horse, the Wheel and Language: How Bronze-Age Riders from the Eurasian Steppes Shaped the Modern World*. Princeton.

Appadurai, A. ed. 1986. *The Social Life of Things: Commodities in Cultural Perspective*. Cambridge.

Appiah, K. A. 2006. *Cosmopolitanism: Ethics in a World of Strangers*. New York.

Arnason, J. P., S. Eisenstadt & B. Wittrock eds. 2004. *Axial Civilizations and World History*. Leiden.

Arnason, J. P. & K. Raaflaub eds. 2011. *The Roman Empire in Context*. Chichester.

Austin, M. M. 2006. *The Hellenistic World from Alexander to the Roman Conquest: A Selection of Ancient Sources in Translation*. 2nd augmented ed. Cambridge.

Auyang, S. Y. 2014. *The Dragon and the Eagle: The Rise and Fall of the Chinese and Roman Empires*. New York.

Baba, H. K. 1994. *The Location of Culture*. New York.

Bagnall, R. 2002. 'Alexandria: Library of Dreams'. *Proceedings of the American Philosophical Society*, Vol. 146, pp. 348–362.

Bakhtin, M. 1984. *Rabelais and His World*. Trans. H. Iswolsky. Bloomington.

Ballantyne, T. & A. Burton. 2012. *Empire and the Reach of the Global, 1870–1945*. Cambridge, MA.

Bang, P. F. 2008. *The Roman Bazaar: A Comparative Study of Trade and Markets in a Tributary Empire*. Cambridge.

   2011a. 'Lord of All the World: The State, Heterogeneous Power and Hegemony in the Roman and Mughal Empires'. In Bang & Bayly, pp. 171–192.

   2011b. 'Court and State in the Roman Empire: Domestication and Tradition in Comparative Perspective'. In Duindam, Artan & Kunt, pp. 103–128.

   2012. 'Between Ásoka and Antiochos: An Essay in World History on Universal Kingship and Cosmopolitan Culture in the Hellenistic Ecumene'. In Bang & Kolodziejczyk, pp. 60–75.

   2013. 'The Roman Empire II: The Monarchy'. In Bang & Scheidel, pp. 412–472.

   2014. *Irregulare Aliquod Corpus? Comparison, World History and the Historical Sociology of the Roman Empire I: Theoretical and Methodological Introduction and Summary*. Copenhagen.

   2015a. 'Tributary Empires and the New Fiscal Sociology: Some Comparative Reflections'. In Monson & Scheidel, pp. 537–556.

   2015b. 'Platonism: Ernest Gellner, Greco-Roman Society and the Comparative Study of the Pre-modern World'. *Thesis Eleven*, Vol. 128, pp. 58–71.

   2016. 'Beyond Capitalism: Conceptualizing Ancient Trade through Friction, World Historical Context and Bazaars'. In J.-C. Morena García ed.,

Dynamics of Production in the Ancient Near East: 1300–500 BC. Oxford, pp. 75–90.

2018a. 'Empire, Civilization, and Trade: The Roman Experience in World History'. In Kristiansen, Lindkvist & Myrdal, pp. 494–514.

2018b. 'Megacity, Cosmopolis, Axis Mundi: Capital Comparisons and World History'. In P. Eich & K. Wojciech eds., *Die Verwaltung der Stadt Rom in der Hohen Kaiserzeit*. Paderborn, pp. 325–333.

2021a. 'Empire: A World History: Anatomy and Concept, Theory and Synthesis'. In Bang, Bayly & Scheidel, Vol. 1, pp. 1–87.

2021b. 'The Roman Empire'. In Bang, Bayly & Scheidel, Vol. 2, pp. 250–289.

Bang, P. F. & C. A. Bayly eds. 2003. 'Tributary Empires in History: Comparative Perspectives from Antiquity to the Late Medieval'. *The Medieval History Journal*, Vol. 6(2), special issue.

2011. *Tributary Empires in Global History*. Basingstoke.

Bang, P. F., C. A. Bayly & W. Scheidel eds. 2021. *The Oxford World History of Empire*. 2 vols. Oxford.

Bang, P. F. & D. Kolodziejczyk eds. 2012. *Universal Empire: A Comparative Approach to Imperial Culture and Representation in Eurasian History*. Cambridge.

Bang, P. F. & W. Scheidel eds. 2013. *The Oxford Handbook of the State in the Ancient Near East and Mediterranean*. Oxford.

Bang, P. F. & K. Turner 2015. 'Kingship and Elite Formation'. In Scheidel, pp. 11–38.

Barfield, T. J. 1992. *The Perilous Frontier: Nomadic Empires and China, 221 BC to AD 1757*. Cambridge.

2001. 'The Shadow Empires: Imperial State Formation along the Chinese-Nomad Frontier'. In Alcock, Altroy, Morrison et al., pp. 10–41.

Barjamovic, G. 2018. 'Interlocking Commercial Networks and Infrastructure of Trade in Western Asia during the Bronze Age'. In Kristiansen, Lindkvist & Myrdal, pp. 113–142.

forthcoming. 'Empire'. In J. Silverman & E. Pfoh eds., *Routledge Handbook of the Ancient Near East and the Social Sciences*. London.

Barjamovic, G. & K. Ryholt eds. 2019. *Libraries before Alexandria: Near Eastern Traditions*. Oxford.

Barker, G. & C. Goucher eds. 2015. *A World with Agriculture, 12,000 BCE–500 CE: The Cambridge World History, Vol. 2*. Cambridge.

Batty, R. 2007. *Rome and the Nomads: The Pontic-Danubian Realm in Antiquity*. Oxford.

Bayly, C. A. 1983. *Rulers, Townsmen and Bazaars: North Indian Society in the Age of British Expansion, 1770–1870*. Cambridge.

1986. 'The Origins of Swadeshi (Home Industry): Cloth and Indian Society, 1700–1930'. In Appadurai, pp. 285–321.

1988. *Indian Society and the Making of the British Empire: The New Cambridge History of India*, Vol. II, 1. Cambridge.

1996. *Empire and Information: Intelligence Gathering and Social Communication in India, 1780–1870*. Cambridge.

2002. '"Archaic" and "Modern" Globalization in the Eurasian and African Arena, 1750–1850'. In Hopkins, pp. 47–73.

2004. *The Birth of the Modern World*. Oxford.

2005. 'From Archaic Globalization to International Networks, circa 1600–2000'. In J. H. Bentley, R. Bridenthal & A. A. Yang eds., *Interactions: Transregional Perspectives on World History*. Honolulu, pp. 14–29.

Beach, M. C. & E. Koch. 1997. *King of the World. The Padshahnama: An Imperial Mughal Manuscript from the Royal Library, Windsor Castle, with New Translations by Wheeler Thackston*. London.

Beard, M. 2015. *SPQR: A History of Ancient Rome*. New York.

Beard, M., J. North & S. Price. 1998. *Religions of Rome: A History*. Cambridge.

Beattie, J. & E. Anderson 2021. 'Ecology: Environments and Empires in World History, 3000 BCE–ca. 1900 CE'. In Bang, Bayly & Scheidel, Vol. 1, pp. 460–493.

Beaujard, P. 2018. 'The Birth of a Single Afro-Eurasian World System (Second Century BC–Sixth Century CE)'. In Kristiansen, Lindkvist & Myrdal, pp. 242–250.

2019. *The Worlds of the Indian Ocean: A Global History*. 2 vols. Cambridge.

Back, H. 2021. 'Registers of "the People" in Greece, Rome and China'. In Beck and Vankeerberghen, pp. 193–224.

Beck, H. & G. Vankeerberghen eds. 2021. *Rulers and Ruled in Ancient Greece, Rome, and China*. Cambridge.

Beecroft, A. 2010. *Authorship and Cultural Identity in Early Greece and China: Patterns of Literary Circulation*. Cambridge.

Belich, J. 2022. *The World the Plague Made: The Black Death and the Rise of Europe*. Princeton.

Belich, J., J. Darwin, M. Frenz and C. Wickham eds. 2016. *The Prospect of Global History*. Oxford.

Benabou, M. 1976. *La résistance africaine à la romanisation*. Paris.

Benedict, R. 1934. *Patterns of Culture*. Boston.

Benjamin, C. ed. 2015. *A World with States: Empires and Networks 1200 BCE–900 CE. The Cambridge World History, Vol. 4*. Cambridge.

2018. *Empires of Ancient Eurasia: The First Silk Roads Era, 100 BCE–250 CE*. Cambridge.

2021. 'The Kushan Empire'. In Bang, Bayly & Scheidel, Vol. 2, pp. 325–446.

Bentley, J. H. 1994. *Old World Encounters: Cross-Cultural Contacts and Exchanges in Pre-modern Times*. Oxford.

Berend, N. 2023. 'Interconnection and Separation: Medieval Perspectives on the Modern Problem of the "Global Middle Ages."' *Medieval Encounters*, Vol. 29, pp. 285–314.

Bergson, L. 1965. *Der griechische Alexanderroman: Rezension B*. Stockholm.

Bernal, I. 1980. *A History of Mexican Archaeology: The Vanished Civilizations of Middle America*. London.

Bernal, M. 1987. *Black Athena. Vol. 1: The Fabrication of Ancient Greece 1785–1985*. New Brunswick.

Bhabha, H. K. 1994. *The Location of Culture*. London.
Bianchi, E., S. Brill & B. Holmes eds. 2019. *Antiquities Beyond Humanism*. Oxford.
Bielenstein, H. 1986. 'Wang Mang, the Restoration of the Han Dynasty, and Later Han'. In Twitchett & Loewe, pp. 223–290.
Bin Wong, R. 1997. *China Transformed: Historical Change and the Limits of European Experience*. London.
Blake, S. P. 1991. *Shahjahanabad: The Sovereign City in Mughal India, 1639–1739*. Cambridge.
Blouin, K. 2014. *Triangular Landscapes: Environment, Society, and the State in the Nile Delta under Roman rule*. Oxford.
Bodde, D. 1986. 'The State and Empire of Ch'in'. In Twitchett & Loewe, pp. 20–102.
Bodel, J. & W. Scheidel eds. 2017. *On Human Bondage: After Slavery and Social Death*. Chichester.
Borges, J. L. 2002 (1970). *The Book of Imaginary Beings*. With M. Guerrero & N. T. di Giovanni. Vintage ed. London.
Borrut, A., M. Ceballos & A. M. Vacca eds. 2024. *Navigating Language in the Early Islamic World: Multilingualism and Language Change in the First Centuries of Islam*. Turnhout.
Boserup, E. 1965. *The Conditions of Agricultural Growth: The Economics of Agrarian Change under Population Pressure*. London.
Bossler, B. & R. Lal 2018. 'Gender Systems: The Exotic Asian and Other Fallacies'. In Elman & Pollock, pp. 93–125.
Bowersock, G. W. 1987. 'The Mechanics of Subversion in the Roman Provinces'. In Giovannini, pp. 291–317.
  2012. *Empires in Collision in Late Antiquity*. Waltham, MA.
Boyce, B. 1991. *The Language of the Freedmen in Petronius' Cena Trimalchionis*. Leiden.
Bradley, K. 1994. *Slavery and Society at Rome*. Cambridge.
Bradley, K. & P. Cartledge eds. 2011. *The Cambridge World History of Slavery. Vol. 1: The Ancient Mediterranean World*. Cambridge.
Bradley, M. ed. 2015. *Smell and the Ancient Senses*. London.
Bransbourg, G. 2015. 'The Later Roman Empire'. In Monson & Scheidel, pp. 258–281.
Braudel, F. 1972. *The Mediterranean and the Mediterranean World in the Age of Philip II*. 2 Vols. Trans. S. Reynolds. London.
Braund, D. 1984. *Rome and the Friendly King: the character of Client Kingship*. London.
  ed. 2005. *Scythians and Greeks: Cultural Interaction in Scythia, Athens and the Early Roman Empire (Sixth Century BC to First Century AD)*. Liverpool.
Brend, B. 1995. *The Emperor Akbar's Khamsah of Nizami*. London.
Briant, P. 2002. *From Cyrus to Alexander: A History of the Persian Empire*. Trans. P. T. Daniels. Winona Lake.
Brosseder, U. B. 2018. 'Xiongnu and Huns: Archaeological Perspectives on a Centuries-Old Debate about Identity and Migration'. In Di Cosmo & Maas, pp. 176–188.

Brown, P. 1971a. 'The Rise and Function of the Holy Man in Late Antiquity'. *Journal of Roman Studies*, Vol. 61, pp. 80–101.
  1971b. *The World of Late Antiquity*. London.
  1981. *The Cult of the Saints in Late Antiquity: Its Rise and Function in Latin Christianity*. Chicago.
  1982. *Society and the Holy in Late Antiquity*. Berkeley.
  2018. '"Charismatic" Goods: Commerce, Diplomacy, and Cultural Contacts along the Silk Road in Late Antiquity'. In Di Cosmo & Maas, pp. 96–107.
Brun, J.-P., T. Faucher, B. Redon et al. eds. 2018. *The Eastern Desert of Egypt during the Greco-Roman Period: Archaeological Reports*. Paris.
Brunt, P. A. 1962. 'The Army and the Land in the Roman Revolution'. *Journal of Roman Studies*, Vol. LII, pp. 69–86 (repr. in *Roman Imperial Themes*, Oxford, 1990).
Bulliet, R. W. 1979. *Conversion to Islam in the Medieval Period: An Essay in Quantitative History*. Cambridge, MA.
Bürgel, J. C. 1986. 'Der Wettstreit zwischen Plato und Aristoteles im Alexander-Epos des persischen Dichters Nizami'. *Die Welt des Orients*, Vol. 17, pp. 95–109.
Burke III, E. 2009. 'The Big Story: Human History, Energy Regimes, and the Environment'. In E. Burke III & K. Pomeranz eds., *The Environment and World History*. Berkeley, pp. 33–53.
Burke III, E. & R. J. Mankin eds. 2019. *Islam and World History: The Ventures of Marshall Hodgson*. Chicago.
Burton, G. P. & K. Hopkins 1983. 'Ambition and Withdrawal: The Senatorial Aristocracy under the Emperors'. In K. Hopkins, *Death and Renewal: Sociological Studies in Roman History*, Cambridge, pp. 120–200.
Busch, A. 2011. *Poetry of Kings: The Classical Hindi Literature of Mughal India*. New York.
Campbell, B. 2012. *Rivers and the Power of Ancient Rome*. Chapell Hill.
Canepa, M. 2009. *The Two Eyes of the Earth: Art and Ritual of Kingship between Rome and Sasanian Iran*. Berkeley.
Cannadine, D. 1983. 'The Context, Performance and Meaning of Ritual: The British Monarchy and the "Invention of Tradition", c. 1820–1977'. In E. Hobsbawm & T. Ranger eds., *The Invention of Tradition*. Cambridge, pp. 101–164.
Cannadine, D. & S. Price eds. 1987. *Rituals of Royalty: Power and Ceremonial in Traditional Societies*. Cambridge.
Cappers, R. T. J. 2006. *Roman Foodprints at Berenike: Archaeobotanical Evidence of Subsistence and Trade in the Eastern Desert of Egypt*. Los Angeles.
Carey, S. 2003. *Pliny's Catalogue of Culture: Art and Empire in the Natural History*. Oxford.
Carneiro, R. L. 1970. 'A Theory of the Origin of the State'. *Science, New Series*, Vol. 169(3947), pp. 733–738.
Cartledge, P. 2024. 'Sparta: Ancient Greece's Foremost Slave State?' In P. F. Bang, A. H. Rasmussen & C. A. Thomsen eds., *Between Athens and Rhodes: A Collection*

of *Studies in Honour of Vincent Gabrielsen on Fleets, Offices, Associations and the Economy of the Ancient Greek World.* Classica & Mediaevalia Supplementum 2. Copenhagen, pp. 189–202.

Casale, G. L. forthcoming. 'Maps, Dictionaries, and Ottoman Romanitas: Cataloging Empire's Past and Present in Sixteenth-Century Istanbul'. In P. F. Bang & C. Høgel eds., *Imperial Languages.*

Caseau, B. 2024. 'The Substance of Incense during Roman Antiquity and the Early Byzantine Period'. In Fricke, pp. 265–282.

Ceci, F. & A. Krause-Kolodziej. 2018. 'Χαῖρε 'Ορφεῦ! Perception of a Mystery: The Images of the Myth of Orpheus on Ancient Coins'. *Acta Antiqua Academicae Scientiarum Hungaricae,* Vol. 58, pp. 721–740.

Chakrabarty, D. 2000. *Provincializing Europe: Postcolonial Thought and Historical Difference.* Princeton.

Chakrabarty, D. & H. Saussy. 2018. 'Afterword: The Act of Comparing (Both Sides, Now)'. In Pollock & Elman, pp. 310–342.

Chase-Dunn, C. & D. Khutkyy 2021. 'The Evolution of Geopolitics and Imperialism in Interpolity Systems'. In Bang, Bayly & Scheidel, Vol. 1, pp. 111–154.

Chaudhuri, K. N. 1985. *Trade and Civilisation in the Indian Ocean: An Economic History from the Rise of Islam to 1750.* Cambridge.

— 1990. *Asia Before Europe: Economy and Civilisation of the Indian Ocean from the Rise of Islam to 1750.* Cambridge.

Chen, S. 2002. 'Son of Heaven and Son of God: Interactions among Ancient Asiatic Cultures Regarding Sacral Kingship and Theophoric Names'. *Journal of the Royal Asiatic Society,* Vol. 12(3), pp. 289–325.

Chida-Razvi, M. M. 2014. 'The Perception of Reception: The Importance of Sir Thomas Roe at the Mughal Court of Jahangir'. *Journal of World History,* Vol. 25(2/3), pp. 263–284.

Christensen, K. K. 2025. *Local and Imperial Culture in the Roman Provinces.* London.

Clarence-Smith, W. G. & D. Eltis 2011. 'White Servitude'. In Eltis & Engerman, pp. 132–159.

Clastres, P. 1987. *Society against the State: Essays in Political Anthropology.* Trans. R. Hurley. New York.

Cobb, M. 2015. 'The Chronology of Roman Trade in the Indian Ocean from Augustus to Early Third Century AD'. *Journal of the Social and Economic History of the Orient,* Vol. 58, pp. 362–418.

— 2018. 'Pepper Consumption in the Roman Empire'. *Journal of the Economic and Social History of the Orient,* Vol. 61, pp. 519–559.

Coe, M. D. 2021. 'The Khmer Empire'. In Bang, Bayly & Scheidel, Vol. 2, pp. 430–449.

Coert, J. forthcoming. *Inservientes reges: Klientelherrscher als Reichselite des frühen Prinzipats.* Stuttgart.

Collins, J. J. & J. G. Manning eds. 2016. *Revolt and Resistance in the Ancient Classical World and the Near East: In the Crucible of Empire.* Leiden.

Conrad, S. 2016. *What Is Global History?* Princeton.
Cooper, F. 2005. *Colonialism in Question: Theory, Knowledge, History*. Berkeley.
Crawford, M. H. & J. M. Reynolds. 1977–1979. 'The Aezani Copy of the Price Edict'. *Zeitschrift für Papyrologie und Epigraphik*, Vol. 26, pp. 125–151, and Vol. 34, pp. 163–210.
Crone, P. 1980. *Slaves on Horses: The Evolution of the Islamic Polity*. Cambridge.
 1986. 'The Tribe and the State'. In John A. Hall ed., *States in History*. Oxford, pp. 48–77.
 1989. *Pre-industrial Societies: Anatomy of the Pre-modern World*. Oxford.
 2006. 'Imperial Trauma: The Case of the Arabs'. In *Common Knowledge*, Vol. 12(1), pp. 107–116.
 2012. *The Nativist Prophets of Early Islamic Iran: Rural Revolt and Local Zoroastrianism*. Cambridge.
Crone, P. & M. Hinds 1986. *God's Caliph: Religious Authority in the First Centuries of Islam*. Cambridge.
Crosby, A. W. 1986. *Ecological Imperialism: The Biological Expansion of Europe, 900–1900*. Cambridge.
Crossley, P. K. 2008. *What Is Global History?* Cambridge.
 2011. 'Slavery in Early Modern China'. In D. Eltis & S. L. Engerman eds., *The Cambridge World History of Slavery, Vol. 3: A.D. 1420–1804*. Cambridge, pp. 186–213.
 2019. *Hammer and Anvil: Nomad Rulers at the Forge of the Modern World*. Lanham.
 2021. 'The Qing Empire: Three Governments in One State and the Stability of Manchu Rule'. In Bang, Bayly & Scheidel, Vol. 2, pp. 810–831.
Csáky, V., D. Gerber, I. Koncz et al. 2020. 'Genetic Insights into the Social Organisation of the Avar Period Elite in the 7th century AD Carpathian Basin'. *Nature: Science Reports*, Vol. 10(948).
Cunliffe, B. 2015. *By Steppe, Desert and Ocean: The Birth of Eurasia*. Oxford.
Darwin, J. 2007. *After Tamerlane: The Rise and Fall of Global Empires, 1400–2000*. London.
Davis, N. Z. 2006. *Trickster Travels: A Sixteenth-Century Muslim Between Worlds*. New York.
Davy, M. & J. White, trans. and ed. 1783. *Institutes Political and Military Written Originally in the Mogul Language by the Great Timour*. Oxford.
De Ligt, L. 2012. *Peasants, Citizens and Soldiers: Studies in the Demographic History of Roman Italy, 225 BC–AD 100*. Cambridge.
De Romanis, F. 2015. 'Comparative Perspectives on the Pepper Trade'. In De Romanis & Maiuro, pp. 127–150.
 2020. *The Indo-Roman Pepper Trade and the Muziris Papyrus*. Oxford.
De Romanis, F. & M. Maiuro eds. 2015. *Across the Ocean: Nine Essays on Indo-Mediterranean Trade*. Leiden.
De Ste Croix, G. E. M. 1981. *The Class Struggle in the Ancient Greek World*. London.

Debie, M. 2024. *Alexandre Le Grand En Syriaque. Maître des lieux, des savoirs et des temps*. Paris.
Dench, E. 2018. *Empire and Political Cultures in the Roman World*. Cambridge.
Di Cosmo, N. 2002. *Ancient China and its Enemies: The Rise of Nomadic Power in East Asian History*. Cambridge.
Di Cosmo, N. & M. Maas eds. 2018. *Empires and Exchanges in Eurasian Late Antiquity: Rome, China, Iran, and the Steppe, ca. 250–750*. Cambridge.
Diamond, J. 1997. *Guns, Germs and Steel: The Fates of Human Societies*. New York.
Dijkstra, K. 1995. *Life and Loyalty: A Study in the Socio-religious Culture of Syria and Mesopotamia in the Graeco-Roman Period Based on Epigraphical Evidence*. Leiden.
Donde, D. 2014. "The Mughal Sikander: Influence of the Romance of Alexander on Mughal Manuscript Painting." Paper delivered to the International Conference on Greek Studies: An Asian Perspective (25th–28th February 2014) Organized by Greek Chair, School of Language, Literature & Culture Studies. Jawaharlal Nehru University, New Delhi.
Dossey, L. 2010. *Peasant and Empire in Christian North Africa*. Berkeley.
Doyle, L. 2020. *Interimperiality: Vying Empires, Gendered Labour, and the Literary Arts of Alliance*. Durham.
Dreyer, E. L. 2007. *Zheng He: China and the Oceans in the Early Ming Dynasty, 1405–1433*. New York.
DuBois, P. 2014. *A Million and One Gods: The Persistence of Polytheism*. Cambridge, MA.
Duindam, J. 2015. *Dynasties: A Global History of Power 1300–1800*. Cambridge.
Duindam, J., T. Artan & M. Kunt eds. 2011. *Royal Courts in Dynastic States and Empires: A Global Perspective*. Leiden.
Durand, J. 1974. Historical Estimates of World Population: An Evaluation. *University of Pennsylvania, Population Center, Analytical and Technical Reports*, No. 10. Philadelphia.
Dyson, S. 1975. 'Native Revolt Patterns in the Roman Empire'. In H. Temporini ed., *Aufstieg und Niedergang der römischen Welt*, Vol. II, Band 3. Berlin, pp. 138–175.
Eaton, R. M. 1993. *The Rise of Islam and the Bengal Frontier, 1204–1760*. Berkeley.
2019. *India in the Persianate Age 1000–1765*. London.
Eberle, L. P. 2018. 'Resistance'. In C. Noreña ed., *A Cultural History of Western Empires in Antiquity*. London, pp. 177–199.
Eckstein, A. M. 2007. *Mediterranean Anarchy, Interstate War, and the Rise of Rome*. Berkeley.
Edelmann, B. 2007. *Religiöse Herrschaftslegitimation in der Antike: Die religiöse Legitimation orientalisch-ägyptischer und griechisch-hellenistischer Herrscher im Vergleich*. St. Katharinen.
Eich, A. 2015. *Die Söhne des Mars: Eine Geschichte des Krieges von der Steinzeit bis zum Ende der Antike*. München.
Eich, P. 2015. 'The Common Denominator: Late Roman Imperial Bureaucracy from a Comparative Perspective'. In Scheidel, pp. 90–149.

Eisenberg, M. & L. Mordechai 2019. 'The Justinianic Plague: An Interdisciplinary Review'. *Byzantine and Modern Greek Studies*, Vol. 43(2), pp. 156–180.
Elias, N. 1969. *Die höfische Gesellschaft: Untersuchungen zur Soziologie des Königtums und der höfischen Aristokratie*. Berlin.
Elliott, C. P. 2016. 'The Antonine Plague, Climate Change and Local Violence in Roman Egypt'. *Past and Present*, Vol. 231, pp. 3–31.
 2024. *Pox Romana: The Plague That Shook the Roman World*. Princeton.
Elliott, M. 2009. *Emperor Qianlong: Son of Heaven, Man of the World*. Upper Saddle River, NJ.
Elm, S. 2012. *Sons of Hellenism, Fathers of the Church: Emperor Julian, Gregory of Nazianzus, and the Vision of Rome*. Berkeley.
Elman, B. A. 2000. *A Cultural History of Civil Examinations in Late Imperial China*. Berkeley.
Elsner, J. ed. 2020. *Empires of Faith in Late Antiquity: Histories of Art and Religion from India to Ireland*. Cambridge.
Elsner, J., S. Lenk & G. Parpulov eds. 2017. *Imagining the Divine: Art and the Rise of World Religions*. Oxford.
Eltis, D. & S. L. Engerman eds. 2011. *The Cambridge World History of Slavery, Vol. 3: A.D. 1420–1804*. Cambridge.
Elvin, M. 1973. *The Pattern of the Chinese Past*. London.
 2006. *The Retreat of the Elephants: An Environmental History of China*. New Haven.
Engels, D. W. 1978. *Alexander the Great and the Logistics of the Macedonian Army*. Berkeley.
Erskine, A. 1995. 'Culture and Power in Ptolemaic Egypt: The Museum and Library of Alexander'. *Greece & Rome*, Vol. 42, pp. 38–48.
Etting, V. 2004. *Queen Margrete I (1353–1412) and the Founding of the Nordic Union*. Leiden.
Evers, K. G. 2018. *Worlds Apart Trading Together: The Organisation of Long-Distance Trade between Rome and India in Antiquity*. Oxford.
Falk, H. 2009. 'The Pious Donation of Wells in Gandhara'. In G. Mevissen & A. Banerji eds., *Prajñādhara: Essays on Asian History, Epigraphy and Culture in Honour of Gouriswar Bhattacharya*. New Delhi, pp. 23–36.
 2015. 'Indian Gold Crossing the Indian Ocean through the Millennia'. In De Romanis & Maiuro, pp. 95–113.
Fantuzzi, M. & R. Hunter 2006. *Tradition and Innovation in Hellenistic Poetry*. Cambridge.
Faruqui, M. D. 2012. *The Princes of the Mughal Empire, 1504–1719*. Cambridge.
Feinman, G. M. & J. C. Moreno García 2022. *Power and Regions in Ancient States: An Egyptian and Mesoamerican Perspective*. Cambridge.
Fejfer, J. 2008. *Roman Portraits in Context*. Berlin.
Feltham, H. B. 2009. Justinian and the International Silk Trade. *Sino-Platonic Papers*, No. 194. Philadelphia.

Filser, W. T. & Klose, W. 2024. 'La villa maritima del Capo di Sorrento'. In L. di Franco ed., *Surrentum/Sorrento: Studi e ricerche per la carta archeologica della città*. Rome, pp. 127–174.

Finer, S. E. 1975. 'State- and Nation-Building in Europe: The Role of the Military'. In Tilly, pp. 84–163.

Finkielkraut, A. 2005. *Nous autres, modernes*. Paris.

Finley, M. I. 1968. *Ancient Sicily to the Arab Conquest*. London.

1975. *The Use and Abuse of History*. New York.

1980. *Ancient Slavery and Modern Ideology*. London.

1983. *Politics in the Ancient World*. Cambridge.

1985. *The Ancient Economy*. 2nd ed. London.

1998. *Ancient Slavery and Modern Ideology*. Expanded edition by B. Shaw. Princeton.

Fischer, G. 2011. *Between Empires: Arabs, Romans, and Sasanians in Late Antiquity*. Oxford.

Flaig, E. 1992. *Den Kaiser Herausfordern: Die Usurpation im Römischen Reich*. Frankfurt.

2019. *Weltgeschichte der Sklaverei*. München.

Fleischer, C. H. 1986. *Bureaucrat and Intellectual in the Ottoman Empire: The Historian Mustafa Ali, 1541–1600*. Princeton.

2018. 'A Mediterranean Apocalypse: Prophecies of Empire in the Fifteenth and Sixteenth Centuries'. *Journal of the Social and Economic History of the Orient*, Vol. 61, pp. 18–90.

Florentino, M. & M. Amantino. 2011. 'Runaways and Quilombolas in the Americas'. In Eltis & Engerman, pp. 708–739.

Flores, J. & S. Subrahmanyam. 2004. 'The Shadow Sultan: Succession and Imposture in the Mughal Empire, 1628–1640'. *Journal of the Social and Economic History of the Orient*, Vol. 47(1), pp. 81–121.

Fogel, R. W. 2004. *The Escape from Hunger and Premature Death, 1700–2100*. Cambridge.

Foltz, R. 1998. *Conversations with Emperor Jahangir by 'Mutribi' al-Assamm of Samarqand*. Trans. from the Persian by R. Foltz. Costa Mesa.

2010. *Religions of the Silk Road: Premodern Patterns of Globalization*. 2nd ed. New York.

Ford, R. B. 2020. *Rome, China, and the Barbarians: Ethnographic Traditions and the Transformation of Empires*. Cambridge.

Forêt, P. 2000. *Mapping Chengde: The Qing Landscape Enterprise*. Honolulu.

Fournet, J. L. 1999. *Hellénisme dans l'Egypte du Vie Siècle: la bibliothèque et l'œuvre de Dioscore d'Aphrodité*, 2 vols. Cairo.

Fowden, G. 1986. *The Egyptian Hermes: A Historical Approach to the Late Antique Mind*. Princeton.

1993. *Empire to Commonwealth: Consequences of Monotheism in Late Antiquity*. Princeton.

2004. *Qusayr 'Amra: Art and the Umayyad Elite in Late Antique Syria*. Berkeley.

2014. *Before and after Muhammad: The First Millennium Refocused*. Princeton.

Fraenkel, C. 2015. *Teaching Plato in Palestine: Philosophy in a Divided World.* Princeton.
Frankfurter, D. 1998. *Religion in Roman Egypt: Assimilation and Resistance.* Princeton.
Frankopan, P. 2015. *The Silk Roads: A New History of the World.* London.
Frazer, J. G. 1890. *The Golden Bough: A Study in Comparative Religion.* 2 Vols. London.
Freedman, P. 2008. *Out of the East: Spices and the Medieval Imagination.* New Haven.
Frederiksen, R. 2011. *Greek City-Walls of the Archaic Period 900–480 BC.* Oxford.
Fricke, B. ed. 2024. *Holy Smoke: Censers across Cultures.* Munich.
Friedman, J. 2018. 'Postscript: Getting the Goods for Civilization'. In Kristiansen, Lindkvist & Myrdal, pp. 534–546.
Friesen, S. J. 2001. *Imperial Cults and the Apocalypse of John: Reading Revelation in the Ruins.* Oxford.
Friesen, S. J. & W. Scheidel. 2009. 'The Size of the Economy and the Distribution of Income in the Roman Empire'. *Journal of Roman Studies*, Vol. 99, pp. 61–91.
Fukuyama, F. 2011. *The Origins of Political Order: From Prehuman Times to the French Revolution.* New York.
Gaddis, J. L. 2019. *On Grand Strategy.* New York.
Gallivan, P. A. 1973. 'The False Neros: A Re-examination'. *Historia*, Vol. 22(2), pp. 364–365.
Gambash, G. 2015. *Rome and Provincial Resistance.* New York.
Gandhi, S. 2020. *The Emperor Who Never Was: Dara Shukoh in Mughal India.* Cambridge, MA.
Garnsey, P. 1988. *Famine and Food-Supply in the Graeco-Roman World: Responses to Risk and Crisis.* Cambridge.
    2017. 'Dem Bones'. In E. Minchin and H. Jackson eds., *Text and the Material World: Essays in Honour of Graeme Clarke.* Uppsala, pp. 199–210.
Garnsey, P. & C. Humfress 2001. *The Evolution of the Late Antique World.* Cambridge.
Garnsey, P. & R. Saller 1986. *The Roman Empire: Economy, Society and Culture.* London.
Garnsey, P. & G. Woolf. 1989. 'Patronage of the Rural Poor in the Roman World'. In Wallace-Hadrill, pp. 153–170.
Gatier, P. L. 1996. 'Des girafes pour l'Empereur'. *Topoi*, Vol. 6(2), pp. 903–941.
Geertz, C. 1980. *Negara: The Theater State in Nineteenth-Century Bali.* Princeton.
    1983. *Local Knowledge: Further Essays in Interpretive Anthropology.* New York.
Gehrke, H. J. ed. 2020. *Making Civilizations: The World before 600.* In P. Lewis. A. Iriye & J. Osterhammel eds., *A History of the World*, Vol. 1, trans. E. Butler. Cambridge, MA.
Gellner, E. 1969. *Saints of the Atlas.* London.
    1981. *Muslim Society.* Cambridge.
    1983. *Nations and Nationalism.* Oxford.
    1988. *Plough, Sword and Book: The Development of Human Ideas and Institutions.* London.

Gschwend, A. J. 2010. *The Story of Süleyman: Celebrity Elephants and Other Exotica in Renaissance Portugal*. Zürich.
Geyer, M. 2018. 'The Invention of World History from the Spirit of Nonviolent Resistance'. In Burke & Mankin, pp. 55–81.
Ghobrial, J.-P. ed. 2019. *Global History and Microhistory*. New York.
Giliberti, G. 1996. *Studi Sulla Massima 'Caesar Omnia Habet'*. Torino.
Giovannini, A. ed. 1987. *Opposition et résistances à l'empire d'Auguste à Trajan*. Geneva.
Gleba, M., B. Marin-Aguílera & B. Dimova eds. *Making Cities: Economies of Production and Urbanization in Mediterranean Europe, 1000–500 BC*. Cambridge.
Golden, P. B. 2011. *Central Asia in World History*. New York.
Gommans, J. & S. R. Huseini 2022. 'Neoplatonic Kingship in the Islamic World: Akbar's Millennial History'. In Moin & Strathern, pp. 192–222.
Goodman, M. 2007. *Rome and Jerusalem: The Clash of Ancient Civilizations*. London.
  2015. 'Enemies of Rome'. In P. Garnsey & R. Saller eds., *The Roman Empire: Economy, Society and Culture*. 2nd ed. Oakland, pp. 55–71.
Goody, J. 1986. *The Logic of Writing and the Organization of Society*. Cambridge.
  1990. *The Oriental, the Ancient and the Primitive: Systems of Marriage and the Family in the Pre-industrial Societies of Eurasia*. Cambridge.
  1996. *The East in the West*. Cambridge.
Gosden, C. 2004. *Archaeology and Colonialism: Cultural Contact from 5000 BC to the Present*. Cambridge.
Gradel, I. 2002. *Emperor Worship and Roman Religion*. Oxford.
Graeber, D. & M. Sahlins. 2017. *On Kings*. Chicago.
Graeber, D. & D. Wengrow. 2021. *The Dawn of Everything: A New History of Humanity*. New York.
Green-Mercado, M. 2018. 'Speaking the End Times: Early Modern Politics and Religion from Iberia to Central Asia'. *Journal of the Social and Economic History of the Orient*, Vol. 61, pp. 1–17.
Grewe, B.-S. & K. Hofmeester eds. 2016. *Luxury in Global Perspective: Objects and Practices, 1600–2000*. Cambridge.
Gruzinski, S. 2012. *L'Aigle et le Dragon. Démesure européenne et mondialisation au XVIe siècle*. Paris.
Guha, R. 1983. *Elementary Aspects of Peasant Insurgency in Colonial India*. Delhi.
  2002. *History at the Limit of World-History*. New York.
Gungwu, W. 1958. *The Nanhai Trade: A Study of the Early History of Chinese Trade in the South China Sea*. Kuala Lumpur.
Habib, I. 1999. *The Agrarian System of Mughal India 1556–1707*. 2nd rev. ed. Oxford.
Haldén, P. 2020. *Family Power: Kinship, War and Political Orders in Eurasia, 500–2018*. Cambridge.
Haldon, J. 1993. *The State and the Tributary Mode of Production*. London.
Haldon, J., Elton, H., Huebner S. R. et al. 2018. 'Plagues, Climate Change, and the End of an Empire: A Response to Kyle Harper's *The Fate of Rome* (1): Climate'. *History Compass*, Vol. 16, p. 12.

Hall, J. A. 1985. *Powers and Liberties: The Causes and Consequences of the Rise of the West*. London.
   2010. *Ernest Gellner: An Intellectual Biography*. London.
   2012. 'Imperial Universalism: Further Thoughts'. In Bang & Kolodziejczyk, pp. 304–309.
   2024. *Nations, States and Empires*. Cambridge.
Hallett, C. H. 2021. 'The Wood Comes to the City: Ancient Trees, Sacred Groves, and the "Greening" of Early Augustan Rome'. *Religion in the Roman Empire*, Vol. 7(2), pp. 221–274.
Haloun, G. & W. B. Henning 1952. 'The Compendium of the Doctrines and Styles of the Teachings of Mani, the Buddha of Light'. *Asia Major*, 3, pp. 184–212.
Hansen, M. H. ed. 2000. *A Comparative Study of Thirty City-State Cultures: An Investigation Conducted by the Copenhagen Polis Centre*. Copenhagen.
   ed. 2002. *A Comparative Study of Six City-State Cultures*. Copenhagen.
   2006. *Polis: An Introduction to the Ancient Greek City-State*. Oxford.
Hansen, V. 2012. *The Silk Road: A New History*. Oxford.
   2020. *The Year 1000: When Explorers Connected the World – and Globalization Began*. New York.
Harder, A. 2012. *Callimachus: Aetia*. 2 vols. New York.
Harker, A. 2008. *Loyalty and Dissidence in Roman Egypt: The Case of the Acta Alexandrinorum*. Cambridge.
Harper, K. 2011. *Slavery in the Late Roman World AD 275–425*. Cambridge.
   2017. *The Fate of Rome: Climate, Disease, and the End of an Empire*. Princeton.
   2021. *Plagues upon the Earth: Disease and the Course of Human History*. Princeton.
Harris, W. V. 1978. *War and Imperialism in Republican Rome, 327–70 BC*. Oxford.
   1989. *Ancient Literacy*. Cambridge, MA.
Hasan, F. 2004. *State and Locality in Mughal India: Power Relations in Western India, c. 1572–1730*. Cambridge.
Hathaway, J. 2018. *The Chief Eunuch of the Ottoman Harem: From African Slave to Power-Broker*. Cambridge.
Hauken, T. 1998. *Petition and Response: An Epigraphic Study of Petitions to Roman Emperors, 181–249*. Bergen.
Healey, J. F. 2010. *Aramaic Inscriptions and Documents of the Roman Period*. Oxford.
Hegel, G. W. F. 2020. *Vorlesungen über die Philosophie der Weltgeschichte*. In Hrgb. W. Jaeschke ed., *Gesammelte Werke*, Vol. 27(4). Hamburg.
Hekster, O. 2022. *Caesar Rules: The Emperor in the Changing Roman World (c. 50 BC – AD 565)*. Cambridge.
Hense, M. 2019. 'The Great Temple of Berenike'. In A. Manzo, C. Zazzaro & D. J. De Falco eds., *Stories of Globalisation: The Red Sea and the Persian Gulf from Late Prehistory to Early Modernity*. Leiden, pp. 246–263.
Heslin, P. 2015. *The Museum of Augustus: The Temple of Apollo in Pompeii, the Portico of Philippus in Rome, and Latin Poetry*. Los Angeles.

Hevia, J. 1995. *Cherishing Men from Afar: Qing Guest Ritual and the Macartney Embassy of 1793*. Durham, NC.
  2012. *The Imperial Security State: British Colonial Knowledge and Empire-Building in Asia*. Cambridge.
Hilsdale, C. 2021. 'Imperial Monumentalism, Ceremony, and Forms of Pageantry: The Inter-Imperial Obelisk in Istanbul'. In Bang, Bayly & Scheidel, Vol. 1, pp. 223–264.
Hingley, R. 2005. *Globalizing Roman Culture: Unity, Diversity and Empire*. Abingdon.
Hintze, A. 1997. *The Mughal Empire and Its Decline: An Interpretation of the Sources of Social Power*. Ashgate.
Hirth, F. 1885. *China and the Roman Orient: Researches into Their Ancient and Medieval Relations as Represented in Old Chinese Records*. Shanghai.
Hobsbawm, E. J. 1959. *Primitive Rebels. Studies in Archaic Forms of Social Movement in the 19th and 20th Centuries*. Manchester.
  1969. *Bandits*. New York.
Hodgson, M. G. S. 1974. *The Venture of Islam. Conscience and History in a World Civilization*, 3 vols. Chicago.
  1993. *Rethinking World History: Essays on Europe, Islam, and World History*. Edited, with an introduction and conclusion, by Edmund Burke III. Cambridge.
Hodos, T. ed. 2017. *The Routledge Handbook of Archaeology and Globalization*. Abingdon.
  2020. *The Archaeology of the Mediterranean Iron Age: A Globalising World c. 1100–600 BCE*. Cambridge.
Holmes, C. & N. Standen eds. 2018. *The Global Middle Ages*. Oxford.
Honigman, S. 2003. *The Septuagint and Homeric Scholarship in Alexandria: Study in the Narrative of the 'Letter of Aristeas'*. London.
Hoo, M. 2022. 'Globalization beyond the Silk Road: Writing Global History of Ancient Economies'. In von Reden, Dwivedi, Fabian et al., Vol. 2, pp. 7–29.
Hopkins, A. G. ed. 2002. *Globalization in World History*. London.
Hopkins, K. 1978. *Conquerors and Slaves*. Cambridge.
  1999. *A World Full of Gods: Pagans, Jews and Christians in the Roman Empire*. London.
  2018. *Sociological Studies in Roman History*. Edited by C. Kelly. Cambridge.
Hopwood, K. 1989. 'Bandits, Elites and Rural Order'. In Wallace-Hadrill, pp. 171–188.
Horden, P. & N. Purcell 2000. *The Corrupting Sea: A Study of Mediterranean History*. Oxford.
Hostetler, L. & Wu Xuemei 2022. *Qing Imperial Illustrations of Tributary Peoples (Huang Qing zhigong tu): A Cultural Cartography of Empire*. Leiden.
Howard-Johnston, J. 2010. *Witnesses to a World Crisis. Historians and Histories of the Middle East in the Seventh Century*. Oxford.
Howse, R. 2014. *Leo Strauss: Man of Peace*. Cambridge.
Hui, V. T. 2005. *War and State Formation in Ancient China and Early Modern Europe*. Cambridge.

Hulsewé, A. F. P. & M. A. N. Loewe 1979. *China in Central Asia: The Early Stage: 125 B.C.–A.D. 23. An Annotated Translation of Chapters 61 and 96 of the History of the Former Han Dynasty*. Leiden.

Hume, D. 1993. *Dialogues Concerning Natural Religion (1779) and Natural History of Religion (1757, 1777)*. Oxford.

Hunt, L. 2014. *Writing History in the Global Era*. New York.

Huyse, P. 1999. *Die dreisprachige Inschrift Šābuhrs I. an der Ka'ba-i Zardušt*. Corpus Inscriptionum Iranicarum, Part III, Vol. 1.1. London.

Hyland, J. 2017. *Persian Interventions: The Achaemenid Empire, Athens and Sparta, 450–386 BCE*. Baltimore.

Inglebert, H. 2018. *Histoire universelle ou Histoire globale?: Les temps du monde*. Paris.

Jarzombek, M. 2024. *The Long Millennium: Affluence, Architecture and Its Dark Matter Economy*. Abingdon.

Jasanof, M. 2005. *Edge of Empire. Conquest and Collecting in the East 1750–1850*. London.

Jaspers, K. 1949. *Vom Ursprung und Ziel der Geschichte*. München.

Jenco, L. 2015. *Changing Referents: Learning across Space and Time in China and the West*. New York.

Jennings, J. 2011. *Globalizations and the Ancient World*. Cambridge.

Jesnick, I. J. 1997. *The Image of Orpheus in Roman Mosaic: An Exploration of the Figure of Orpheus in Graeco-Roman Art and Culture with Special Reference to Its Expression in the Medium of Mosaic in Late Antiquity*. Oxford.

Johanning, K. forthcoming. *Reading the Signs: Hierarchy, Ambiguity, and Cosmopolitanism in the Roman Empire and Early India*. Potsdamer Altertumswissenschaftliche Beiträge. Stuttgart.

Johnson, W. A. 2012. *Readers and Reading Culture in the High Roman Empire: A Study of Elite Communities*. Oxford.

Johnson, W. J. 1994. *The Bhagavad Gita: A New Translation*. Oxford.

Johnston, A. C. 2017. *The Sons of Remus: Identity in Roman Gaul and Spain*. Cambridge, MA.

Jolowicz, D. & J. Elsner eds. 2023. *Articulating Resistance under the Roman Empire*. Cambridge.

Jones, A. H. M. 1964. *The Later Roman Empire, 284–602: A Social Economic and Administrative Survey*. 2 Vols. Norman, OK.

Kafadar, C. 2007. 'A Rome of One's Own: Reflections on Cultural Geography and Identity in the Lands of Rum'. *Muqarnas*, Vol. 24, pp. 7–21.

Katsari, C. & E. Dal Lago eds. 2008. *Slave Systems: Ancient and Modern*. Cambridge.

Keay, J. 2006. *The Spice Route: A History*. Berkeley.

Kelly, B. 2011. *Petitions, Litigation, and Social Control in Roman Egypt*. Oxford Studies in Ancient Documents. Oxford.

Kelly, C. 2004. *Ruling the Later Roman Empire*. Cambridge, MA.

Kennedy, P. 1988. *The Rise and Fall of the Great Powers: Economic Change and Military Conflict from 1500 to 2000*. London.

Kia, M. 2020. *Persianate Selves: Memories of Place and Origin before Nationalism*. Stanford.
Kim, H. J. 2013. *The Huns, Rome and the Birth of Europe*. Cambridge.
Kinoshita, S. 2012. 'Animals and the Medieval Culture of Empire'. In J. J. Cohen ed., *Animal, Vegetable, Mineral: Ethics and Objects*. Santa Barbara, pp. 35–63.
Kinra, R. 2015. *Writing Self, Writing Empire: Chandar Bhan Brahman and the Cultural World of the Indo-Persian State Secretary*. Oakland.
  2021. 'The Mughal Empire'. In Bang, Bayly & Scheidel, Vol. 2, pp. 751–788.
Koch, E. 1988. *Shah Jahan and Orpheus*. Graz.
  2006. *The Complete Taj Mahal and the Riverfront Gardens of Agra*. London.
  2010. 'The Mughal Emperor as Solomon, Majnun, and Orpheus or the Album as a Think Tank for Allegory'. *Muqarnas*, Vol. 27, pp. 277–311.
  2012. 'How the Mughal *Pādshāhs* Referenced Iran in Their Visual Construction of Universal Rule'. In Bang & Koloziejczyk, pp. 194–209.
Kolodziejczyk, D. 2012. 'Khan, Caliph, Tsar and Imperator: The Multiple Identities of the Ottoman Sultan'. In Bang & Kolodziejczyk, pp. 175–193.
König, J. & G. Woolf eds. 2013. *Encyclopedism from Antiquity to the Renaissance*. Cambridge.
Konstan, D. & K. Raaflaub eds. 2009. *Epic and History*. Chichester.
Kosmin, P. J. 2014. *The Land of the Elephant Kings: Space, Territory, and Ideology in the Seleucid Empire*. Cambridge, MA.
Kradin, N. N. 2014. *Nomads of Inner Asia in Transition*. Moscow.
Kristiansen, K. 2018a. 'Theorising Trade and Civilization'. In Kristiansen, Lindkvist & Myrdal, pp. 1–24.
  2018b. 'The Rise of Bronze Age Peripheries and the Expansion of International Trade, 1950–1100 BCE'. In Kristiansen, Linkvist & Myrdal, pp. 87–112.
Kristiansen, K., T. Lindkvist & J. Myrdal eds. 2018. *Trade and Civilisation: Economic Networks and Cultural Ties, from Prehistory to the Early Modern Era*. Cambridge.
Kropff, A. 2016. 'An English Translation of the Edict on Maximum Prices, Also Known as the Price Edict of Diocletian'. http://kark.uib.no/antikk/dias/priceedict.pdf.
Kuhn, P. A. 1977. 'Origins of the Taiping Vision: Cross-Cultural Dimensions of a Chinese Rebellion'. *Comparative Studies in Society and History*, Vol. 19(3), pp. 350–366.
  1978. 'The Taiping Rebellion'. In J. K. Fairbank ed., *The Cambridge History of China*. Vol. 10. Cambridge, pp. 264–317.
  1990. *Soulstealers: The Chinese Sorcery Scare of 1768*. Cambridge, MA.
  2002. *Origins of the Modern Chinese State*. Stanford.
Kuhrt, A. & S. Sherwin-White. 1993. *From Samarkhand to Sardis: A New Approach to the Seleucid Empire*. London.
Kumar, K. 2017. *Visions of Empire: How Five Imperial Regimes Shaped the World*. Princeton.
  2021. *Empires: A Historical and Political Sociology*. Cambridge.
Kutchner, N. A. 2018. *Eunuch and Emperor in the Great Age of Qing Rule*. Oakland.

Lal, R. 2005. *Domesticity and Power in the Early Mughal World*. Cambridge.
Lane, F. C. 1958. 'Economic Consequences of Organised Violence'. *Journal of Economic History*, Vol. 18(4), pp. 401–417.
Lane Fox, R. 1986. *Pagans and Christians*. London.
Larsen, M. D. C. 2018. *Gospels before the Book*. Oxford.
Larsen, M. T. 1996. *The Conquest of Assyria: Excavations in an Antique Land*. London.
   2000. 'The Old Assyrian City-State'. In Hansen, pp. 77–88.
   2015. *Ancient Kanesh: A Merchant Colony in Bronze Age Anatolia*. Cambridge.
Lattimore, O. 1940. *Inner Asian Frontiers of China*. New York.
   1962. *Studies in Frontier History: Collected Papers 1928–1958*. Paris.
Lauffer, S. 1971. *Diokletians Preisedikt*. Berlin.
Lavan, M. 2017. 'Writing Revolt in the Early Roman Empire'. In J. Firnhaber-Baker & D. Schoenars eds., *The Routledge History Handbook of Medieval Revolt*. New York, pp. 19–38.
Lavan, M., R. Payne & J. Weisweiler eds. 2016. *Cosmopolitanism and Empire*. New York.
Lee, A. D. 1997. 'The Army'. In A. Cameron & P. Garnsey eds., *The Cambridge Ancient History, Vol. 13: The Late Empire, 337–425AD*. Cambridge, pp. 211–237.
Lefevre, C. 2019. 'Mughal Early Modernity and Royal Ādāb: Shaykh ʿAbd al-Ḥaqq Muḥaddith Dihlawī's Sufi Voice of Reform'. In C. Mayeur-Jaouen ed., *Adab and Modernity. A 'Civilising Process'? (Sixteenth–Twenty-First Century)*. Leiden, pp. 63–92.
Lendon, J. E. 1997. *Empire of Honour: The Art of Government in the Roman World*. Oxford.
   2005. *Soldiers and Ghosts: A History of Battle in Classical Antiquity*. New Haven.
Lenowitz, H. 1998. *The Jewish Messiahs: From the Galilee to Crown Heights*. Oxford.
Lenski, N. 2016. *Constantine and the Cities: Imperial Authority and Civic Politics*. Philadelphia.
   2018. 'Framing the Question: What Is a Slave Society?' In Lenski & Cameron, pp. 15–60.
Lenski, N. & C. M. Cameron eds. 2018. *What Is a Slave Society? The Practice of Slavery in Global Perspective*. Cambridge.
Leppin, H. 2017. 'Globalisierung des Altertums in zweierlei Gestalt'. *Historische Zeitschrift*, Vol. 304, pp. 147–156.
Letteney, M. 2023. *The Christianization of Knowledge in Late Antiquity: Intellectual and Material Transformations*. Cambridge.
Lewis, D. M. 2018. *Greek Slave Systems in their Eastern Mediterranean Context, c. 800–146 BC*. Oxford.
Lewis, M. E. 2007. *The Early Chinese Empires: Qin and Han*. Cambridge, MA.
Lieberman, V. 2003–2009. *Strange Parallels: South East Asia in Global Context, c. 800–1830*. 2 vols. Cambridge.

2010. 'A Zone of Refuge in South East Asia? Reconceptualizing Interior Spaces'. *Journal of Global History*, Vol. 5, pp. 333–346.
Lieven, D. 2000. *Empire: The Russian Empire and Its Rivals*. London.
2022. *In the Shadow of the Gods: The Emperor in World History*. London.
Lim, R. 2018. 'Trade and Exchanges along the Silk and Steppe Routes in Late Antique Eurasia'. In Di Cosmo & Mass, pp. 70–83.
Lloyd, G. E. R. 1996. *Adversaries and Authorities: Investigations into Ancient Greek and Chinese Science*. Cambridge.
2015. *Analogical Investigations: Historical and Cross-cultural Perspectives on Human Reasoning*. Cambridge.
Lloyd, G. E. R. & N. Sivin. 2002. *The Way and the Word: Science and Medicine in Early China and Greece*. New Haven.
Lloyd, G. E. R. & J. J. Zhao eds. 2018. *Ancient Greece and China Compared*. Cambridge.
Lo Cascio, E. 2000. *Il Princeps e Il Suo Impero. Studi di storia amministrativa e finanziaria romana*. Bari.
Loewe, M. 1986. 'The Concept of Sovereignty'. In Twitchett & Loewe, pp. 726–746.
2006. *The Government of the Qin and Han Empires 221 BCE – 220 CE*. Cambridge.
Longworth, P. 1975. 'The Pretender Phenomenon in Eighteenth-Century Russia'. *Past & Present*, Vol. 66, pp. 61–83.
Lovejoy, P. E. 2011. *Transformations in Slavery: A History of Slavery in Africa*. 3rd ed. Cambridge.
Ludlow, F. & J. G. Manning. 2014. 'Revolts under the Ptolemies: A Paleoclimatological Perspective'. In Collins & Manning, pp. 154–171.
Lukacs, J. R. 2002. 'Hunting and Gathering Strategies in Prehistoric India: A Biocultural Perspective on Trade and Subsistence'. In K. D. Morrison & J. L. Junker eds., *Forager-Traders in South and Southeast Asia Long-Term Histories*. Cambridge, pp. 42–61.
Ma, J. 2013. 'Hellenistic Empires'. In Bang & Scheidel, pp. 324–357.
2024. *Polis: A New History of the Ancient Greek City-State from the Early Iron Age to the End of Antiquity*. Princeton.
MacGregor, N. 2021. *À monde nouveau, nouveaux musées. Les musées, les monuments et la communauté réinventée*. Paris.
MacMullen, R. 1966. *Enemies of the Roman Order: Treason, Unrest, and Alienation in the Empire*. Cambridge, MA.
MacKenzie, J. M. 1995. *History, Theory and the Arts*. Manchester.
Maier, C. S. 2007. *Among Empires: American Ascendancy and Its Predecessors*. Cambridge, MA.
Maine, H. S. 1861. *Ancient Law: Its Connection to the History of Early Society*. New York.
Majeed, J. 2021. 'Literature of Empire: Difference, Creativity, and Cosmopolitanism'. In Bang, Bayly & Scheidel, Vol. 1, pp. 342–371.
Malamud, M. 2009. *Ancient Rome and Modern America*. Chichester.

Malinowski, B. 1922. *Argonauts of the Western Pacific*. New York.
Malkin, I. 2011. *A Small Greek World: Networks in the Ancient Mediterranean*. Oxford.
Mallette, K. 2021. *Lives of the Great Languages: Arabic and Latin in the Medieval Mediterranean*. Chicago.
Mann, M. 1986. *The Sources of Social Power*. Vol. 1. Cambridge.
  2012. *The Sources of Social Power*. Vol. 3. Cambridge.
Manning, J. G. 2018. *The Open Sea: The Economic Life of the Ancient Mediterranean World from the Iron Age to the Rise of Rome*. Princeton.
Marriott, M. ed. 1955. *Village India: Studies in the Little Community*. Chicago.
Marsham, A. 2021. 'The Caliphate'. In Bang, Bayly & Scheidel, pp. 355–379.
Marsili, F. 2003. 'The Myth of Huangdi, the Ding Vases, and the Quest for Immortality in the *Shiji*: Some Aspects of Sima Qian's "Laicism"'. *Rivista Degli Studi Orientali*, Vol. 77, pp. 135–168.
Marx, K. 1859. *Zur Kritik der Politischen Ökonomie*. Berlin.
  1964. *Pre-capitalist Economic Formations*. With an introduction by Eric Hobsbawm. New York.
Mattern, S. 1999. *Rome and the Enemy: Imperial Strategy in the Principate*. Berkeley.
  2008. *Galen and the Rhetoric of Healing*. Baltimore.
Mattingly, D. ed. 2013. *The Archaeology of Fazzān. Vol. 4: Survey and Excavations at Old Jarma (Ancient Garama) Carried Out by C. M. Daniels (1962–69) and the Fazzān Project (1997–2001)*. London.
Maxfield, V. & Peacock, D. 2001–2007. *The Roman Imperial Quarries: Survey and Excavation at Mons Porphyrites 1994–1998*. 2 vols. London.
Mayer, E. E. 2012. *The Ancient Middle Classes: Urban Life and Aesthetics in the Roman Empire, 100 BCE–250 CE*. Cambridge, MA.
  2018. 'Tanti non emo, Sexte, Piper: Pepper Prices, Roman Consumer Culture, and the Bulk of Indo-Roman Trade'. *Journal of the Social and Economic History of the Orient*, Vol. 61(4), pp. 560–589.
McAnany, P. & N. Yoffee eds. 2010. *Questioning Collapse: Human Resilience, Ecological Vulnerability, and the Aftermath of Empire*. Cambridge.
McCormick, M. 2003. 'Rats, Communications, and Plague: Toward an Ecological History'. *Journal of Interdisciplinary History*, Vol. 34, pp. 1–25.
McEvedy, C. & R. E. Jones 1978. *Atlas of World Population History*. London.
McGing, B. 2016. 'Revolting Subjects: Empires and Insurrection, Ancient and Modern'. In Collins & Manning, pp. 139–153.
McKeown, A. 2012. 'What Are the Units of World History?' In D. Northrop ed., *A Companion to World History*. Chichester, pp. 79–93.
McKitterick, R. 2008. *Charlemagne: The Formation of a European Identity*. Cambridge.
McNeill, J. R. 1992. *The Mountains of the Mediterranean World: An Environmental History*. Cambridge.
McNeill, W. H. 1976. *Plagues and Peoples*. New York.
  1982. *The Pursuit of Power*. Chicago.

Mearsheimer, J. J. 2001. *The Tragedy of Great Power Politics*. New York.
Meier, M. 2019. *Geschichte der Völkerwanderung: Europa, Asien und Afrika vom 3. bis zum 8. Jahrhundert*. München.
Metcalf, B. D. ed. 1984. *Moral Conduct and Authority: The Place of Adab in South Asian Islam*. Berkeley.
Meyer-Zwiffelhoffer, E. 2002. Πολιτικῶς ἀρχειν. *Zum Regierungsstil der senatorischen Statthalter in den kaiserzeitlichen griechischen Provinzen*. Stuttgart.
Mikkelsen, G. 2003. 'Dunhuang I: The Cave Sites; Manichean Texts'. *Encyclopedia Iranica*. Leiden.
Miksic, J. 2021. 'Srivijaya'. In Bang, Bayly & Scheidel, Vol. 2, pp. 401–429.
Millar, F. 1977. *The Emperor in the Roman World*. London.
  1993. *The Roman Near East, 31 BC–AD 337*. Cambridge, MA.
  1998. *The Crowd in Rome in the Late Republic*. Ann Arbor.
Miller, J. I. 1969. *The Spice Trade of the Roman Empire, 29 B.C.–A.D. 641*. Oxford.
Minissale, G. 2009. *Images of Thought: Visuality in Islamic India*. 2nd ed. Newcastle.
Mitchell, S. & P. van Nuffelen eds. 2010. *One God: Pagan Monotheism in the Roman Empire*. Cambridge.
Moin A. A. 2012. *The Millennial Sovereign: Sacred Kingship and Sainthood in Islam*. New York.
Moin, A. A. & A. Strathern eds. 2022. *Sacred Kingship in World History: Between Immanence and Transcendence*. New York.
Möller, A. 2000. *Naukratis: Trade in Archaic Greece*. Oxford.
Momigliano, A. 1977. *Alien Wisdom: The Limits of Hellenization*. Cambridge.
  1987. 'Some Preliminary Remarks on the "Religious Opposition" to the Roman Empire'. In Giovannini, pp. 103–129.
Monson, A. & W. Scheidel eds. 2015. *Fiscal Regimes and the Political Economy of Premodern States*. Cambridge.
Monroe, C. M. 2018. 'Marginalizing Civilization: The Phoenician Redefinition of Power circa 1300–800 BC'. In Kristiansen, Lindkvist & Myrdal, pp. 195–241.
Moore, B., Jr. 1966. *Social Origins of Dictatorship and Democracy: Lord and Peasant in the Making of the Modern World*. Boston.
Moore, R. I. 2000. *The First European Revolution, c. 970–1215*. Oxford.
Moreno García, J.-C. 2021. 'Egypt, Old to New Kingdom (2686–1069 BCE)'. In Bang, Bayly & Scheidel, Vol. 2, pp. 13–42.
Morris, I. 2010. *Why the West Rules – For Now*. New York.
  2013. 'Greek Multicity States'. In Bang & Scheidel, pp. 279–303.
Morris, I. & W. Scheidel eds. 2009. *Dynamics of Ancient Empires: State-Power from Assyria to Byzantium*. New York.
Morris, L. 2021. *The Begram Hoard and Its Context*. München.
Morrison, K. D. 2002. 'Pepper in the Hills: Upland–Lowland Exchange and the Intensification of the Spice Trade'. In K. D. Morrison & J. L. Junker eds., *Forager-Traders in South and Southeast Asia Long-Term Histories*. Cambridge, pp. 105–128.

Motyl, A. J. 2001. *Imperial Ends: The Decay, Collapse, and Revival of Empires.* New York.
Moule, M. C. & Pelliott, P. 1938. *Marco Polo. The Description of the World.* London.
Mouritsen, H. 2011. *The Freedman in the Roman World.* Cambridge.
Moyer, I. S. 2011. *Egypt and the Limits of Hellenism.* Cambridge.
Mullen, A. ed. 2024. *Social Factors in the Latinization of the Roman West.* Oxford.
Münkler, H. 2006. *Imperien: Die Logik der Weltherrschaft – vom alten Rom bis zu den Vereinigten Staaten.* Berlin.
Murphy, T. 2004. *Pliny's Natural History: The Empire in the Encyclopedia.* Oxford.
Mutschler, F.-H. & A. Mittag eds. 2008. *Conceiving the Empire: China and Rome Compared.* Oxford.
Naas, V. 2011. 'Imperialism, *Mirabilia*, and Knowledge: Some Paradoxes in *The Naturalis Historia*'. In R. Gibson & R. Morello eds., *Pliny the Elder: Themes and Contexts.* Leiden, pp. 57–70.
Nabhan, G. P. 2014. *Cumin, Camels, and Caravans: A Spice Odyssey.* Berkeley.
Naerebout, F. G. & H. W. Singor 2014. *Antiquity: Greeks and Romans in Context.* Chichester.
Naipaul, V. S. 1982. *Among the Believers: An Islamic Journey.* New York.
Nappo, D. 2015. 'Roman Policy on the Red Sea in the Second Century CE'. In De Romanis & Maiuro, pp. 55–72.
N'Diaye, T. 2008. *Le génocide voilé.* Paris.
Necipoğlu, G. 1989. 'Süleyman the Magnificent and the Representation of Power in the Context of Ottoman-Habsburg-Papal Rivalry'. *The Art Bulletin*, Vol. 71, pp. 401–427.
  1992. *Architecture, Ceremonial, and Power: The Topkapi Palace in the Fifteenth and Sixteenth Centuries.* Boston.
  2005. *The Age of Sinan: Architectural Culture in the Ottoman Empire.* Princeton.
Nelis, D. P. 2012. 'Poetry and Politics in Vergil's Georgics'. In *Mythe et pouvoir à l'époque hellénistique.* Lyon, pp. 397–413.
Netz, R. 2020. *Scale, Space and Canon in Ancient Literary Culture.* Cambridge.
Neuwirth, A. 2014. *Koranforschung: Eine politische Philologie? Bibel, Koran und Islamentstehung im Spiegel Spätantiker Textpolitik und moderner Philologie.* Berlin.
Nussbaum, M. C. 2018. *The Cosmopolitan Tradition: A Noble but Flawed Ideal.* Cambridge, MA.
O'Brien, P. K. 2012. 'Fiscal and Financial Preconditions for the Formation of Developmental States in the West and the East from the Conquest of Ceuta (1415) to the Opium War (1839)'. *Journal of World History*, Vol. 23, pp. 513–553.
O'Meara, D. J. 2003. *Platonopolis: Platonic Political Philosophy in Late Antiquity.* Oxford.
Ober, J. 2017. *Demopolis: Democracy before Liberalism in Theory and Practice.* Cambridge.

Oka, R. 2018. 'Trade, Traders, and Trading Systems: Macromodelling of Trade, Commerce, and Civilization in the Indian Ocean'. In Kristiansen, Lindkvist & Myrdal, pp. 279–319.

Olko, J. 2012. 'Aztec Universalism: Ideology and Status Symbols in the Service of Empire-Building'. In Bang & Kolodziejczyk, pp. 253–279.

Omissi, A. 2018. *Emperors and Usurpers in the Later Roman Empire: Civil War, Panegyric, and the Construction of Legitimacy*. Oxford.

Osborne, R. 1987. *Classical Landscape with Figures: The Ancient Greek City and Its Countryside*. London.

Osborne, R. & B. Cunliffe eds. 2005. *Mediterranean Urbanization 800–600 BC*. Oxford.

Østergaard, U. 1991. *Akropolis Persepolis Tur/Retur: Hellenismeforskningen Mellem Orientalisme, Hellenisme, Imperialisme og Afkolonisering*. Aarhus.

Otis, B. 1964. *Virgil: A Study in Civilized Poetry*. Oxford.

Palombo, C. 2021. 'Studying Trade and Local Economies in Early Islamicate Societies: Responses to the "Long-Divergence" Debate from Islamic History'. *Cromohs*, Vol. 24, pp. 161–181.

Papathomas, A. 2000. 'Der erste Beleg für die "historische Quelle" des Alexanderromans: Identifizierung und Neuedition der Vorlage für Pseudo-Kallisthenes, Historia Alexandri Magni I 42'. *Philologus*, Vol. 144, pp. 217–226.

Pappano, A. E. 1937. 'The False Neros'. *The Classical Journal*, Vol. 32(7), pp. 385–392.

Parker, G. 1998. *The Grand Strategy of the Philip II*. New Haven.

Parker, G. 2008. *The Making of Roman India*. Cambridge.

Paschalis, M. 2007. 'The Greek and the Latin Alexander Romance: Comparative Readings'. In M. Paschalis, S. Frangoulidis, S. Harrison et al., eds., *The Greek and the Roman Novel: Parallel Readings*. Groningen, pp. 70–102.

Patterson, O. 1982. *Slavery and Social Death*. Cambridge, MA.

Payne, R. E. 2016. *A State of Mixture: Christians, Zoroastrians, and Iranian Political Culture in Late Antiquity*. Berkeley.

Peacock, D. & D. Williams eds. 2007. *Food for the Gods: New Light on the Ancient Incense Trade*. Oxford.

Peacock, D. & L. Blue eds. 2006–2011. *Myos Hormos: Quseir al-Qadim, Roman and Islamic Ports on the Red Sea*. 2 Vols. Oxford.

Pekáry, T. 1987. '*Seditio*: Unruhen und Revolten im römischen Reich von Augustus bis Commodus'. *Ancient Society*, Vol. 18, pp. 133–150.

Peterson, T. 1980. 'The Arab Influence on Western European Cooking'. *Journal of Medieval History*, Vol. 6, pp. 317–340.

Pezzolo, L. 2021. 'The Venetian Empire'. In Bang, Bayly & Scheidel, Vol. 2, pp. 621–647.

Pfeiffer, R. 1968. *History of Classical Scholarship: From the Beginnings to the End of the Hellenistic Age*. Oxford.

Pfeiffer, S. & H. Klinkott 2021. 'Legitimizing the Foreign King in the Ptolemaic and Seleucid Empires: The Role of Local Elites and Priests'. In C. Fisher-Bovet &

S. von Reden eds., *Comparing the Ptolemaic and Seleucid Empires*. Cambridge, pp. 233–261.
Pines, Y. 2012. *The Everlasting Empire: The Political Culture of Ancient China and Its Imperial Legacy*. Princeton.
Pines, Y. & J. Rüpke eds. 2021. *The Limits of Universal Rule: Eurasian Empires Compared*. Cambridge.
Pippidi, D. M. ed. 1976. *Assimilation et résistance à la culture Gréco-Romaine dans le monde ancien. Travaux du VIe Congrès international d'études classiques (Madrid, Septembre 1974)*. Paris.
Pitts, M. 2018. *The Roman Object Revolution: Objectscapes and Intra-Cultural Connectivity in Northwest Europe*. Amsterdam.
Pitts, M. & M. J. Versluys eds. 2015. *Globalisation and the Roman World: World History, Connectivity and Material Culture*. Cambridge.
Pollock, S. ed. 2003. *Literary Cultures in History: Reconstructions from South Asia*. Berkeley.
　2006. *The Language of the Gods in the World of Men: Sanskrit, Culture, and Power in Premodern India*. Berkeley.
Pollock, S. I. & B. Elman eds. 2018. *What China and India Once Were: The Pasts That May Shape the Global Future*. New York.
Pomeranz, K. 2000. *The Great Divergence: China, Europe, and the Making of the Modern World Economy*. Princeton.
Pomeranz, M., F. Bellino, C. Mayeur-Jaouen et al., eds. 2018. *L'Adab, Toujours Recommence: 'Origins', Transmissions, and Metamorphoses of Adab Literature*. Leiden.
Porter, D. L. ed. 2012. *Comparative Early Modernities*. New York.
Poser, R. 2021. 'He Wants to Save Classics from Whiteness: Can the Field Survive?' *New York Times Magazine*, 2 Feb.
Potter, D. S. 1990. *Prophecy and History in the Crisis of the Roman Empire: A Historical Commentary on the Thirteenth Sibylline Oracle*. Oxford.
　1994. *Prophets and Emperors: Human and Divine Authority from Augustus to Theodosius*. Cambridge, MA.
Price, R. ed. 1996. *Maroon Societies: Rebel Slave Communities in the Americas*. Baltimore.
Price, S. 1984. *Rituals and Power: The Roman Imperial Cult in Asia Minor*. Cambridge.
　1987. 'From Noble Funerals to Divine Cult: The Consecration of Roman Emperors'. In Cannadine & Price, pp. 56–105.
Pu Yi 1987. *The Last Manchu: The Autobiography of Henry Pu Yi, Last Emperor of China*. Edited, with a revised preface and epilogue, by Paul Kramer. New York.
Puett, M. 2015. 'Ghosts, Gods, and the Coming Apocalypse: Empire and Religion in Early China and Ancient Rome'. In Scheidel, pp. 230–260.
Quinn, J. 2024. *How the World Made the West: A 4000-Year History*. London.
Raaflaub, K. A. 2011. 'From City-State to Empire: Rome in Comparative Perspective'. In Arnason & Raaflaub, pp. 39–67.

Ram-Prasad, K. 2019. 'Reclaiming the Ancient World: Towards a Decolonised Classics'. *Eidolon*. https://eidolon.pub/reclaiming-the-ancient-world-c481fc19c0e3.

Raschke M. G. 1978. 'New Studies in Roman Commerce with the East'. In H. Temporini & W. Haase eds., *Aufstieg und Niedergang der Römischen Welt*. Vol. 2.9.2. Berlin, pp. 604–1378.

Rathbone, D. 2001. 'The "Muziris" Papyrus (SB XVIII 13167): Financing Roman Trade with India'. In *Alexandrian Studies II in Honour of Mostafa el Abbadi. Bulletin de la Société Archéologique d'Alexandrie*, Vol. 46. Alexandria, pp. 39–50.

Rawson, J. 1999. 'The Eternal Palaces of the Western Han: A New View of the Universe'. *Artibus Asiae*, Vol. 59, pp. 5–58.

Reinink, G. J. 2002. 'Heraclius, the New Alexander: Apocalyptic Prophecies during the Reign of Heraclius'. In G. J. Reinink & B. H. Stolte eds., *The Reign of Heraclius (610–641): Crisis and Confrontation*. Leuven, pp. 81–94.

Ray, H. P. 2007. *Colonial Archaeology in South Asia*. Oxford.

Rezakhani, K. 2010. 'The Road That Never Was: The Silk Road and Trans-Eurasian Exchange'. *Comparative Studies of South Asia, Africa and the Middle East*, Vol. 30(3), pp. 420–433.

2017. *ReOrienting the Sasanians: East Iran in Late Antiquity*. Edinburgh.

Richards, J. F. 1975. *Mughal Administration in Golconda*. Oxford.

1993. *The Mughal Empire*. Cambridge.

Richardson, S. 2017. 'Before Things Worked: A "Low-Power" Model of Early Mesopotamia'. In Ando & Richardson, pp. 17–62.

Richter, D. S. 2011. *Cosmopolis: Imagining Community in Late Classical Athens and the Early Roman Empire*. New York.

Rieber, A. J. 2014. *The Struggle for the Eurasian Borderlands: From the Rise of Early Modern Empires to the End of the First World War*. Cambridge.

Ripat, P. 2011. 'Expelling Misconceptions: Astrologers at Rome'. *Classical Philology*, Vol. 106, pp. 115–154.

Robinson, C. F. 2013. 'The First Islamic'. In Bang & Scheidel, pp. 518–538.

Robinson, D. M. 2021. 'The Ming Empire'. In Bang, Bayly & Scheidel, Vol. 2, pp. 533–570.

Roller, D. W. 2003. *The World of Juba II and Kleopatra Selene: Royal Scholarship on Rome's African Frontier*. New York.

Rollinger, R. 2021. 'Herodotus and Empire: Ancient Near Eastern Monuments and Their Cultural Recycling in Herodotus' Histories'. In J. Ben-Dov & F. Rojas eds., *Afterlives of Ancient Rock-Cut Monuments in the Near East: Carvings in and out of Time*. Leiden, pp. 186–220.

Rosenstein, N. 2004. *Rome at War: Farms, Families and Death in the Middle Republic*. Chapel Hill.

2009. 'War, State Formation, and the Evolution of Military Institutions in Ancient China and Rome'. In Scheidel, pp. 24–51.

Rostovtzeff, M. 1926. *The Social and Economic History of the Roman Empire*. Oxford.

Rowlands, M. & D. Fuller 2018. 'Deconstructing Civilization: A "Neolithic" Alternative'. In Kristiansen, Lindkvist & Myrdal, pp. 172–194.
Rushdie, S. 1982. 'Imaginary Homelands'. *London Review of Books*, Vol. 4(18) (7 October), pp. 18–19.
Ruffini, G. R. 2018. *Life in an Egyptian Village in Late Antiquity: Aphrodito before and after the Islamic Conquest*. Cambridge.
Ruffino, L. & E. Vidal 2010. 'Early Colonization of Mediterranean Islands by Rattus Rattus: A Review of Zooarcheological Data'. *Biological Invasions*, Vol. 12(8), pp. 2389–2394.
Sachsenmaier, D. 2018. *Global Entanglements of a Man Who Never Travelled: A Seventeenth-Century Chinese Christian and His Conflicted Worlds*. New York.
Şahin, K. 2013. *Empire and Power in the Reign of Süleyman: Narrating the Sixteenth-Century Ottoman World*. Cambridge.
Sahlins, M. 1972. *Stone Age Economics*. Chicago.
Said, E. 1978. *Orientalism*. New York.
Sallares, R. 2014. 'Disease'. In P. Horden & S. Kinoshita eds., *A Companion to Mediterranean History*. Chichester, pp. 250–262.
Saller, R. 1982. *Personal Patronage in the Early Empire*. Cambridge.
Salmeri, G. 1997. 'Dell'Uso Dell'Incenso in Epoca Romana'. In A. Avanzini ed., *Profumi d'Arabia: Atti del convegno Pisa 1995*. Roma, pp. 529–540.
Salvatore, A. 2021. 'More (or Less) Than a Civilizational "Formation"? Islam as the "Black Hole" of Comparative Civilizational Analysis'. In S. A. Arjomand & S. Kalberg eds., *From World Religions to Axial Civilizations and Beyond*. New York, pp. 161–182.
Sarris, P. 2011. *Empires of Faith: The Fall of Rome to the Rise of Islam, 500–700*. Oxford.
Schafer, E. H. 1963. *The Golden Peaches of Samarkand: A Study of T'ang Exotics*. Berkeley.
Scheidel, W. 2005. 'Human Mobility in Roman Italy, II: The Slave Population'. *Journal of Roman Studies*, Vol. 95, pp. 64–79.
  ed. 2009. *Rome and China: Comparative Perspectives on Ancient World Empires*. New York.
  2011. 'The Roman Slave Supply'. In Bradley & Cartledge, pp. 287–310.
  2013. 'Studying the State'. In Bang & Scheidel, pp. 5–57.
  ed. 2015a. *State Power in Ancient China and Rome*. New York.
  2015b. 'The Early Roman Monarchy'. In Monson & Scheidel, pp. 229–257.
  2015c. 'State Revenue and Expenditure in the Han and Roman Empires'. In Scheidel 2015a, pp. 150–180.
  2017. The Great Leveler: Violence and the History of Inequality from the Stone Age to the Twenty-First Century. Princeton.
  ed. 2018. *The Science of Roman History: Biology, Climate, and the Future of the Past*. Princeton.
  2019. *Escape from Rome: The Failure of Empire and the Road to Prosperity*. Princeton.
  2022. 'Resetting History's Dial? A Critique of David Graeber and David Wengrow, *The Dawn of Everything: A New History of Humanity*'.

Cliodynamics SI: Leading Scholars of the Past Comment on Dawn of Everything. Review, Vol. 4, pp. 1–27.
2025. *What Is Ancient History?* Princeton.
Schmidt-Colinet, A., A. Stauffer & K. As'ad 2000. *Die Textilien aus Palmyra: Neue und alte Funde*. Tadmur.
Schneider, R. M. 2006. 'Orientalism in Late Antiquity. The Oriental in Imperial and Christian Imagery'. In J. Wiesehöfer & P. Huyse eds., *Eran und Aneran. Studien zu den Beziehungen zwischen dem Sasanidenreich und der Mittelmeerwelt*. München, pp. 241–278.
2012. 'The Making of Oriental Rome: Shaping the Trojan Legend'. In Bang & Kolodziejczyk, pp. 76–129.
Schoemaker, S. J. 2014. '"The Reign of God Has Come": Eschatology and Empire in Late Antiquity and Early Islam'. *Arabica*, Vol. 61, pp. 514–558.
Schulz, R. J. 2024. *To the Ends of the Earth: How Ancient Explorers, Scientists, and Traders Connected the World*. Trans. R. Savage. Oxford.
Schwartz, A. 2009. *Reinstating the Hoplite: Arms, Armour and Phalanx Fighting in Archaic and Classical Greece*. Stuttgart.
Scott, J. C. 1985. *Weapons of the Weak: Everyday Forms of Peasant Resistance*. New Haven, CT.
2009. *The Art of Not Being Governed: An Anarchist History of Upland Southeast Asia*. New Haven, CT.
2017. *Against the Grain: A Deep History of the Earliest States*. New Haven.
Scullard, H. H. 1974. *The Elephant in the Greek and Roman World*. London.
Seland, E. H. 2011. 'The Persian Gulf or the Red Sea? Two Axes in Ancient Indian Ocean Trade, Where to Go and Why'. *World Archaeology*, Vol 43(3), pp. 398–409.
2012. 'The *Liber Pontificalis* and the Red Sea Trade of the Early to Mid-4th Century AD'. In D. A. Aigius et al. eds., *Navigated Spaces, Connected Places*. Oxford, pp. 117–126.
2014a. 'Archaeology of Trade in the Western Indian Ocean, 300 BC–AD 700'. *Journal of Archaeological Research* 22, pp. 367–402.
2014b. 'Caravans, Smugglers and Trading Fairs: Organizing Textile Trade on the Syrian Frontier'. In K. Droß-Krüpe ed., *Textile Trading and Distribution in Antiquity: Textilhandel und -distribution in der Antike*. Wiesbaden, pp. 83–90.
2022. *A Global History of the Ancient World: Asia, Europe and Africa before Islam*. Abingdon.
Sen, T. 2003. *Buddhism, Diplomacy, and Trade: The Realignment of India-China Relations, 600–1400*. Honolulu.
Shahbazi, A. S. 2014. *Persepolis: Die altpersische Residenzstadt*. Darmstadt.
Shaw, B. D. 1984. 'Bandits in the Roman Empire'. *Past and Present*, Vol. 105, pp. 3–52.
1995. *Rulers, Nomads, and Christians in Roman North Africa*. Aldershot.
1999. 'War and Violence'. In G. W. Bowersock, P. Brown & O. Grabar eds., *Late Antiquity: A Guide to the Postclassical World*. Cambridge, MA, pp. 130–169.

2011. *Sacred Violence: African Christians and Sectarian Hatred in the Age of Augustine*. Cambridge.
Shelach-Lavi, G. 2015. *The Archaeology of Early China: From Prehistory to the Han Dynasty*. Cambridge.
Sherratt, S. 2016. 'From "Institutional" to "Private": Traders, Routes and Commerce from the Late Bronze to the Iron Age'. In J.-C. Moreno García ed., *Dynamics of Production in the Ancient Near East*. Oxford, pp. 289–301.
Sidebotham, S. E. 1996. 'Roman Interests in the Red Sea and Indian Ocean'. In J. Reade ed., *The Indian Ocean in Antiquity*. London, pp. 287–312.
    2011. *Berenike and the Ancient Maritime Spice Route*. Berkeley.
Sijpesteijn, P. M. 2013. *Shaping a Muslim State: The World of a Mid-Eighth-Century Egyptian Official*. Oxford.
Silver, L. 2008. *Marketing Maximilian: The Visual Ideology of a Holy Roman Emperor*. Princeton.
Sim, M. 2007. *Remastering Morals with Aristotle and Confucius*. Cambridge.
Sommer, M. 2005. *Roms orientalische Steppengrenze: Palmyra – Edessa – Dura Europos – Hatra. Eine Kulturgeschichte von Pompeius bis Diocletian*. Stuttgart.
Spawforth, A. J. S. ed. 2007. *The Court and Court Society in Ancient Monarchies*. Cambridge.
Spence, J. D. 1974. *Emperor of China: Self-Portrait of K'anghsi*. New York.
    1999. *God's Chinese Son: The Taiping Heavenly Kingdom of Hong Xiuquan*. London.
Spyrou, M. A., L. Musralina, G. A. Gnecchi Ruscone et al. 2022. 'The Source of the Black Death in 14th-Century Central Eurasia'. *Nature*, 15 June 2022.
Steensgaard, N. 1974. *The Asian Trade Revolution of the 17th Century: The East India Companies and the Decline of the Caravan Trade*. Chicago.
Steinkeller, P. 2021. 'The Sargonic and Ur III Empires'. In Bang, Bayly & Scheidel 2021, Vol. 2, pp. 43–72.
Stephens, S. A. 2003. *Seeing Double: Intercultural Poetics in Ptolemaic Alexandria*. Berkeley.
Stevens, K. 2016. 'Empire Begins at Home: Local Elites and Imperial Ideologies in Hellenistic Greece and Babylonia'. In Lavan, Payne & Weisweiler, pp. 65–88.
Stockton, D. 1979. *The Gracchi*. Oxford.
Stoneman, R., K. Erickson & I. Netton eds. 2012. *The Alexander Romance in Persia and the East*. Groningen.
Strathern, A. 2019. *Unearthly Powers: Religious and Political Change in World History*. Cambridge.
Strauch, I. ed. 2012. *Foreign Sailors on Socotra: The Inscriptions and Drawings from the Cave Hoq*. Bremen.
Stroh, W. 2007. *Latein ist tot, es lebe Latein: kleine Geschichte einer grossen Sprache*. Berlin.
Strootman, R. 2017. *The Birdcage of the Muses: Patronage of the Arts and Sciences at the Ptolemaic Imperial Court, 305–222 BCE*. Leuven.
Stroumsa, G. G. 2015. *The Making of the Abrahamic Religions in Late Antiquity*. Oxford.

Subrahmanyam, S. 1997. 'Connected Histories: Notes towards a Reconfiguration of Early Modern Eurasia'. In *Modern Asian Studies*, Vol. 31(3), pp. 735–762.

1998. 'Hearing Voices: Vignettes of Early Modernity in South Asia, 1400–1750'. *Daedalus*, Vol. 127(3), pp. 75–104.

2003. 'Turning the Stones Over: Sixteenth-Century Millenarianism from the Tagus to Ganges'. *Indian Economic and Social History Review*, Vol. 40, pp. 129–161.

2012. *From Tagus to the Ganges: Explorations in Connected History*. Oxford.

2022. *Connected History: Essays and Arguments*. London.

Swain, S. 1996. *Hellenism and Empire: Language, Classicism, and Power in the Greek World, AD 50–250*. Oxford.

Syros, V. 2012. 'An Early Modern South Asian Thinker on the Rise and Decline of Empires: Shāh Walī Allāh of Delhi, the Mughals, and the Byzantines'. *Journal of World History*, Vol. 23(4), pp. 793–840.

Táíwò, O. 2022. *Against Decolonization: Taking African Agency Seriously*. London.

Tambiah, S. J. 1976. *World Conqueror and World Renouncer: A Study of Buddhism and Polity in Thailand against a Historical Background*. Cambridge.

Terrenato, N. 2019. *The Early Roman Expansion into Italy: Elite Negotiation and Family Agendas*. Cambridge.

Tezcan, B. 2010. *The Second Ottoman Empire: Political and Social Transformation in the Early Modern World*. Cambridge.

Thackston, W. M. 1999. *The Jahangirnama: Memoirs of Jahangir, Emperor of India*. Translated, edited and annotated by W. M. Thackston. Oxford.

2002. *The Baburnama: Memoirs of Babur, Prince and Emperor*. Translated, edited and annotated by W. H. Thackston. Introduction by Salman Rushdie. New York.

Thapar, R. 1997. *Aśoka and the Decline of the Mauryas*. 2nd ed. Oxford.

1999. *Śakuntalā: Texts, Readings, Histories*. New York.

Thomas, N. 1994. *Colonialism's Culture: Anthropology, Travel and Government*. Princeton.

Thompson, E. A. 1952. 'Peasant Revolts in Late Roman Gaul and Spain'. *Past & Present*, Vol. 2, pp. 11–23.

Thompson, R. W., J. Howard-Johnston & P. Greenwood 1999. *The Armenian History Attributed to Sebeos. Part I, Translation and Notes*. Liverpool.

Thorner, D. 1965. 'Peasant Economy as a Category in Economic History'. In M. I. Finley ed., *Deuxième Conférence Internationale d'Histoire Économique, Aix-en-Provence*, Vol 2. Paris, pp. 287–300.

Tiersch, C. 2015. 'Zwischen Resistenz und Integration. Lokale Clanchefs im römischen Nordafrika'. In E. Baltrusch & J. Wilker eds., *Amici – socii – clientes? Abhängige Herrschaft im Imperium Romanum*. Berlin, pp. 243–273.

Tilly, C. ed. 1975. *The Formation of National States in Western Europe*. Princeton.

1985. 'War Making and State Making as Organised Crime'. In R. B. Evans, D. Rueschemeyer & T. Skocpol eds., *Bringing the State Back In*. Cambridge, pp. 169–191.

1992. *Coercion, Capital, and European States, AD 990–1992*. Oxford.

Tokarczuk, O. 2021. *The Books of Jacob*. Trans. Jennifer Croft. London. (Polish edition, *Księgi Jakubowe*, Cracow, 2014.)
Toledano, E. R. 2011. 'Enslavement in the Ottoman Empire in the Early Modern Period'. In Eltis & Engerman, pp. 25–46.
Tomber, R. 2008. *Indo-Roman Trade: From Pots to Pepper*. London.
Tougher, S. 2020. *The Roman Castrati: Eunuchs in the Roman Empire*. London.
Toynbee, A. 1962–1964 (1934–1961). *A Study of History*. Vols. 1–12, paperback edition. Oxford.
Trautman, T. R. 2015. *Elephants and Kings: An Environmental History*. Chicago.
Trigger, B. 2006. *A History of Archaeological Thought*. 2nd ed. Cambridge.
Truschke, A. 2016. *Culture of Encounters: Sanskrit at the Mughal Court*. New York.
Tsing, A. 2015. *The Mushroom at the End of the World: On the Possibility of Life in Capitalist Ruins*. Princeton.
Twitchett, D. & M. Loewe eds. 1986. *The Cambridge History of China. Vol. 1: The Ch'in and Han Empires, 221 BC–AD 220*. Cambridge.
Van Berkel, M. & J. Duindam eds. 2018. *Prince, Pen and Sword: Eurasian Perspectives*. Leiden.
Van Creveld, M. 1999. *The Rise and Decline of the State*. Cambridge.
Van Dam, R. 1985. *Leadership and Community in Late Antique Gaul*. Berkeley.
  2007. *The Roman Revolution of Constantine*. Cambridge.
  2010. *Rome and Constantinople: Rewriting Roman History During Late Antiquity*. Waco.
Van der Veen, M. & J. Morales. 2015. 'The Roman and Islamic Spice Trade: New Archaeological Evidence'. *Journal of Ethnopharmacology*, Vol. 167, pp. 54–63.
Vankeerberghen, G. 2021. 'Of Gold and Purple: Nobles in Western Han China and Republican Rome'. In Beck and Vankeerberghen, pp. 25–69.
Van Oyen, A. 2020. *The Socio-economics of Roman Storage: Agriculture, Trade, and Family*. Cambridge.
Van Thiel, H. 1974. *Leben und Taten Alexanders von Makedonien: Der griechische Alexanderroman nach der Handschrift L*. Darmstadt.
Vasunia, P., A. Blanshard, M. Leonard et al. (The Postclassicisms Collective). 2020. *Postclassicisms*. Chicago.
Veblen, T. 1899. *The Theory of the Leisure Class: An Economic Study of Institutions*. New York.
Veïsse, A.-E. 2022. 'The "Great Theban Revolt", 206–186'. In P. J. Kosmin & I. S. Moyer eds., *Cultures of Resistance in the Hellenistic East*. Oxford, pp. 57–73.
Versluys, M. J. 2017. *Visual Style and Constructing Identity in the Hellenistic World: Nemrud Dağ and Commagene under Antiochos I*. Cambridge.
Veyne, P. 1976. *Le pain e le cirque: Sociologie historique d'un pluralisme politique*. Paris.
Vlassopoulos, K. 2014. 'Which Comparative Histories for Ancient Historians'. *Synthesis*, Vol. 21, pp. 31–47.
  2021. *Historicising Ancient Slavery*. Edinburgh.
Vogel, H. U. 2013. *Marco Polo Was in China: New Evidence from Currencies, Salts and Revenues*. Leiden.

Von Reden, S. 2015. 'Global Economic History'. In Benjamin, pp. 29–54.
Von Reden, S., D. Dwivedi, L. Fabian et al. eds. 2020. *Handbook of Ancient Afro-Eurasian Economies. Vol. 1: Contexts.* Boston.
Von Reden, S., L. Fabian & E. J. S. Weaverdyck eds. 2022. *Handbook of Ancient Afro-Eurasian Economies. Vol. 2: Local, Regional, and Imperial Economies.* Boston.
Von Reden, S., D. Dwivedi, L. Fabian et al. eds. 2023. *Handbook of Ancient Afro-Eurasian Economies. Vol. 3: Frontier-Zone Processes and Transimperial Exchange.* Boston.
Wagner, K. A. 2007. *Thuggee: Banditry and the British in Early Nineteenth Century India.* Basingstoke.
  2010. *The Great Fear of 1857: Rumours, Conspiracies and the Making of the Indian Uprising.* Oxford.
  2021. 'Resistance, Rebellion, and the Subaltern'. In Bang, Bayly & Scheidel, Vol. 1, pp. 416–436.
Waguespack, N. 2012. 'Early Paleoindians, from Colonization to Folsom'. In T. R. Pauketat ed., *The Oxford Handbook of North American Archaeology.* Oxford, pp. 86–95.
Wallace-Hadrill, A. ed. 1989. *Patronage in Ancient Society.* London.
  1994. *Houses and Society in Pompeii and Herculaneum.* Princeton.
  1996. 'The Imperial Court'. In A. Bowman, E. Champlin & A. Lintott eds., *The Cambridge Ancient History, Vol. 10: The Augustan Empire, 43 BC–AD 69.* 2nd ed. Cambridge, pp. 283–308.
  2008. *Rome's Cultural Revolution.* Cambridge.
Wallerstein, I. 1974. *The Modern World System, Vol. 1: Capitalist Agriculture and the Origins of the European World Economy in the Sixteenth Century.* New York.
Walter, G. 1966. *Die Völkerschaften auf den Reliefs von Persepolis: Historische Studien über den sogenannten Tributzug an der Apadanatreppe.* Berlin.
Waltz, K. 1979. *Theory of International Politics.* Reading.
Wang, G. 1958. *The Nanhai Trade: A Study of the Early History of Chinese Trade in the South China Sea.* Kuala Lumpur.
Watanabe-O'Kelly, H. 2021. *Projecting Imperial Power: New Nineteenth-Century Emperors and the Public Sphere.* Oxford.
Waters, M. W. 2021. 'The Achaemenid Persian Empire: From the Medes to Alexander'. In Bang, Bayly & Scheidel, Vol. 2, pp. 111–136.
Watson, A. 1992. *The Evolution of International Society: A Comparative Historical Analysis.* London.
Weaver, P. R. C. 1972. *Familia Caesaris: A Social Study of the Emperor's Freedmen and Slaves.* Cambridge.
Weaverdyck, E. J. S., L. Fabian, L. Morris et al. 2022. 'Constituting Local and Imperial Landscapes'. In Von Reden, Fabian and Weaverdyck, Vol. 2, pp. 301–338.
Weber, M. 1920–1921. *Gesammelte Aufsätze zur Religionssoziologie.* 3 vols. Tübingen.

1980 (1921). *Wirtschaft und Gesellschaft: Fünfte Revidierte Auflage v. J. Winckelmann.* Tübingen.
Weisweiler, J. 2020. 'The Heredity of Senatorial Status in the Early Empire'. *Journal of Roman Studies*, Vol. 110, pp. 29–56.
Whitfield, S. 2018. 'On the Silk Road: Trade in the Tarim?' In Kristiansen, Lindkvist & Myrdal, pp. 251–278.
Whittaker, C. R. 1994. *The Frontiers of the Roman Empire: A Social and Economic Study.* Baltimore.
Whittow, M. 1996. *The Making of Byzantium, 600–1025.* Berkeley.
   2018. 'Byzantium's Eurasian Policy in the Age of the Türk Empire'. In Di Cosmo & Maas, pp. 271–286.
Wickham, C. 2005. *Framing the Early Middle Ages: Europe and the Mediterranean 400–800.* Oxford.
   2023. *The Donkey and the Boat: Reinterpreting the Mediterranean Economy, 950–1180.* Oxford.
Wiesehöfer, J. 1978. *Der Aufstand Gaumātas und die Anfänge Dareios' I.* Bonn.
Will, Ernest. 1992. *Les Palmyréniens: La Venise des sables (Ier siècle avant – IIIéme après J.-C.).* Paris.
Wills, J. E. Jr. 1984. *Embassies and Illusions: Dutch and Portuguese Envoys to K'ang-hsi, 1666–1687.* Cambridge, MA.
Wills, J. E. Jr. ed. 2011. *China and Maritime Europe, 1500–1800: Trade, Settlement, Diplomacy, and Missions.* Cambridge.
Wink, A. 1986. *Land and Sovereignty in India: Agrarian Society and Politics under the Eighteenth-Century Maratha Svarājya.* Cambridge.
Winterling, A. 2003. *Caligula: Eine Biographie.* München.
Wittrock, B. 2015. 'The Axial Age in World History'. In Benjamin, pp. 101–119.
Wolf, E. R. 1966. *Peasants.* Englewood Cliffs, New Jersey.
   1982. *Europe and the People without History.* Berkeley.
Woolf, G. 1994. 'Becoming Roman, Staying Greek'. *Proceedings of the Cambridge Philological Society*, Vol. 40, pp. 116–143.
   2008. 'Divinity and Power in Ancient Rome'. In N. Brisch ed., *Religion and Power: Divine Kingship in the Ancient World and Beyond.* Chicago, pp. 243–260.
   2011. 'Provincial Revolts in the Early Roman Empire'. In M. Popovic ed., *The Jewish Revolt against Rome.* Leiden, pp. 27–44.
   2012. *Rome: An Empire's Story.* Oxford.
   2020. *The Life and Death of Ancient Cities: A Natural History.* Oxford.
Xin Fan 2021. *World History and National Identity in China: The Twentieth Century.* Cambridge.
Yaffe, D. 2021. 'The Color of Classics: A Discipline Focused on the Ancient World Faces a Contemporary Racial Reckoning'. *Princeton Alumni Weekly.* https://paw.princeton.edu/article/color-classics.
Yarrow, S. 2018. 'Economic Imaginaries of the Global Middle Ages'. *Past and Present, Supplement*, Vol. 13, pp. 214–231.

Yates, R.D.S. 1997. 'The City-State in Ancient China'. In D. L. Nichols & T. H. Charlton eds., *The Archaeology of City-States: Cross-Cultural Approaches*. Washington, DC, pp. 71–90.

Yoffee, N. 2005. *Myths of the Archaic State: Evolution of the Earliest Cities, States, and Civilizations*. Cambridge.

  ed. 2015. *Early Cities in Comparative Perspective, 4000 BCE–1200 CE: The Cambridge World History, Vol. 3*. Cambridge.

Yu, H., A. Jamieson, A. Hulme-Beaman et al. 2022. 'Palaeogenomic Analysis of Black Rat (*Rattus rattus*) Reveals Multiple European Introductions Associated with Human Economic History'. *Nature Communications*, May 3, Vol. 13 (1), 2399.

Yü, Y.-S. 1967. *Trade and Expansion in Han China: A Study in the Structure of Sino-Barbarian Economic Relations*. Berkeley.

Zanker, G. 2023. *Fate and the Hero in Virgil's Aeneid: Stoic World Fate and Human Responsibility*. Cambridge.

Zanker, P. 1988 *The Power of Images in the Age of Augustus*. Ann Arbor.

Zarakol, A. 2022. *Before the West: The Rise and Fall of Eastern World Orders*. Cambridge.

Zarrow, P. 2004. 'The Imperial Word in Stone. Stele Inscriptions at Chengde'. In R. W. Dunnell, M. C. Elliott, P. Forêt et al. eds., *New Qing Imperial History: The Making of Inner Asian Empire at Qing Chengde*. London, pp. 146–164.

Zelin, M. 1984. *The Magistrate's Tael: Rationalizing Fiscal Reform in Eighteenth-Century Ch'ing China*. Berkeley.

Zhao, D. 2015a. *The Confucian-Legalist State: A New Theory of Chinese History*. Oxford.

  2015b. 'The Han Bureaucracy: Its Origin, Nature, and Development'. In Scheidel, pp. 56–89.

Zhao, T. 2021. *All Under Heaven: The Tianxia System for a Possible World Order*. Trans. J. E. Harroff. Oakland.

Zielonka, J. 2006. *Europe as Empire: The Nature of the Enlarged Union*. Oxford.

Zinkina, J., D. Christian, L. Grinin et al. 2019. *A Big History of Globalization: The Emergence of a Global World System*. Cham.

Index

'archaic' globalization, 124, 130, 132, 137, 147, 151
Abbasids, the, xiii
Abraham, 92, 113, 175
Abu Tauleb Hossaini, 23
Achaemenid dynasty and empire, 25–26, 31, 38, 43, 58–60, 67, 110, 127, 179–180, 184
Acropolis, 60
Adab, 104–105
Adam, 15, 113, 150
administration, 62, 76–78, 81–82, 105–106
Adriatic, the, 138, 142
Adulis, 151
Aegean, the, 30, 38, 180
Aemilius Scaurus, Marcus, 133, 135
Aeneas, epic hero, 102
Aeneid, the, 102, 164
Afghanistan, 58, 60, 94, 103, 133, 137
Africa, xiii, 5, 7, 9, 29, 34, 49–50, 52–53, 121, 123, 133, 141, 148, 152, 161, 167–169, 172–174
African, xii, 48–49, 52, 71, 89, 125, 145, 147, 151, 167–168
Afro-Eurasia, 12, 14, 16, 20, 22, 25–26, 30–31, 36, 38, 53, 55, 61, 66, 83, 87, 99, 138, 140, 146, 149, 152, 165, 180–181, 186
Afro-Eurasian arena, 25, 40, 48, 55, 57, 77, 87, 98, 112, 123–124, 130, 147, 150, 157, 187
Afro-Eurasian history, xii, 51, 153, 155, 177, 179
Afro-Eurasian landmass, 25, 35, 57, 60, 100
Afro-Eurasian societies, 48, 61
Afro-Eurasian state making, 54, 59
Afro-Eurasian world, 26, 31, 51, 56–57, 67, 76, 79, 98, 118, 121, 125, 127, 136, 148–149, 164, 176, 182, 185–186, 188
agrarian civilizations, 12
agrarian societies, 20, 25, 160, 181, 185
agrarian world, 155–156
agricultural intensification, 33
agricultural plains, 37, 157
agricultural society, 37, 72, 131, 154, 158–160, 168, 173
agriculturalists, 31–32, 34–36, 41, 45, 173

Akbar, Mughal emperor, xiii, 94–95, 165
Alaric, 174
Alexander, the Great, 2, 28, 30, 60–61, 64, 67, 86–90, 93–96, 98, 121, 165, 180, 187–188
Alexander Romance, 86–87
Alexandria, 86, 89–90, 94, 100, 106, 108, 138, 140, 149, 164–165, 180
Algeria, 53
Ali, the fourth Caliph, 103, 168
"all under heaven", 61, 67, 78, 155
alligator, 136
alphabet, 45
Alps, 29
Altare della Patria, 3
altars, 137, 142, 167
Americas, the, 10, 14, 20–22, 31, 36, 48–49, 51, 53, 67, 123, 130, 186, 189
Ammianus Marcellinus, 144
amphitheatre, 166
Anabasis, 43, 60, 86
anachoresis, 158
anarchy, 66
Anatolia, 30, 44, 53, 140, 158
Anderson, Perry, 31, 106–108, 111–112
animal husbandry, 32–33, 70, 92, 173
anomaly, 2, 47, 55
Antropology and anthropologists, 13, 19–20, 37, 40, 49, 74, 103, 115, 134
anti-colonial struggle, 9
Antonine emperors, 122
Antonine plague, 37–38, 163
Antoninus Pius, Roman emperor, 89–90, 122
Aphrodito, the Egyptian village, 105
Apollonius of Tyana, 93, 151
Appiah, Kwame Anthony, xiii
Arabia, xiii, 145
Arabic armies, 69
Arabic conquests, 34
Arabic language, 87–88, 106
Arc de Triomphe, 2–3
archaeological, 36, 140, 142, 145, 183

223

archaeology and archaeologists, 10, 21, 123, 143, 147, 149
archaic globalization, 123–124, 132, 136–138
aristocrats, 36, 42, 45–48, 70, 73–75, 77–81, 92, 98, 103–104, 107, 110, 122, 124, 127, 131, 136–137, 163, 184
Aristotle, 43, 47, 93–94, 98
Arjuna, hero of the Bhagavad Gita, 102
Armenia, xiii
Armenian, 87–89, 117, 172, 175
armies, 34, 42, 47, 50, 60, 68, 70, 81, 83–84, 105, 121, 144, 154, 174, 184
Arminius, the Germanic rebel leader, 163
aromatics, 121, 136, 141–142, 145
artists, 96, 98
Ashoka, Mauryan emperor, xiii, 10, 61, 111
assembly, 45, 81
Assyr and Assyria, 10, 22, 30, 45
Athenian, 38, 47, 60, 66
Athens, 25, 37, 49, 66–67, 108, 179
Atlantic, the, 25, 36, 141
Atlantic Europe, 14, 137, 181
Attila, the Hun, 69, 183
Augustus, the Roman emperor, 57, 69, 73, 91, 98, 104, 134–135, 140, 156, 160, 164
    Augustan, 92, 96, 98, 135
Augustine, Saint, 53, 167
Aurangzeb, Mughal emperor, 171
Aurelian, Roman emperor, 144
Avars, the, 184–185
Avicenna, 98
axial age, the, 23, 25, 99–100, 188
axis in world history, 23, 67, 99
Azerbaijan, 88
Aztec Triple Alliance, 186
Aztecs, 68, 130

Babur, Mughal emperor, xiii, 103
Babylon, 28
Babylonian exile, 112
Babylonian Ishtar Gate, 10
Bactria, 151
Bagaudae, 156
Baghdad, xiii, 184
Bakhtin, Mikhail, 161
Balkans, the, 52, 183, 185
bandits, 156, 159
Bar Kochba, Simon, 166
barbarian, 86, 128, 150
Barbarikon, 149
Barberini Diptych, 127–128, 150
Basra, 49
Batne, 144

Bay of Bengal, 138
Bayly, C. A., xiv, 2, 15, 17, 21, 23, 25, 68, 85, 96, 110, 119, 123–124, 131–132, 135, 149, 153, 160–161, 187–188
Begram hoard, 133
Beijing, xv, xvi, 125–126, 128
Benedict, 106, 135
Bengal, 132, 146
Berenike, 141, 143, 145
Berlin, 1, 10
Bethlehem, 130
Bhabha, Homi, 111
Bhagavad Gita, 102
Bible, the
    New Testament, 112, 153
    Old Testament, 10, 175
bishops, 117, 167–168
Bithynia-Pontus, Roman province, 160
Black Death, 37–38, 187
Boas, Franz, 135
Book of Daniel, 175
Borges, Jorge Luis, 125
Boserup, Ester, 32–33
Bosporus, the, 5, 51
Boukoloi, 163, 165, 167
Brandenburger Tor, 2–3
Braudel, 182
Brazil, 48
Bronze Age, 10, 22, 30, 35–36, 38, 40–42, 45, 61, 99–100, 137–138, 140, 147, 152, 185–186
bronze alloy, 138
Brown, Peter, xiii, 114–116, 124–125, 132
Buddha, 23, 99, 113
Buddhism, 112, 118
bureaucracy, 74, 77–78
Byron, Lord, 5

Caesar (name and title), 25, 43, 58, 65, 77, 104, 125, 127, 160
caging, social, 31, 34, 37, 41, 55
Cahokia, 123
caliph, 26, 50, 114, 168, 176
    as successor of Muhammad, 75
Caliphate, xiii, 49, 168
Callimachus, 91–92
Cambyses, Achaemenid emperor, 179
camelopard, 125–126
camels, 70
Campania, 49
canon formation, 91, 100, 102
capitalism, 11, 148
Capitoline Hill, 165
captives, 52, 70
Caracalla, Roman emperor, 162
Caribbean, the, 21, 48, 53, 148

Index

plantation economies, 21, 48, 53, 148
Carthage, 2, 22, 29, 34, 45, 49, 54, 59, 61, 65
Caspian Sea., 184
Cassius Dio, 164
caste, 7
castration, 51, 78
castratoin, 79
Catholic Chruch and Christianity, 78, 110, 115, 167, 169
cavalry, 34, 70, 182
ceremonial, 51, 62, 64, 75, 85, 105, 127, 135–136, 143, 146
ceremony, 68, 75, 96, 104, 131
Chakrabarty, Dipesh, 12
Chandragupta, Mauryan emperor, xiii, 10
charismatic, 74, 132, 156–157
Charlemagne, 124, 176
Charles V, Holy Roman emperor, 164
Chengde, 110
China, 25, 58, 65, 83, 88
  agricultural expansion, 39
  and Greco-Roman antiquity, 16
  and Rome, 21
  and the frontier, 173
  and world history, 14–16
  first imperial unification, 100
  trade from, 146, 149, 153
Chinggis Khan, 69, 71
Chios, 49
Christianity, 5, 92, 98, 101, 112–113, 115–118, 169, 171, 175, 180, 188
  Protestant, 11, 153
  Nestorian, 10
Christians, 10, 112–114, 160, 167–168
chronologies, xiii, 10, 16, 22
Church, 79, 110, 117, 145, 167–169
churches, 116
Cicero, Marcus Tullius, 104, 137
Cilicia, 159
cinnamon, 146
circumnavigation of the globe, 122–123, 137, 141, 179
Circus Maximus, 76
city-state, the, 21–22, 31, 44–45, 47, 50, 65, 67
civilization, *passim*
Claudius, Roman emperor, 79
Cleopatra, Ptolemaic Queen of Egypt, 92
climate, 35–36, 39, 43
cloves, 145–146
collectors and collecting, 132–134
colonialism, 7, 12–13, 22, 26, 69, 96, 98, 111, 154, 156, 178, 180, 188
colonies, 2
Colosseum, 76, 89, 127

communication, 18, 20, 82, 105, 107, 112, 121, 154, 159, 162
comparison, xiii
  a method of contextualization, 17
  and connection, a false dichotomy, 181
  and connections, 177
  and empire, 21
  and the history of slavery, 21, 49
  as sociology, 21
  as world history, 22
  fundamental similarities, 14
  polarizing, inverse eurocentrism, 9
  risk of, 8
  vs connections, 16
  Weberian, 12
competition, 2, 30, 66–67, 69, 130, 141, 154, 168, 171
Confucianism, 112, 118
Confucius, 23, 99, 107
connected histories, 7
  before modern globalization, 178
  global connection rather than comparison, 16
  global connections, 17
  global cultural connections, 87
  marvel and wonder, 178
  the Alexander Romance, 87
connectivity, 16–17, 27, 82, 180
conquest, 2, 5–6, 29, 43, 52, 65, 69, 71–73, 75, 80, 87, 98, 106, 113, 117, 134, 147, 172
Constantine, the Great (Roman emperor), 115, 145
Constantinople, xiii, 5–6, 83, 125, 128, 151, 168, 172, 185
constitutions, 43, 47, 110
consumers, 132
consumption of diversity, 132–133, 136
context, 20–21, 27, 40, 44, 50–51, 55, 61, 91, 96, 98, 110, 113, 118, 122, 137, 152, 162, 168, 175–177, 179–180, 184
contextualize, 31, 182
contextualization, xii, 22
convergence, 17, 64, 96
Coptic, 117
Coptos, 140
core-periphery relations, 148–149
Corinth, 45
Coromandel Coast, 147–148
corruption, 72, 75, 153
cosmopolis, 86, 102–103, 107, 111–112, 117, 123
cosmopolitan, 26, 80–81, 87, 100–101, 103–107, 109–112, 116, 118, 124, 162, 170, 176, 180, 188
cosmopolitanism, 18, 87
  translocality, 100, 107, 112, 118
cosmos, 41, 74, 121
countryside, 92, 134, 154, 158, 161, 167

court, the, 75–76
  courtly languages, 87–106
  ritual constraints, 75
crocodiles, 125, 133
cult, 18, 41, 74, 114, 116, 142, 160, 166–167
Cyrus, the Great, Achaemenid emperor, 60, 184

Damascus, xiii, 56
Danube, 39, 52, 174, 183
Darah Shukoh, Mughal prince, 103
Dareios, Achaemenid emperor, 179
David, king, xv, 37, 92–93, 96, 114
debt, 158, 161, 167
decolonization, 8
decolonize, xi
decorum, 104–105
Delhi. *See* Shahjahanabad
Delian League, 66
democracy, 47
demographers, 36
demography, 18, 31–32
dhamma, 61, 111
dharma, 58
dialect, 91, 100, 109
dialects, 87, 101, 108–109, 169
dialogue, xiii, 14, 26, 42, 65, 102, 112, 114, 116, 118, 169, 186
differences, 16, 20, 22, 102, 117, 181
Diocletian, Roman emperor, 144, 167, 189
Diodorus Siculus, 45–46, 55
Dionysus, 89
Dioscorus of Aphrodito, 105
disease, 38–41, 48, 187
dispossessed, 158, 163
dissidence, 169
distinction, 72, 98, 103, 112, 132, 181
distribution of land and wealth, 46, 80, 135, 157
divine kingship, 73–74
divinity, 74, 88, 114
division, 1, 42, 68, 117, 148, 170, 172, 175–176
domesticated animals, 14, 33, 37, 48, 185
Domitian, Roman emperor, 89
Donatism, 167–169
Donatus, 167
drudgery, 33, 41, 53, 137
Druids, 165
Duketios, 45
Dunhuang, 113, 120
dynasties, xiii, 26, 61, 69, 81, 87–88, 102, 111, 146
Dürer, Albrecht, 125–126

East India companies, 122
ecology, 14, 26–28, 31–32, 56, 182
ecumene, 98, 117
ecumenic, 26, 132, 180, 182, 185

ecumenical, 96, 110
Edessa, 56
education, 104, 106
Egypt, xiii, 9, 30, 35, 38, 45, 76, 87, 89, 91–92, 105, 121, 132, 138, 140, 143, 146–147, 149, 158, 163, 165, 167, 170, 172, 179
Elagabalus, Roman emperor, 111, 142
elephants, 28–30, 39, 121, 124, 127–128, 150, 180
elites, *passim*
Elvin, Mark, 14
embassies, 64, 122, 151
empire, *passim* (see also universal empire)
emulation, 1, 58, 64, 103, 124
England, 108, 177
Enlightenment, 113
environments, 32, 36, 49, 138
epics, 88, 91–93, 99, 101–102, 104, 118
epidemic, 14, 38–39, 48, 163, 187
eschatological expectation, 153, 175
Eskandarnameh, 88
Ethiopia, 125, 145
ethnicities, 89, 121, 183
Etruria, 49
Etruscan, 45
euergetism, 58, 135
Eunuchs, 50–51, 79
Euphrates, the, 140
eurocentrism, 9, 12, 15
European trading companies, 26
Europeans, 1, 5, 7, 9, 14, 48, 96, 127–128, 150
Eurydice, 89, 92
exoticism, 121, 125, 166
  exotic goods, 141, 151
  exotic rarities, 121, 130
  exotic tributaries, 127
  exotic tributes, 62, 127
  goods, 152
  marvels of empire, 133
  medicine, 131
expansion (see also conquest)
  agricultural, 35–36, 39–40, 184
  of nineteenth century colonialism, 9
  of cosmopolitan languages, 103
  of state-making societies, 31, 180
expansionism, militarist, 65
exploitation, 49, 51, 157, 164
extraction, 82, 171

families, 32, 35, 40, 42, 49, 52, 75, 79, 81–82, 111, 163, 185
Fanon, Frantz, 111
farmers, 32–33, 36, 158
farmland, 70
Farsi, 88
Fatehpur Sikri, 94, 165

Index

Ferghana valley, 119
festivals, 118, 159, 169
feudalism, 7, 44
Finkielkraut, Alain, xii
Finley, Moses, 20–21, 23, 43, 46–47, 49, 70, 137
Firdausi, Persian poet, 88
fiscal challenges, 144, 171
fixity of writing, 100, 102
floodplains, 58, 138, 170
Florence, 94
forests, 33, 142, 151–152, 157, 171, 182
  forest people, 151
  jungle, 10, 39
Frazer, James G., 74
freedmen, 79, 109
freedom, 48
frontier, 21, 34, 37, 40, 52, 60, 69, 73, 149–152, 154, 157–158, 170–171, 173–176, 183, 185
Fronto, Marcus Cornelius, 89
Fukuyama, Francis, 15

Galen, 98
Gandhi, 9
Ganges, the, 36, 42, 61
Ganja, 88
Garamantes, the, 173–174
Gaugamela, Battle of, 28
Gaul, 43, 156, 165–166, 172
Gellner, Ernest, 13, 42, 72, 78, 114–117, 169–170
  stallions or geldings, 78
gemstones, 121, 134
gentleman, the, 81–82, 104
gentry classes, 77, 83, 109, 154, 162
Germanic Warriors, 163, 174, 176
Germs, 14
gifts, 62, 96, 124–125, 127–128, 130, 145, 149–150
  gift-giving, 135
Gilgamesh, the epic of, 99
ginger, 146
giraffes, 125
globalization, xii, xiv, 17, 45, 99, 130–131, 152, 180
Goa, 178
god and gods, 75, 94, 113, 115–116, 153, 175
  divine kingship, 73
Gok Turks, 184–185
Goody, Jack, 40, 99, 182, 187
Gordian III, Roman emperor, 56
Gospel of Matthew, 127
government and rule, 40, 42, 68, 73–75, 77–80, 83–84, 116–117, 156–157, 159, 163, 168–172, 179
Gracchi brothers, the, 46
grammars of language and kingship, 64, 101–102, 109
great powers, 21, 58, 127

Greeks, xi, xiv, 7, 9, 16, 19, 28, 31, 45, 127
Guangzhou, 153
Gulf of Aden, 141
Guptas, Indian imperial dynasty, xiii, 61, 103

Habsburgs, the, 64
Hadrian, 104, 156, 177
Hagia Sophia, 5–6
Hakkas, the, 154
Han dynasty and empire, xiii, 63, 69, 77–78, 83, 107, 119–122, 126, 131, 140, 149–150, 155, 176, 183
Hangzhou, xiv, 138, 184
Hannibal, 29, 34, 65
Harappa civilization, 10
Harun Al Rashid, 124
Hegel, G. W. F., 7, 23, 99
hegemony, 11–12, 14–15, 17, 57, 61–62, 67, 122, 149, 178
Hellenistic civilization, xiii, 61
  Hellenistic Central Asia, 31
  Hellenistic court culture, 91, 98, 100
  Hellenistic courts, 87
  Hellenistic warfare, 29
  successor monarchies, 2, 30, 61
Hellenistic rulers and elites, 28, 61, 106
Hellenistic world, 30, 39, 90, 103
Helots, the, 53, 55
Heraclea, battle of, 28
Heraclius, Roman emperor, 165
Herculaneum, 142
Hermes Trismegistus, 93
Herod, the Great, king od Judea, 62, 130
Herodotus, 44–45, 60, 179, 184
Hieroglyphs, 10, 110
Hilly regions, 142, 151–152, 157, 171
Hinduism, 112, 118
hippopotamus, 125, 133
Hodgson, Marshall, 15, 19–20, 23, 25, 185, 187
Homer, 88, 91, 108–109, 112
hoplites, 46
Horace, (Quintus Horatius Flaccus), 91
horses, 33–34, 43, 70, 119, 121, 131, 136, 149–150, 180, 182
households, 40, 50, 75, 77, 79, 83, 108, 163
  elite households, 51, 77, 122
  imperial households, 75–76
  patrimonial households, 79–80
humanitas, 104
Hume, David, 114, 116
Huns, the, 183–184
hunter-gatherers, 32–33, 36

Iberian merchants, 181
Iberian powers, the, 122

Ibn Khaldun, 71–73, 117
Iliad, the, 108–109
illiterate, the, 109, 115
imagination, xiii, 21, 125, 160
immanence, 114, 116
imperial capitals, 76, 83
imperial government
  limitations of, 84, 157
imperialism (see also conquest, universal empire), 14
import of exotic rarities, 133, 138
imports of slaves, 48, 52
imports of spices, 121, 141–143, 180
impostor, the royal, 177–179
Incas, the, 68, 186
incense, 137, 142, 189
  frankincense, 130
independence, 47, 154, 157, 161–162
India, xii, xiv, 1, 7, 10–11, 13, 15, 23, 26, 30–31, 36, 38–39, 42, 44, 53, 57–58, 61, 65, 84, 88, 94–95, 101, 103, 105, 115, 121–122, 124, 138, 140–141, 143–148, 151, 159, 170, 180
Indian Ocean, 15, 17, 96, 136–138, 140–143, 146–147, 149, 151–152, 180, 188
Indonesia, 138, 146
Indus, the, 10, 35–36, 60–61, 149
information, 99, 151, 156, 158–160
infrastructure, 30, 50, 82, 106, 154, 183
inscriptions, 58, 64, 79, 110, 142
inter-imperiality, 64
Ionians, 127
Iran, xiii, 26, 88, 110, 178, 189
Iraq, 49
irrigation, 35–36, 163
Ishmaelites, the, 175
Isidorus, 164–165, 167
Isis, the god, 114, 164
Islam, xiii, xv, 13, 15, 20, 72, 75, 92, 98, 101, 112–116, 118, 168–169, 171, 180, 185–186, 188
Istanbul. *See* Constantinople
Italy, 28–29, 45, 49, 52, 76, 156, 161, 172, 180
  Roman subject allies, 71
ivory, 121, 128, 133, 136, 150

Jahangir, Mughal Emperor, 103, 178
Jaspers, Karl, 23, 25, 99
Jerusalem, 112, 130
Jesus, 98, 112–114, 127, 153, 156
Jews, the, 90, 165–166
Jhelu, 28
John of Antioch, 177
Judaea, 62, 165–166
Judaism, 11, 112–113, 175
Julian, Roman emperor, 104, 113, 115
Jupiter, 165

justice, 93, 163, 167–168
Justinianic plague, 37–39

Kaisar-i Rum (Roman Emperor in Persian), 23, 58
Kanishka III (Kushan ruler), 58, 60
khagan, Turk and Mongol title of emperor, 25
Khmers, the, 103
Khuldabad, 171
king of kings, the, 23, 26–26, 56, 58, 62
kingship
  models of, 92, 146
  paradisiacal kingship, 96
  universal kingship, 65, 73, 87, 89, 95, 130
Kuhrt, Amelie, xiii
Kula, the, 134
Kushan dynasty, 26, 36, 58, 60, 133, 149
Kushanas, xiii, 103
Kyrgyzstan, 119

lacquer-ware, 133
Laila va Majnun (Persian epic), 92
landlords, 19, 158–159, 167, 173
landowners, 47, 84, 116, 157, 159, 162, 168
Lane, Frederic C., 68–69, 72, 116
lapis lazuli, 137
Lebanon, 45, 138
Leo X, pope, 124
Lepcis Magna, 174
libraries, 90, 100, 108
lions, 125
literacy, 109
literati, 86, 107
localism, forces of, 82, 169–170
logistical constraints, 43–44, 82, 151
London, 1, 3, 13, 137

mace, 146
Macedon, kingdom of, 29
macro-history, 12, 22, 179
  of regions, 17, 182
Magadha, kingdom of, 61
Maghreb, 71
Magi, the, 127
Mahabharata (the Sanskrit epic), 101–102
Malabar Coast, 141, 147–148
malaria, 38
Malinowski, Bronislaw, 134–135
mandate of heaven, 74, 153
Mani, the prophet, 112–113
mansabdar, 80
Mantinium, 168
Manuel I, king of Portugal, 126
manuscript culture, 87, 92, 94
  compared with printed books, 107–108

Mao, 155
Marathas, the, 171
Marathon, 67, 180
Marcus Aurelius, 89, 104, 122
Margrete I, queen and regent of Scandinavia, 177
Mariccus, rebel leader in Gaul, 165
Martial (Marcus Valerius Martialis), 89, 127, 164
martyrs, 116, 131
marvels and world history, 180
marvels, the culture of, 76, 121, 125, 127, 130–131, 133–134, 178
Marx, Karl, 7
Marxism, 13, 44, 161
Mauryan dynasty, xiii, 61
Mauryan Empire, 54, 59
Mayan archaeology, 10
Mayan language, 10
Mayas, the, 44
McNeill, William H., 14, 37–38, 41, 81, 122, 182, 187
Mecca, 88, 147, 175
medieval period, 5, 44, 88, 147, 177
Memphis (in Egypt), 165
menagerie, 125
Mendesian nome, the, 163
mercenaries, 43, 45, 71
merchants, 144, 151
　European, 140, 147
　Greco-Egyptian, 140
　Indian, 140, 145
　Islamic, 147
　Muslim, 147
　of Adulis, 151
　of the Atlantic, 141, 152
　Palmyrene, 140, 150
　Roman, 140
　Romano-Egyptian, 143
　Sogdian, 151
Mesoamerica, 44, 67
Mesopotamia, 9, 28, 30, 38, 44, 60, 140, 172
Messiah, the, 166
metals, 34, 42, 138
metre (poetic), 102
metropole, the, 2, 111, 154
　metropolitan perspective, 111
　metropolitan powers, 2
micro-history, 178–179
migrant workers, 167
migrants, 38, 45, 182
militarism, 66, 102
military
　manpower, 48, 69, 71, 174
　mobilization, 15, 48, 70–71, 176, 184
　military capacity, 171, 175, 184
millenarianism, 153, 155, 164–166, 176, 189

mimicry, 111
Ming Dynasty, xiii, 64, 77, 125–126
Mississippi, the, 123
mobile populations, 32, 34, 69–70, 152, 158, 160, 168, 173, 182
mobility of populations, 182
modernity, 12, 16, 19, 21, 180, 187
　anti-modernity, 19
modernization, 111, 161–162, 181
Moluccas, 146
monarchy, 22, 42, 46–47, 67, 69–70, 72–73, 91, 98, 110, 115, 125, 136, 157, 164
Mongols, the, 69
　conquests, 25, 184
　language, 110
monkeys, 151
monopoly
　global trade, 147
　on violence, 40, 68, 72
monotheism, 86–87, 92, 112–115, 117–118, 131, 188
monuments, xvi, 1–3, 76
Moses, the prophet, 20, 47, 113
Mosques, in Roman imperial style, 5–6
mountains, 34, 182
Mu'awiya, the Umayyad caliph, 168
Mughals, the, xii, xiii, 21, 23, 64, 76–77, 84, 94, 96, 103, 110, 127, 170
Muhammad, 75, 92, 113, 168, 175–176
multilingualism, 88, 110
Murad IV, Ottoman Emperor, 178
Museum, the, xvi, 10, 29, 59, 91, 93, 106, 126, 128, 150
Myos Hormos, 141, 145
myrrh, 130
mythological display, 89, 91–92, 94, 125, 127

Naipaul, V. S., 1, 15
Nanjing, 154–155
Naqsh-e Rostam, 26, 58–59, 110
Narcissus, freedman of the Roman emperor, 79
narratives, big and structuring, xi, xii, 51, 101, 180
nationalism, 42, 112
nations, 2–3, 8, 12
Naukratis, 45
Nelson Column, 3
Neoplatonism, 93
Nero, Roman emperor, 57, 78, 156, 165–166, 170, 177–178, 182
Netherlands, the, 11
new world history, xii, 16
Nicaea, 117
Nile, the, 35, 60, 106, 108, 138, 140, 145
Nineveh, 60
Nizami Ganjavi, 88, 92–95

nomads and nomadism, 34, 70–73, 149, 151, 183–184, 188
Numidia, 167
nutmeg, 146

Oceania, 14
Odainathus, Septimius, 56
Oea, 174
oecumene. *See* ecumene
officials and officeholders, 62, 77, 82–83, 116, 160, 163, 170
Oracle of the Potter, 165
oracles, 164
orality, 99–101, 109, 118, 169
organizational capacity, 13, 30
Orient, the, 8–9
oriental spices and textiles, 138
Orientalism, 8–9
Orpheus, 86–90, 92–94, 96–97, 103, 180
ostriches, 127
Ottomans, xiii, 5, 21, 52, 64, 76
Ovid (Publius Ovidius Naso), 62, 91

pageantry, 2, 76, 89, 91, 121, 125
paideia, 104
Palatine hill, the, 76
Palestine, 172
Pallas, freedman of the Roman emperor, 79
Palmyra, 56, 81, 140, 144, 165
Parentium, 142
Paris, 1, 3
Parthenon Marbles, the, 10
Parthian Empire, 63
  Parthian language, 110
pastoralism, 173
patrimonial empire, 77
patrimonial power, 78
patronage, 50, 77, 79–81, 84, 90, 98, 105, 115–116, 159, 168–169, 171
Patterson, Orlando, 49–50, 79
pearls, 121, 136
peasant society, 31, 34, 37, 39, 182
peasantries, 26, 32, 34–39, 46, 53, 55, 146, 152, 156, 180, 187
  military recruitment, 46, 174
  runaways, 163, 167
Peloponnesian War, the, 66
pepper, 121–122, 137, 140–148, 151, 180
Pergamon Altar, 10
Perikles, 37
Persepolis, 58, 97, 127
Persian Empire, 58, 60
Persian Gulf, the, 140–141, 145, 149–151
Persian language, 23, 92, 103
Persius, the satirist, 143

Peter, the Apostle, 153
Petronius, 109
pharaohs, the, 22, 45, 137–138, 165
Philip the Arab, Roman emperor, 59
philosophy and kingship, 93, 95
philosophy and monotheism, 112
Philostratus, 93, 107, 151
Phoenician alphabet, 45
Phoenician city-states, 45
Phoenician trading stations, 140
Piacenza, 29
pirates, 53
Plato, 42, 93–95, 98
Pliny the Elder, 28, 133–135, 144
Pliny the Younger, 160
poetry, 88, 91–94, 104–105, 108
  poetics, 92, 98
poets, 86, 88, 91–92, 96, 103
polis, the, 21, 43–46, 162
political fragmentation, 2, 18, 30, 44, 66, 85, 117, 152
Polo, Marco, 138
Polybios, the Greek historian, 47
Polybius, freedman of the Roman emperor, 79
polytheism, 115–116
Pompeii, 142
Pontos, Kingdom of, 62
population, *passim*
population growth, 22
Poros, king, 28
Porphyry, 93, 135
postcolonialism, 8–9, 100, 111, 159, 161
postmodernism, xi, xii
potlach. *See* distribution of land and wealth
praetorian guard, 50, 78
precolonial
  the Americas, 20, 67
  world history, xiv, 13, 15, 17, 87, 182
pre-industrial conditions, 5, 13, 17, 20, 40, 42–43, 49, 83, 107, 135, 174, 182–183, 186–187
premodern
  cultural connections, 18
  cultures of consumption, 137
  government and elite wealth, 80
  government expenditure, 68
  warfare, 65
  weaponry, 166
  world trade, 123–124
prestige goods, 33, 135–136, 149, 180
pretender. *See* royal impostor, the; impostor, the royal
priesthoods, 41, 131, 142, 164, 167
progressive crescent, the, 7, 13
prophecy, 155, 164–166, 175, 177, 180
prophets, 113, 164

protection, 41, 50, 68, 114, 159, 168
  a protective bargain, 41
provincial elites, 84–85, 105, 117
provincial government, 83
provincial society, 77, 81, 84, 118, 167, 169, 171
provincialization, 12, 170
Ptolemaic dynasty, 89, 106
Ptolemies, 165
Ptolemy V, 110
Punic language, 169
Punic wars, the, 30–31, 34, 61
Punt, land of, 138
Pyrrhus, king of Epirus, 28–29

Qianlong, the Qing emperor, 104, 127–128, 150
qilin. *See* giraffes
Qin dynasty and empire, xiii, 42, 46, 61, 67,
  69–72, 77–78, 100–101, 122, 125, 136, 140
Qing dynasty and empire, xiii, 15–16, 24, 53, 64,
  76–77, 85, 96, 104, 110, 122, 126–128, 154, 160
queens, 2, 10, 56–57, 144

Rajasthan, 110
Ramayana, the, 101
Raphael, 124
rarities, 124
Ravenna, 172, 174
Realpolitik, 66
rebellion
  and resistance, chapter, 6 *passim*
  restorationist, 155, 162, 164
  peasant, 161–170
recontextualization, xii, 5, 26, 87
Red Sea, 140–141, 143, 145, 147, 151
regionalization of power, 85, 117, 171
Republican politics, 47
resistance, 157–161
revelation, divine, 113, 153, 175–176
revenue and tribute, 72, 77, 80, 83, 171–172
revolution
  Bronze Age, 40
  city-state, 47
  global politics of, 154
  international revolutionaries, 155
  liberal enlightenment, 162
  modern critics of power, 9
  national or worker, 154, 161
  poetry, 90
  politics of, 155
  scientific, 125
  the military revolution, 15
rhetorical education, 101–102, 104
Rhine, the river, 39, 52, 174, 183
rhinoceros, 125, 127
Rhône, the river, 29

rice paddies, 39, 146
Richthofen, Ferdinand von, 17
ritual community, 41, 114–115, 118, 169–170
  language, 101
ritual goods, 134–135, 146, 149
ritual offering, 143
rituals of power and healing, 152
Roman Republic, 31, 42, 70, 72–73, 174, 180
  agrarian state as an aristocratic collective, 47
Rosetta Stone, the, 110
rulership, 65, 74, 88, 94
Rushdie, Salman, 19
Russia, 177

Safavid dynasty, 178
saffron, 137
Sahel, the, 39
saints, 114–116, 167–169
Sakuntala, the (a Sanskrit play), 109
Salamis, 67, 180
Samarkand, xiii, 23
Sanskrit cosmopolis, 102
Sanskrit language, 87, 101–103, 105, 109–110,
  118, 180
  cosmopolis, 102
  culture, 101–102, 118
  Sanskritization, 118, 146
Sardis, xiii
Sasanian Empire, 26, 58–60, 64, 88, 110, 113,
  172, 175
Scandinavia, 39, 177
schism, 117, 169
sedentary agriculture and society, 26, 31–35, 37,
  69–70, 72–73, 152, 158–159, 173–174, 180,
  182, 184–185, 187
Seianus, Lucius Aelius, 78
Seneca, Lucius Annaeus, 77–79, 137
Shahanshah, the, 25, 56, 58, 65
Shahjahan, Mughal emperor, xiii, 94, 97, 103,
  128, 150
Shahjahanabad, 83–84, 128
Shahnameh, the Book of Kings, 88
Shapur, the Great Sasanian emperor, 56,
  58–60, 110
Sherwin-White, Susan, xiii
Sibyl, the, 164
Sicily, 29, 45–46, 49, 156, 161
Silius Italicus, Roman poet, 89
Silk Roads, 149–150
silks, 121–122, 136, 140, 149, 151, 174, 180
Sima Qian, 43, 46, 72, 78, 101, 107, 119, 131, 136
similarities, 12, 102
slash and burn agriculture, 32
slavery, 7, 26
  and peasant freedom, 48

slavery (cont.)
　　and social death, 49
　　Islamic, 50
　　Levantine background, 50
　　manumission, 51
　　maroon communities, 158
　　military, 50
　　plantation, 49
　　Ottoman, 51
　　urban, 51
small pox, 163
Smerdis, 179
sociology, historical, xiv, 7, 11–13, 21, 33, 41–42, 77, 87, 99, 106, 116
Socotra, island of, 141, 145
Socrates, 23, 93, 99
Sokoto Caliphate, 49
soldiers, 43, 46, 50, 71, 73, 80–81, 144, 163, 174
　　land allotments, 46
　　logistics, 43
　　slave, 50
Solomon, 92–94, 96
son of heaven, 58, 77
Sophistic, the Second, 107
South China Sea, 146
Soviet communism, 155
Spain, 29, 98, 172
Sparta, 42, 53, 55, 66–67, 179
Spartacus, 155
spices in world trade, 137–147
spices, the magic of, 136–137
splinter churches, 117, 167–168
Sri Lanka, 146–147
state formation, 22, 26–28, 31, 35, 40, 42, 44, 54–56, 59–60, 66, 68–69, 146, 152, 175, 182, 186–187
　　rivalries, 41, 57, 64, 68, 100, 164, 178
　　rivalry, 103
statehood, 40, 62, 91, 106
state making, 40, 182
　　and population, 22, 31
　　and social caging, 35
　　elites, 30, 76, 88, 180
　　societies, 60
　　slavery, 53
state system, 66, 69
steppe lands of Central Asia, 25, 34, 71, 73, 140, 149, 152, 182–185
Strabo, the geographer, 55
Strait of Malacca, 146–147
subaltern voices, 9, 185
Sub-Saharan Africa, 39–40, 53
subsistence needs, 83

succession of power and authority, 5, 25, 69, 113, 167–168, 175, 178
Sudan, the, 125
Suetonius, 64, 134, 177
Sufi saints, 115
Sumerians, the, 45, 185
Sumner Maine, H. J., 7
surplus, the agrarian, 31, 35, 38–39, 83–84
Süleyman the Magnificent, Ottoman emperor, 164
synthesis, 18, 188
Syracuse, 45
Syria, xiii, 126, 164, 170, 172–173
Syriac, 87–89, 117

Tacitus, 57, 78, 164, 166, 177, 183
Taiping movement and rebellion, 154–155
Taklamakan Desert, 149
Tang dynasty and empire, xiii, 146, 176
Tarim Basin, 10, 119–120, 140, 149, 151
taxation, xii, 46, 82, 106, 148
　　payment capacity and arrears, 62, 83
　　resistance, 163
　　tithes and fifths, 83
Teimur Lenk, 23, 71, 94
temples
　　as a basis of power, 41, 101, 110, 112
Teutoburg Forest, battle of, 163
textiles, 132, 136, 140–141
Thales, 93
Theban, the rising, 165
Thebes, in Egypt, 110
theology, 103, 114, 117, 145, 153, 167–169
theory, 13, 19–20, 23, 44, 66, 79, 99, 111, 122, 147, 155, 183
Thermopylae, battle of, 180
Thucydides, 38, 66–67
Tiber, the river, 2, 65, 91
Tiberius, Roman emperor, 78
Tibetan language, 110
tigers, 127–128, 150
Tigris, the river, 60
Tilly, Charles, 42
tin, 138
Titus, Roman Emperor, 112, 166
Tokarczuk, Olga, xi
tournaments of value, 134
Toynbee, Arnold, 10–11, 18
Trafalgar Square, 2–3
Trajan, 156, 160
transcendentalism, 112, 115–116, 118
transhumance, 34
translation, xi, xii, 19, 23, 28, 55–56, 86, 88–91, 94, 109–110, 122, 144, 165–166, 168, 177

transport
  railroads, 82
  rivers and sea, 43, 173, 182
  Roman roads, 182
Trebia, battle of the, 29
tributary submission, 55, 59, 62, 76, 86, 88, 127, 130, 149
  rituals of tribute, 132
Trobriand Islands, the, 134
truth languages, 106–112
tyranny, 66, 70, 72, 156

Ulpian, Roman jurist, 81
Umayyads, the, xiii, 106, 168
UN, the, 8
unity. *See also* China, first imperial unification
  Arab, 176
  of Europe, 2
  of the church, 168–169
  of the Roman Empire, 1, 116
universal empire, 26
  provincial elites, 84–85
  quest for supremacy, 57, 61, 69, 113
  sovereignty, 62
  stability of, 69
  the quest for supremacy, 57–58, 64, 69
  universalism, 60–61, 96
  universality in diversity, 110
  universalist religion, 112, 115, 118
uprisings, apocalyptic and millenarian, 153, 156, 162–164, 167, 170, 189
urbanism, 36, 38, 44, 143
urbanization, 37–40, 187

Vaballathus, imperial claimant and son of Zenobia, 56–57
Valerian, Roman emperor, 56, 59
Vancouver Island, 135
Varus, Publius Quinctilius, 163
Venice, 68, 138, 140

Vergil (Publius Vergilius Maro), 88, 92, 96, 102, 112, 164
  the Georgics, 92
Verus, Lucius, Roman emperor, 38
Vespasian, Roman emperor, 166
Vindolanda, 143
violence, use of, 48
  as enterprise, 68
  low-level, 159
viruses, 8, 37
Vitellius, Roman emperor, 166
Vittorio Emmanuele, monument, 2

Wallerstein, Immanuel, 148
Wang Mang, Chinese emperor, 78
warfare, 18, 30, 42, 68, 71, 171, 173
warlords, 71, 162, 174
warrior coalition, 151, 174–175, 184
warriors, 41, 46, 110, 151, 163, 174, 176, 183–184
Weber, Max, 11–13, 40, 77
  Weberian theory, 13
wonders, 87, 124, 127, 133–134
world history, the new, 7–16
  and Rome, 16–26
world systems, 147–149
world religion, 112, 118
worship, cultic and divine, 73, 113, 167, 175
Wudi, Chinese emperor, 119, 131

Xenophon, 43
Xiongnu, the, 183

Yangtze, the river, 39, 154
Yersinia Pestis, 38
Yongzheng, emperor of the Qing dynasty, 83

Zama, the battle of, 34
Zenobia, of Palmyra, 56, 81, 144
Zoroaster, the prophet, 113
Zoroastrian religion, 113, 179

For EU product safety concerns, contact us at Calle de José Abascal, 56–1°, 28003 Madrid, Spain or eugpsr@cambridge.org.

www.ingramcontent.com/pod-product-compliance
Ingram Content Group UK Ltd.
Pitfield, Milton Keynes, MK11 3LW, UK
UKHW022138110226
467941UK00014B/217